THE CLOSED SHOP

The Closed Shop

A Comparative Study in Public Policy and Trade Union Security in Britain, the USA and West Germany

CHARLES HANSON
SHEILA JACKSON
University of Newcastle upon Tyne

DOUGLAS MILLER
Newcastle upon Tyne Polytechnic

Gower

Published by

Gower Publishing Company Limited,
Gower House, Croft Road,
Aldershot, Hants GU11 3HR, England

British Library Cataloguing in Publication Data

Hanson, Charles
    The closed shop.
    1. Open and closed shop
    2. Open and closed shop — United States
    3. Open and closed shop — West Germany
    I. Title   II. Jackson, Sheila
    III. Miller, Douglas
    331.88'92   HD6488
    ISBN 0-566-00414-3

Reproduced from copy supplied
Printed and bound in Great Britain
by Billing and Sons Limited and Kemp Hall Bindery
Guildford, London, Oxford, Worcester

Contents

Acknowledgements

A book of this kind cannot be written without the accumulation of many debts. Only the largest will be acknowledged here, but we are also grateful to many others who have helped us in a variety of ways. The service of librarians, for example, including those who operate the inter-library loan service, has been indispensable to us.

In Britain we are especially grateful to Charles Rowley, David Dale Professor of Economics in the University of Newcastle upon Tyne. He encouraged the project from its inception and ensured that accommodation was provided in the Centre for Research in Public and Industrial Economics. Lord Harris of High Cross also gave invaluable advice in the early stages of the project. Professor Charles Drake and his colleague Gwyneth Pitt of the Faculty of Law at the University of Leeds have assisted and advised us in a variety of ways and made constructive comments on a draft of Part II. Graham Smith, too, has taken endless trouble to provide us with accurate information about UMAs and dismissal for non-membership of a union, and Anne Staines and Helen Jackson have shared the fruits of their research.

In the USA we are much in debt to Dan Heldman who has valiantly tried to keep us aware of the latest research on union security in that country, has given up many hours of his time to answer particular requests and has criticised a draft of Part II in detail. Harry Cohany, of the Bureau of Labor Statistics, has made available to us the latest statistics relevant to this Part and read a draft of chapters 11 and 13 and Professor Thomas Haggard of the University of South Carolina has also read a draft of Part III and made many helpful comments.

In Germany we express our thanks to Herrn Wisskirchen and Krichel of the BDA, Ulrich Zachert of the DGB, Horst Föhr of the IG Bergbau, Wolfgang Streeck of the International Institute of Management at Berlin, and Hermann Bayer and Eckbert Treu of the University of Münster. Ingo Böbel, Leverhulme Research Fellow at the University of Newcastle upon Tyne 1978-79, was a constant source of inspiration to us and ensured that the research never became dull during that academic year. Maria Hackmann, a labour court judge, read a draft of Part IV and made several helpful comments about it.

Then it is our pleasure and duty to thank the governing bodies of the Dicey Trust, the Headley Trust, the National Right to Work Legal Defence Foundation and the Wincott Foundation. It was the generosity of their financial support which made possible the research on which this book is based.

Finally, our thanks are due to Anne Hanson, Judith Oxley and Diane Thompson, who typed various drafts of three more or less difficult handwritings with amazing patience and efficiency. Without their dedicated efforts this book would never have been produced.

It only remains to be said that all fallacies, omissions and errors are, of course, entirely the responsibility of the authors.

Charles Hanson
Sheila Jackson
Douglas Miller

Preface

Whenever two or more collaborate to write a book the question immediately arises: how is the work to be shared out? It is right that our readers should know how we answered this question.

Because the book falls into three main parts it made sense for each of us to be concerned with one of those parts. Charles Hanson, who had the overall responsibility for the project, took particular responsibility for the introductory chapter and the British section. Since Sheila Jackson had concerned herself with the law and practice of the closed shop in the USA at an early stage, it seemed wise for her to write up that part. And it was natural for Douglas Miller, with his practical experience and linguistic expertise, to concentrate on the German section.

Thus in one sense different parts of the book have been written by different authors. Consequently the reader will find differences in emphasis, not to say different points of view, coming through in the various sections. This may cause some difficulties, but in a book on a controversial topic which evolved through a voluntary compact between three authors, rather than by the dictation of one of them, it is inevitable.

But, in another sense, although the introduction and the conclusion are the only chapters to which we all fully subscribe, the whole book is a co-operative production. We have worked closely together over a period of two years. We have shared ideas and literary material originating in all three countries. And we have frankly criticised each other's drafts and suggested ways of improving them.

Our hope is that this combination of independence and co-operation has enabled us to produce a book which sheds some light on one of the most contentious issues of our time.

Charles Hanson
Sheila Jackson
Douglas Miller
Newcastle upon Tyne, 1981.

PART I

INTRODUCTION

1 The nature of the problem

An important target for most trade unions is organisational security; for some unions this means the achievement of 100 per cent membership, or as near to that as possible. Nevertheless, the closed shop, the main method employed to attain 'union security',[1] 'has been banned in all or in some of its numerous manifestations in a large part of the world'.[2] Strangely, there appears to be no intelligible principle which would explain the widely divergent policies existing in different countries, even when they possess similar social structures and legal traditions. Thus, while in West Germany all forms of union security are considered unlawful, the same is not true for some other countries using the continental system of law, for example the Netherlands and Switzerland.[3] Nor is it easier to find a 'visible common policy among the English-speaking nations with a common law background'.[4] Thus, in Britain all closed shop practices are permitted while in the USA only the less stringent forms are allowed. Obviously, the law of every country is a particular response to its own customs, practices and institutions, however similar these may seem to arrangements in existence elsewhere.

This study is concerned with the way in which union security in general and the closed shop in particular have developed in three countries, Britain, the USA and West Germany. The differences in public policy as expressed in the law of each of these countries are considerable. The most recent comparative study on the subject of the closed shop, covering six countries, was undertaken by Lord

Wedderburn in 1978[5] and it was confined to exploration of the legal aspects of the rights to associate and dissociate. This study attempts to take the process one important step further by considering the translation of the law into industrial reality, and the custom and practice of the closed shop in each of the three countries will, therefore, be examined as far as information exists. It is, of course, dangerous to make simplistic comparisons between different countries; nevertheless, a close look at what happens in theory and practice in the USA, West Germany and Britain may help to place the often emotive subject of the closed shop in perspective.

Britain and the USA have often been described as two nations divided by a common language, and certainly there are very great differences between the English-speaking old world and the new. This is true of their constitutional arrangements and many of their customs and practices; it is also true of their industrial relations systems. The same must be said about the industrial relations systems of these two countries and that of West Germany. All three countries have large, wealthy trade unions and powerful, well-developed labour movements which take an active part in the political process as well as engaging in collective bargaining. But the differences between their industrial relations systems are often greater than the similarities. The Anglo-Saxon model of industrial relations followed chiefly by Britain, but also to a large extent by the USA, places more emphasis upon direct union representation than upon employee participation. However, whereas US unions have a legally defined role to play in employee representation at plant level, and the works council, not the union, is the collective representative of employees within a plant in West Germany, the involvement of British unions in collective bargaining is relatively informal and undefined.

Both the West German and American systems of collective bargaining are highly formalised, although again there exist substantial differences. Collective agreements negotiated by West German unions apply only to members of those unions, although there may be extension, whereas in the United States it is a legal requirement that such an agreement apply to all employees in a given plant or defined group, irrespective of union membership.[6] It is normal for such collective agreements to be legally binding in both the USA and West Germany; but, while agreements tend to have the same practical effect in Britain as in the USA, any legally binding arrangement is an anathema to British trade unionists.

It is important to note that there are differences in trade union structure and development in the three countries. Both Britain and the USA have organically uninterrupted labour movements, whereas the West German movement was destroyed during the Nazi regime and rebuilt to a new pattern afterwards. Thus in the United States and Britain there are many more unions, of both craft and industrial kinds, whereas West German unions are structured almost entirely upon industrial lines. Therefore, in Germany each industry, or group of related industries, is encompassed by one large industrial union;[7] this degree of industrial unionism is non-existent in the USA, where no union can claim to represent any industry in its entirety, and relatively rare in Britain. Similarly, although trade union development has progressed along roughly parallel lines in Britain and America the British movement has never been divided, as the American one was between 1935 and 1955,[8] and is, therefore, the more integrated of the two.

Both the British and American unions have emphasised the importance of achieving organisational security, which has often meant the introduction of the closed shop and other union security practices. US unions have had to accept more legal restraints with regard to security, chiefly because they initially needed the support of the law to gain recognition. To a large extent the UK unions established themselves without legal support, although recently they have acknowledged the benefits to be gained from legislation, most notably in the Employment Protection Act 1975. Whether or not they will also accept the restraints embodied in the new Employment Act 1980 has yet to be seen. It is intriguing that some of the artificially created West German unions, although they have not needed to gain recognition for collective bargaining purposes, still emphasise the need to achieve organisational security. In Germany this has usually taken the form of differentiation between the union and non-union members, rather than an insistence that a closed shop be established.[9] But before going any further, some preliminary questions need to be asked. What is the closed shop? Is it a problem? And if so, why?

What is the closed shop?

The closed shop is a generic term. It covers a variety of practices which contain a common element. That element is that to obtain or retain a job an employee must join a trade union, or in other words, union membership is a condition of employment. Attitudes towards the closed shop and the ways in which governments attempt to regulate it, or not, differ widely from country to country. The consequence is that the nature of the closed shop varies and so does the terminology. For example, in the USA the term 'closed shop' refers to what in Britain would be described as a 'pre-entry closed shop', or a situation in which only existing union members may be engaged by the employer. The Americans prefer to apply the wide-ranging term 'union security' to their many different arrangements which require some or all of the workers in a bargaining unit to become and remain members of the union as a condition of employment or to pay the equivalent of membership dues in lieu of actual membership. In West Germany, by contrast, no native term exists, because in theory constitutional law and the nature of the industrial relations system make the closed shop impossible. Thus the Germans use the British term 'closed shop' to describe the practice.

Although definitions of the different kinds of closed shops only apply inside national boundaries, it is useful at this stage to consider the British varieties, adopting the pattern laid down by McCarthy.[10]

He remarks that the most significant variations in the closed shop in Britain relate to (a) the form which it takes, (b) the manner of its enforcement and (c) the scope of its application.

(a)   Variations in form

The crucial distinction here is between the pre-entry closed shop, where the worker has to join a union *before* he can be engaged by the employer, and the post-entry closed shop, where the non-unionist may be engaged on condition that he joins the union within a stipulated time.

The pre-entry closed shop, which has been outlawed in the USA, is always associated with job control by the union. It is more easily practised by a union of skilled workers, especially where entry to a craft is only through accredited apprenticeship schemes, as among skilled printing workers. McCarthy calls it the 'craft qualification shop'. But relatively unskilled workers, too, may regulate job entry so that employment is restricted to existing trade unionists. For example, newspaper proprietors in London have to apply to the union office when they require unskilled labour, and only members will be considered for employment. This has been called a labour supply closed shop; its equivalent in the USA is the discriminatory hiring hall, but in West Germany, as far as can be ascertained, this kind of practice simply does not exist.

However, it may be that the union does not have complete control of the labour supply, but has formed a recognised pool of labour in co-operation with the employers. The National Dock Labour Board scheme is an example of this arrangement, which may be called a labour pool shop.

Finally there is the promotion veto shop which exists among iron and steel workers. Unskilled men are promoted on a seniority ladder and at various points on that ladder there will be a pre-entry closed shop, which ensures that non-unionists are passed over for promotion.

(b) Variations in the manner of enforcement

The crucial factors here may be the role of the employer and the structure of management. The employer may be a willing or reluctant party to a formal, written agreement or an informal arrangement to the effect that all employees of a particular class or classes must be and remain union members. A large number of such union membership agreements have been signed in the UK since the passage of the Trade Union and Labour Relations Act 1974, and in these circumstances we may speak of the formally recognised closed shop. In terms of the structure of management the involvement of trade unions in corporate decision-making, especially as in the codetermination (Montan) system in West Germany, may have an important bearing on the degree of union security within a company. However, the test of acceptance is whether the employer is willing to threaten to dismiss non-unionists unless they join the union or to exclude them from employment in the first place. If so, it can be said that a closed shop exists.

However, a closed shop may be effectively imposed without any employer co-operation. If a strike is threatened unless non-unionists join the union or leave the shop-floor, and if it actually takes place, non-unionists are normally forced to stop working or join the union. The closed shop is then unilaterally enforced, although management may eventually come to terms with it. Thus we may speak of the unilaterally enforced, or union enforced, closed shop. McCarthy suggests that the unrecognised closed shop becomes recognised as soon as management agrees to take action to enforce it without the need for a strike. But management is normally aware that, without its co-operation, a strike would take place. To say that management is a willing partner in imposing a closed shop is often to say that it sees it as the course of least industrial friction, although many employers who operate closed shops, particularly in Britain, see them as an acceptable rationalisation of the collective bargaining process whereby employee claims are centralised in one representative body.

(c) Variations in scope

The scope of the closed shop varies considerably from one industry to another and from one region to another. It may also vary from plant to plant in the same industry and even within a plant. But there are a number of factors which affect levels of organisation in all countries, in particular establishment size, the nature of the production process, the structure of the workforce, and the extent to which the workforce can also be identified as social community. Consequently, certain groups of workers may be described as 'closed shop prone'.

Craftsmen: historically craft organisation, for example in printing, has been associated with closed shop arrangements as a method of job control.

Casual labour: because of the unstable employment conditions in some industries, notably the docks and entertainment, the closed shop, often in conjunction with the hiring hall, has been used as a method of allocating labour.

Community based labour: union membership in this case is linked to social identity within the local community. Refusal to join may mean ostracism for the individual employee, for example in mining.

The professions: although this study is concerned with trade unions and the closed shop, in all three countries there are examples among certain professional groups such as lawyers and doctors of compulsory membership in the relevant organisation and/or job security practices similar to those operated by skilled and craft unions.

Thus in many countries there are common reasons why certain groups of employees, which have inherent organising ability, may be described as closed shop prone. Clearly such groups will be resistant to measures which attempt to restrict the possibility of forming and maintaining closed shops, but the degree of resistance will depend upon the nature of the collective bargaining system in a particular country. This raises the question of whether or not the law and public policy can affect these groups. The same question is applicable to other groups of employees who, while seeking a similar level of organisation, lack the ability to achieve it without formal assistance.

The way in which the law and public policy with regard to the closed shop is shaped in each country will be a reflection of the state of the debate about the rights to associate and dissociate in that country. It is useful, therefore, to consider the main elements in that debate.

The debate about the closed shop

By its very nature the debate about the closed shop arouses intense controversy. Various philosophical and pragmatic arguments are used by the two sides to the debate and even the term 'closed shop' is a matter of contention. Those who dislike the closed shop in principle may prefer to use the term 'compulsory unionism', emphasising the coercive element of the closed shop,[11] while those who see it as a perfectly reasonable way of enabling trade unions to achieve some degree of organisational strength may prefer to talk about 'union security'. The issue has been described 'as a sharp and emotion-packed one, both for union-management relations and for public policy'[12] and this is not surprising because both parties to the debate accept that it is about economic power. Those who favour the development of the closed shop see it as one of the ways — perhaps the main way — by which trade unions can increase their power in relation to employers and for them all but the most modest restrictions on the device are seen as 'employer-inspired subterfuges for "union-busting" '.[13] But those who consider that the unions already possess monopoly status and excessive power see the closed shop as a main cause of this thoroughly undesirable state of affairs.

The argument about the balance of economic power between the union and the employer is important, but as Haggard has pointed out, 'underlying this union power issue is a deeper and more important philosophical division. What is at issue are the circumstances, if any, under which individual rights and interests should be subordinated to that of the group in order to achieve a so-called common good'.[14]

Those whose sympathies lie with the closed shop tend to rest their philosophical case on the social utility of strong labour unions. Because powerful unions, in their view, produce benefits for society, the law should not attempt to ban those activities which, like compulsory membership, strengthen trade unionism. Leaving aside the question of whether laws which ban the closed shop can be made effective, they are bad in themselves because they work against the interests of society.

In Britain McCarthy has been the most persuasive spokesman for this school. He argues that the closed shop is generally justifiable despite certain disadvantages.

> Undoubtedly the practice sometimes results in a restriction of individual liberty, and probably it sometimes has disadvantageous economic effects. Non-unionists and employers are often coerced, and existing members are forced to obey union rules and orders by means of the threat of expulsion from the job. In its pre-entry form the practice is sometimes used to deny whole classes of workers the right to compete for particular jobs. But in the great majority of cases, these things are done in order to assist in the maintenance and improvement of the unions' powers of job regulation, and in order to make possible greater opportunities for group protection and advancement.[15]

For McCarthy the interests of the union and the group take precedence over those of certain individuals. And the basic reason why he believes that the closed shop is justifiable and that the law should not try to prevent it is his conviction that unions are weak in relation to employers. Thus the fundamental assumptions of some of those who believe that a 'good' law will permit or encourage compulsory unionism are first, that trade unions are currently too weak and, secondly, that on balance their activities are beneficial.

On the other side of the philosophical divide are those who stand in the tradition of classical liberalism as refined and brought up to date by Hayek and other contemporary thinkers. This school of thought places the highest possible value on freedom, which has been defined as 'that condition of men in which coercion of some by others is reduced as much as is possible'.[16] It has recently been said that liberals pass judgement upon the unions fundamentally in terms of their impact on certain freedoms, and especially individual freedom,

> and on this basis they find them wanting. The fault does not lie in unionisation and collective bargaining itself, which is justifiable by reference to the handicap of labour when negotiating with capital owing to relative lack of capital reserves. Rather, unions are to be condemned for acts of coercion, which are not central to their existence, but which occur in the pursuit of their objectives.[17]

Liberals are mindful that where public policy has encouraged or condoned the closed shop 'the coercion which unions have been permitted to exercise contrary to all principles of freedom under the law is primarily the coercion of fellow workers'.[18] They lay the strongest possible emphasis on individual rights, and especially on the right not to be coerced by other individuals or groups. This philosophy is, perhaps, explicitly reflected in certain articles of the West German Constitution (Basic Law). For example Article 1(1) states that 'the dignity of man is inviolable. To respect and protect it shall be the duty of all state authority'; and Article 2(2) asserts that 'everyone shall have the right to life and to inviolability of his person. The freedom of the individual shall be inviolable. These rights may only be encroached upon pursuant to a law'.[19]

But to insist upon the supreme value of individual rights is not necessarily to deny the right to associate, although it certainly calls *compulsory* association into question. One writer who stands firmly against *compulsory* association argues that 'free association is a property right of all men in the free society, and the voluntary associations which men form raise no insoluble problems of principle for such a society'.[20] In the same way, Article 9 of the German Constitution states emphatically that 'all Germans shall have the right to form associations and societies' and goes on to guarantee that right 'to everyone and to all trades and professions'.[21] However, some constitutional experts on the continent have long argued that this positive right to associate must include, by implication, the negative right *not* to associate. How can there be a genuine right to associate where association is obligatory? As an American lawyer has put it: 'Freedom rests on choice, and where choice is denied freedom is destroyed as well'.[22]

How is the individual to be seen in relation to the social group or society as a whole? Is man an individual or a social being? Does it make sense to think of the individual as supremely important in himself? Or does individual personality only develop through a man's contact with his fellows? Should a man best be seen both as an individual and as a member of a family and the other social groups to which all men belong at one time or another? These are the kind of questions raised by the issue of compulsory unionism, which is closely linked to the nature of the right of association, the wider problem of how far the state should allow individuals to associate.

In his classic analysis of this problem Dicey pointed out that the right of association raises difficulties in every civilised country. He remarked that

> the problem to be solved, either as a matter of theory or as a matter of practical necessity, is at bottom always and everywhere the same. How can the right of combined action be curtailed without depriving individual liberty of half its value; how can it be left unrestricted without destroying either the liberty of individual citizens, or the power of the Government?[23]

And he went on to suggest 'that the most which can be achieved by way of bringing into harmony two essentially conflicting rights, namely the right to individual freedom and the right of association, is to effect a rough compromise between them'.[24] Dicey used the law of libel, which he saw as a rough compromise between the right of X to say or write what he chooses and the right of A not to be injured in property or character by X's free utterance of his opinions, as an example of 'a practical solution of a theoretically insoluble problem'.[25]

We may now return to the two questions posed earlier — is the closed shop a problem? And if so, why? The first question demands an affirmative answer at the philosophical level because compulsory unionism involves a basic conflict of rights between a group which wishes to impose its views on all fellow employees by refusing to work with non-unionists, and those who see this kind of compulsion (the others would call it an exercise of their rights) as infringing *their* basic rights as individuals. It has been said that these opposing views are 'irreconcilable value judgements' and that in these circumstances 'one should not be surprised that public policy concerning it' (compulsory unionism in the USA) 'reflects both many compromises and hard fought legal questions'.[26]

Some of the writers whose views have already been quoted in this chapter see the debate about the closed shop as part of a wide philosophical debate about the right relationship between the individual and the group. But the debate is often more pragmatic than philosophical and it is perhaps less obvious to some employers and trade unions and the closed shop is a problem at this level. What pragmatic arguments may be used for and against the practice?

Much the most common argument in favour of the closed shop is that 'he who benefits should pay'. In other words, because all employees in a particular firm benefit from collective bargaining through a trade union, all should be compelled to contribute to the cost of the union. The argument is often based on the premise that a trade union is analogous to the state and that union contributions should be compulsory, like taxes. It is sometimes further suggested that the services provided by trade unions are of a 'public goods' character, i.e. that they cannot be denied to employees who refuse to pay for them. Thus compulsory payments are necessary to overcome the problem of these 'free-riders'.

The argument assumes that the activities of unions are always beneficial. But union-imposed restrictive practices may reduce output and real wages and even destroy a firm. The argument does not necessarily hold even where unions have achieved higher real wages and/or fringe benefits. Most people benefit from voluntary activities to which they do not contribute (e.g. privately financed medical research). The analogy with the state is untenable because taxation must be compulsory, but union membership may be voluntary. Again, it is difficult to see why trade union services should be regarded as public goods. Non-members could negotiate different terms individually or, where they accepted some of the terms and conditions negotiated by the union, pay a bargaining fee.[27] In the USA the free-rider problem has been exacerbated by the insistence *by the unions* that they should be obliged to represent *all* employees, including those who do not desire such representation (Section 9(a) of the Wagner Act).

For some, the main justification for the closed shop is that it adds to the power of the unions and thus creates a more effective counterbalance to the naturally superior economic power of the corporate employer. It does this by preventing the defection of members during wage-bargaining, which may lead to strike action, and it is especially important that unions should possess this extra bargaining power where employment is usually temporary or casual and trade union organisation is, therefore, inherently difficult.

Others will insist that in many countries, for example Britain, the unions are far too powerful, and that where the closed shop is not in any way unlawful the balance of power is tipped unduly in favour of the unions, against the public interest and the interests of individual employees. Protection of the right to associate should enable unions to bargain with employers on roughly equal terms; and the coercive power of unions against employers can never be justified where it is primarily based on the coercion of fellow workers.

Then there is the view that the closed shop encourages 'responsible' unionism. It is said that it gives union organisers a sense of security and enables them to devote themselves to the long-term interests of the members instead of collecting subscriptions and trying to persuade reluctant employees to join. Trade unionists are, therefore, less militant and aggressive, the emergence of rival unions is prevented and employers can rely on collective agreements being kept, because union negotiators have more authority over their members. It is, then, not surprising that some employers favour a closed shop and are very uneasy about laws which attempt to restrict or ban it.

It may be true that some employers welcome the closed shop because they expect it to lead to efficient labour relations. But there is no guarantee that it will have that effect. Because it secures the position of trade union negotiators it may cause them to neglect the interests of their members who cannot show their dissatisfaction by resigning from the union. Thus the result of this dissatisfaction may show itself in unofficial strikes, which have been a central problem of British labour relations since 1945 and particularly prevalent in some industries, e.g. the docks and coalmining, where the closed shop is virtually complete.[28]

Again, endorsement of the closed shop by some employers does not generally justify it. Perhaps it should be permitted in certain special cases where there is overwhelming support from employers, the trade union and employees; but individuals must be safeguarded and the general presumption should be that this kind of restrictive agreement is against the public interest. The emergence of rival unions can be prevented in other ways, e.g. by negotiating a sole bargaining agency.

Another argument used to support the pre-entry closed shop in skilled trades is that this device, through the system of craft apprenticeships, ensures the competence of new employees and prevents the dilution of skills. In addition it prevents the labour market being flooded with skilled craftsmen for whom there is no work. Schemes of this kind, it is said, are very similar to the vetting or licensing arrangements of professional associations which restrict the number of new entrants by examinations and in other ways.

In reply it might be agreed that tests for competence are necessary, but as the Donovan Commission pointed out, apprenticeship was often 'a farce and provides less training than a properly constructed course lasting only a few months'.[29] Restriction on entry into a trade has always been the key to producing monopoly returns for those who are fortunate enough to get through the barrier. Shortage of skilled labour is one of the main reasons for slow economic growth and these practices may distort the labour market, prevent the introduction of new techniques and cause misallocation of resources. Therefore, instead of arguing from professional associations to trade unions, it may make more sense to consider all restriction on entry to be against the public interest.

Finally, those who favour the closed shop may insist that closed shop agreements are freely entered into by employers because they consider them to be to their advantage. Thus they are simply an exercise of the freedom of contract and thoroughly consistent with the philosophy of the free society. At the same time, there is a basic right for trade unionists not to work with non-unionists if they so choose, and for a majority of trade unionists to exercise this right is simply to act in accordance with the normal tenets of a democracy. It follows that legal restrictions on the closed shop cut across the freedom of contract and the formal right not to work with non-unionists, leaving aside the fact that no law can effectively prevent a group from refusing to work with others.

This final argument practically takes us back from the pragmatic to the philosophical debate, and raises some basic questions about the nature of the 'democratic' and 'free' society. Most 'freedoms' and 'rights' in a free society cannot be absolute, because they clash with other freedoms and rights. This is true of freedom of contract. It is generally accepted that 'yellow dog' contracts, whereby an employee agrees not to join a union during his term of employment, should be outlawed. Does it not follow that agreements which make union membership compulsory should also be prohibited? The right of trade unionists to refuse to work with non-members may be accepted, but it is not an absolute right. It is a very crude idea of democracy which equates that system with a situation where the majority always have the right to impose their will on the minority. It has been well said that the American system of government 'embodies a great many constitutional safeguards to prevent majoritarian democracy from degenerating into a people's tyranny'[30] and the same writer went on to assert that the 'system is at the same time one of majority rule and minority rights. The never ending challenge is to maintain the essence of both, while avoiding the fanatical excesses of anarchy and authoritarianism at each extreme'.[31]

Some will perhaps see the problem of the closed shop largely in terms of philosophical arguments about the positive and negative rights to associate. Others may be more concerned with the custom and practice of labour relations in their own countries and with the constitutional arrangements, possibly including a binding international convention, and the balance of economic and political power. But there is no need to be tied to one or other of these different approaches to the problem. They are not mutually exclusive. It may be that good public policy-making involves a judicious mixture of philosophical and pragmatic arguments and in this study an attempt will be made to take a broad view of the closed shop in Britain, the USA and West Germany.

References

1   This term has been broadly defined as '. . . conditions in collective agreements designed to protect the institutional life of the union . . . '. Marsh, A., *A Concise Encyclopedia of Industrial Relations,* Gower Publishing Co. Ltd., Aldershot, 1979, p.325.
2   Kahn-Freund, O., *Labour and the Law*, Stevens, 2nd edn. 1977, p.194.
3   Kassalow, E.M., 'Will West European Unions Embrace the Closed Shop?' *Monthly Labor Review*, July 1979, pp 35-8.
4   Kahn-Freund, O., op.cit., p.194.
5   As Part 6 entitled 'Discrimination in the Right to Organise and the Right to be a Non-Unionist' of Schmidt, F. (ed.), *Discrimination in Employment*, Almquist and Wiksell International, Stockholm 1978.
6   NLRA 1935, section 9(a).
7   One exception is the DAG which cuts across industrial lines.
8   After the industrial-based CIO broke away from the craft-based AFL.
9   See Kahn-Freund, O., *Labour Relations, Heritage and Adjustment*, Oxford University Press 1979, pp. 54-6.
10   McCarthy, W.E.J., *The Closed Shop in Britain*, Blackwell 1964.
11   See, for example, Allen, V.L., *Power in Trade Unions*, Longmans Green 1954, ch.4, pp. 56-9. McCarthy considers the question of terminology in pp. 7-16 of his book (note 10 above).
12   Northrup, H.R., in the foreword to Haggard, T.R., *Compulsory Unionism, the NLRB and the Courts*, University of Pennsylvania, 1977, p.iii.
13   Haggard, T.R., ibid., p.8.
14   Ibid. The philosophical implications of the controversy are thoughtfully considered in the concluding chapter of Haggard's study.

15   McCarthy, W.E.J., op.cit., p.260.
16   Hayek, F.A., *The Constitution of Liberty*, Routledge and Kegan Paul 1960, p.11.
17   Rowley, C.K. and Peacock, A.T., *Welfare Economics: A Liberal Restatement*, Martin Robertson 1975, p.187.
18   Hayek, F.A., op.cit., p.269.
19   Brownlie, I. (ed.), *Basic Documents on Human Rights*, Oxford University Press 1971, pp. 18-19.
20   Petro, S., *The Labor Policy of the Free Society*, Ronald Press 1957, p.71. Chapter 6 of this book is a classic analysis of the right to associate in a free society.
21   Brownlie, I., op.cit., p.21.
22   Dirksen, E.M., 'Individual Freedom versus Compulsory Unionism: A Constitutional Problem', *De Paul Law Review*, vol.XV, no.2, 1966, p.265.
23   Dicey, A.V., *Lectures on the Relation between Law and Public Opinion in England during the Nineteenth Century*, 2nd edn., re-issued by Macmillan 1962, p.468.
24   Ibid.
25   Ibid.
26   Northrup, H.R., op.cit., p.vii.
27   See the discussion of this issue by Burton, J. in IEA Readings 17, Trade Unions: Public Goods or Public 'Bads'? Institute of Economic Affairs 1978, pp. 43-52.
28   To argue in this way is not, of course, to suggest that the existence of the closed shop in certain industries is the main reason, or the only one, for their strike-proneness.
29   *Report of the Royal Commission on Trade Unions and Employers' Associations 1965-68*, Cmnd 3623, HMSO, para. 339, p.88.
30   McAlister, A., 'Labor, Liberalism and Majoritarian Democracy', *Fordham Law Review*, vol.31, p.661.
31   Ibid.

PART II

THE CLOSED SHOP IN BRITAIN

2 The origins until 1965

There is nothing new about compulsory unionism in Britain. The Webbs found that trade unions originated in the second half of the seventeenth century and they argued that 'the exclusion of non-unionists is . . . co-eval with Trade Unionism itself'.[1] Writing in the 1890s they gave various examples of groups of craftsmen, including boilermakers, flint glass makers, tape-sizers, stuff-pressers, and platers and riveters in Tyneside shipyards, among whom compulsion to join the union was 'so complete that it ceases to be apparent' and they went on to say that 'this silent and unseen, but absolutely complete compulsion, is the ideal of every Trade Union'.[2] At the same time when they stated that the practice of compulsory unionism was far more characteristic of the older forms of trade unionism 'than of any society formed in the present generation'[3] they were indicating that some contemporary unions found it impossible to achieve this ideal.

This is not surprising, for until the end of the second decade of the twentieth century trade unionists were a small minority of the labour force in Britain. No total figures can be given with any confidence before 1892, but it seems likely that membership grew slowly and erratically from a base of less than 100,000 in the early 1840s[4] to about a million in the mid 1870s. Numbers fell in the depression of 1878-80, but then recovered to reach a million and a half, or about one in ten of the working population, by 1892. From then onwards the picture is relatively clear, as table 2.1 shows. The long-term trend, upset by the severe unemployment of 1921-33, is of an increase in density so that by the mid 1970s over half of those at work in Britain were organised in trade unions.

Table 2.1
Trade union membership and density in the UK, 1901-78[5]

Year	Civilian labour force (millions)	Total union membership (millions)	Density of union membership (per cent)
1901	16.1	2.0	12.6
1911	17.8	3.1	17.7
1920	18.5	8.3	45.2
1933	19.4	4.4	22.6
1938	19.8	6.1	30.5
1945	20.4	7.9	38.6
1950	21.1	9.3	44.1
1955	21.9	9.7	44.5
1960	22.8	9.8	43.1
1965	23.9	10.3	43.2
1970	23.4	11.2	47.7
1975	23.5	12.0	51.1
1978	23.7	13.1	55.3

With the chief exception of the period 1921-33, trade union density in Britain has been growing since the 1870s and the past hundred years has also seen very large changes in trade union structure. The implication of this kind of growth and change is a mixture of compulsory and voluntary unionism. Some members may be determined to protect and extend the compulsory element, but growth in new industries, services and firms means that, for a time at least, many trade unionists must be prepared to work with non-members.

It might seem that legislators and public policy makers would hardly have been concerned with the problem of coercion of non-members by trade unionists at times when only a very small proportion of the workforce was engaged in trade union activities, but that was not the case. From 1824 onwards, when the unions in Britain emerged from the darkness of total illegality into the shadow of a semi-legality which allowed workers to associate together solely for the purpose of determining wages and hours of work, there was a clear understanding that the right to associate freely always carried with it the risk of coercion against those who did not wish to associate. J.R. McCulloch expressed this view most plainly and because he was a champion of the right to associate he deserves to be listened to with special respect. McCulloch argued that 'nothing can apparently be more reasonable than that workmen should be allowed freely to combine or associate together, for the purpose of adjusting the terms on which they will sell their labour',[6] but he made it clear that for him the only acceptable kind of combination was a voluntary one, unaccompanied by violence.[7] McCulloch knew the problems of making labour laws effective; he must have known of the tendency for trade unions to achieve compulsory membership in their trade, but he thought that a way could be devised to allow freedom of association while preventing that freedom from being abused. These views were widely shared and formed the basis of the majority report of the 1867 Royal Commission on Trade Unions, which preceded a major reform of trade union law.

The 1867 Commission and the legislation of 1871-75

The Trade Union Act of 1871 — the 'Charter of Trade Unions'[8] — marked a turning point in trade union law and attitudes towards trade unions in Britain. It was preceded by an exhaustive Royal Commission which investigated all aspects of the unions with Victorian thoroughness and was seen by the trade unions as a golden opportunity to justify their existence. In making their case before the Commission the trade union lobby, brilliantly advised by Frederic Harrison, a skilful labour lawyer, called for complete freedom of association in response to the employers' claim for freedom of competition.

But how did Harrison rebut the allegations of the employers, supported by an immense amount of evidence, that unions engaged in many restrictive practices and in particular that they excluded 'from work as far as practicable workmen not belonging to the union'?[9] It was impossible to deny that unions acted in these ways. Instead, the trade unionists insisted that 'nearly all the condemned practices of the men's societies have a very close parallel in those of the employers'[10] and that practices of this kind were the necessary price of freedom of association. The trade union advocates, then, did not defend the closed shop *per se*; indeed, they accepted that it was an unsocial practice. But they argued, first, that trade unions must be allowed to engage in such practices because others did so too; second, that the practice would gradually die out; and third, that the unions must have complete freedom to pursue their own interests as they saw them, even if this had certain undesirable side effects.

The claim for freedom to pursue their own interests was at the heart of the trade union case. As the Webbs put it, 'The working men had, in fact, picked up the weapon of their opponents';[11] but they went on to say, 'In so doing the leading Trade Unionists of the time drifted into a position no less inconsistent than that of the employers. When they contended that the Union should be as free to bargain as the individual, they had not the slightest intention of permitting the individual to bargain freely if they could prevent him'.[12] In the Webbs' view, 'the insistence upon the Englishman's right to freedom of contract was, in fact, in the mouths of staunch Trade Unionists, perilously near cant'[13] because 'no Trade Unionist can deny that, without some method of enforcing the decision of the majority, effective trade combination is impossible'.[14]

The majority accepted that there was 'no ground of justice or of policy for withholding such a right (to combine) from the workmen'[15] but they were faced with abundant evidence that trade unionists habitually exercised coercion 'over their fellow workmen who do not belong to the union'.[16] It was this kind of evidence which led them to emphasise that the new privileges should only be made available to voluntary combinations, and that

> whilst conceding to such workmen as desire to exercise it an extended right to combine against their employers, especial care should be taken that an equal right be secured to those workmen who desire to keep aloof from the combination, to dispose of their labour with perfect freedom as they severally think fit.[17]

Thus for the majority the extension of the right to combine and the fullest possible protection of individual rights went hand in hand.

How did the government react to the majority and minority reports? W.E. Gladstone, the Prime Minister, was unwilling to concede the vigorous trade union demands for the complete adoption of the minority proposals, but he admitted the need for legislative change. On the one hand the general principles of the minority report — that unions should be legally recognised and fully protected against the common law doctrines of restraint of trade and conspiracy — were accepted. But on the other hand effective strike action was made virtually impossible. From the trade union point of view the benefits of the Trade Union Act 1871 were nullified by the Criminal Law Amendment Act of the same year. Their view was confirmed in 1872 when it was held that a threat to strike by some gas-stokers, unless their employer reinstated a workman discharged for union activity, was a criminal conspiracy to coerce[18] and the men were sentenced to twelve months' hard labour. The trade union lobby, led by the newly formed Parliamentary Committee of the Trades Union Congress, redoubled their efforts and by 1875 their campaign had achieved complete success.

In the general election of 1874 the trade unionists made it clear that their votes would go to candidates who supported their campaign, and the new Tory government, led by Disraeli, quickly passed two Acts — The Conspiracy and Protection of Property Act and the Employers and Workmen Act — which totally satisfied the trade union demands. Thus, by the use of the political process the unions had achieved their objective of legal recognition and protection from the common law. Or had they? Some early clashes between the courts and Parliament set the pattern for the subsequent development of British labour law which has been appropriately described as 'a see-saw vendetta between the courts and legislature'.[19]

From 1876 to 1905

One of the main reasons why the courts have frequently found themselves at loggerheads with Parliament over labour law is the tradition that the law abhors compulsory labour. Thus it insists on upholding the freedom of contract between the employer and the individual employee and sees protective legislation in favour of the employee as a threat to this freedom. Again, it has been said that 'concern for the unorganised individual citizen lies at the heart of the common law tradition in our courts'.[20] It is, then, not surprising that attempts by the trade unions to secure complete legal protection have led to major battles in the courts with employers and individuals. The security which the unions thought they had achieved in 1875 had disappeared by 1901 following a series of decisions in the courts, and their growing vulnerability forced them to seek additional protection from Parliament. How did this situation come about?

In 1892 the House of Lords, in the case of *Mogul Steamship Co.* v *McGregor Gow*,[21] found in favour of a group of shipowners who had formed an association to secure a trading monopoly on the grounds that it was impossible to distinguish between fair and unfair competition and that the defendants' sole motive was to defend their trading interests. But would this principle be extended to the labour market? Would the courts hold that what was right for a cartel of shipowners was also right for a trade union of workers? That question was answered in the affirmative in 1898 in the case of *Allen* v *Flood*,[22] when the House of Lords found in favour of Allen, an official of the boilermakers, who had threatened the employer that there would be a strike unless he dismissed some shipwrights who had done work which the boilermakers regarded as their own. But three years later the protection which *Allen* v *Flood* appeared to have provided for the closed shop was substantially undermined by *Quinn* v *Leathem*[23] in which it was decided that the defendants, officials of the local butchers' assistants' union, were liable for tortiously interfering in the plaintiff's (Leathem's) business.

The Conspiracy and Protection of Property Act 1875 had excluded the law of *criminal* conspiracy from trade disputes; but the House of Lords judgement in *Quinn* v *Leathem* extended the doctrine of conspiracy into the realm of *civil* law as a separate species of tort and 'rendered illegal a combination to effect any purpose which a court considered 'unjustifiable' or not in pursuit of the legitimate interests of those combining'.[24]

Clearly the judgement in *Quinn* v *Leathem* made it difficult for trade unionists to know in advance what kind of activity would be lawful, and taken together with other decisions on picketing and inducing breaches of contract the legal position of the unions was becoming hazardous. But these decisions were all overshadowed by the *Taff Vale* case[25] in which the House of Lords held that a registered trade union possessed sufficient of the attributes of corporate personality to enable it to be sued in its registered name for the torts of its servants or agents. This reversed the verdict of the Court of Appeal and the widely held view that unions were unincorporated associations having no legal entity, and meant that the central funds of registered unions were generally at risk for the acts of branch officials all over the country. The consequence of *Quinn* v *Leathem* taken together with *Taff Vale* was that the complete protection which the unions thought that Parliament had given them in the 1870s had been swept aside by the courts, and effective trade union activity became virtually impossible. Once again the unions decided to use their growing political strength to persuade Parliament to give them the complete legal protection which they thought they needed and deserved, and in 1906 these tactics were entirely successful. The Trade Disputes Act of that year completely satisfied the trade union demands and provided even greater legal immunity than they thought they had been given in 1875.

Section 1 of this Act removed the risk to trade unions of an action for civil conspiracy in trade disputes, thus reversing *Quinn* v *Leathem*. Section 3 gave persons acting in trade disputes immunity from procuring breaches of contracts of employment; and Section 4 gave trade unions complete immunity from all torts committed by them, either in a trade dispute or at any other time. It was of this clause that the Webbs wrote that it gave the unions 'an extraordinary and unlimited immunity, however great may be the damage caused, and however unwarranted the act, which most lawyers, as well as all employers, regard as nothing less than monstrous'.[26]

Thus the 1906 Act, which reflected the political power of the unions, was of considerable significance for those wishing to impose a closed shop. But the common law, too, soon began to develop in favour of the unions. In *White* v *Riley*[27] an action for conspiracy to injure in a closed shop case was dismissed not merely by references to the 1906 Act, but also by reference to the common law doctrine of action in defence of trading interests. Three years later, in a similar case, the judge found in favour of a closed shop agreement and relied entirely on common law principles.[28] Subsequent decisions[29] upheld and developed this public policy, so that by 1964 McCarthy could write:

> Any man may refuse to work with another who is not a member of a specified trade union, and may persuade others to do likewise. Any man, or group of men, may threaten to strike if non-members are not removed. Such acts are legal, *and would be so if the Act of 1906 were repealed.*[30] (italics provided)

In other words, the development of the common law in favour of the enforcement of the closed shop meant that by 1964 the statutory immunities of the 1906 Act were unnecessary.

But it must be remembered that if the common law allowed the enforcement of the closed shop, it also allowed an employee to be dismissed instantly, without any redress, for joining a trade union. The strong tradition of 'voluntarism' or legal abstention, in British industrial relations meant that trade unions had been unwilling to petition the state for a statutory right to trade union membership. In other words there was a balance, even if it was a rough and ready balance, between the right to join and the right not to join a union. All this was to change in the 1970s.

Rookes v *Barnard* and the Trade Disputes Act 1965

The decision of the House of Lords in the famous case of *Rookes* v *Barnard*[31] 'drove what counsel called "a coach and four" through the Trade Disputes Act of 1906 by extending the common law of tort again'.[32] The plaintiff had lost his job because he had left the union which had a closed shop agreement with the employer. The other employees, under the leadership of the three defendants, had informed the employer that they would refuse to work alongside the plaintiff. The threat to strike was held to be a threat to break the contracts of employment, and this on the particular ground that a no-strike understanding between the union and the employer was admitted to be incorporated in those contracts. In other words it was held that the defendants were liable for the tort of civil intimidation, without having threatened to commit either a crime or a tort, by reason of having threatened to break a contract. It has been argued that in legal terms *Rookes* v *Barnard* was 'a case about the "right to strike", not just about the "closed shop"',[33] and that the decision of the House of Lords 'knocked the bottom out of the certainty of the right to strike and to take other industrial action'.[34] How did the newly elected Labour government react to this judgement? In two particular ways. First, it swiftly mended the hole which had been made in the legal umbrella of the Trade Disputes Act 1906 by passing the Trade Disputes Act 1965. Thus once again there was no doubt that it was not unlawful to threaten a strike or call one to impose a closed shop. But secondly, the government conceded the need for a thorough consideration of the state of labour relations. It therefore decided to appoint a Royal Commission to examine these problems on a longer term basis and to make recommendations for changes in the law in due course.

References

1   Webb, S. and B., *Industrial Democracy*, Longmans Green, 1902 edn., p.214.
2   Ibid., p.215.
3   Ibid., p.214.
4   For estimates of early membership see Webb, S. and B., *History of Trade Unionism*, 1920 edn., appendix vi, pp. 744-50.
5   Sources: up to and including 1970 see Price, R. and Bain, G.S., 'Union Growth Revisited: 1948-1974 in Perspective', *British Journal of Industrial Relations*, vol. xiv, no.3, November 1976. The figures for 1975 and 1978 are taken from the relevant issues of the *Department of Employment Gazette*, maintaining continuity with the earlier figures as far as possible.
6   McCulloch, J.R., *A Treatise on the Circumstances which Determine the Rate of Wages and the Condition of the Labouring Classes*, G. Routledge, 2nd edn., 1854, p.78.
7   Ibid., p.91.
8   Citrine, N.A., *Trade Union Law*, Stevens and Sons 1960, p.10.
9   Majority Report, p.xv.
10   Minority Report, p.xlviii.
11   Webb, S. and B., *History of Trade Unionism*, 1920 edn., p.295.
12   Ibid.
13   Ibid., p.296.
14   Ibid., p.297.
15   Majority Report, p.xx.
16   Ibid., p.xviii.

17   Ibid., p.xx.
18   *R. v Bunn* (1872) 12 Cox c.c.87.
19   Carrothers, A.W.R., *Collective Bargaining Law in Canada*, p.57, quoted in Kahn-Freund, O., *Labour and the Law,* Stevens and Sons, 2nd edn. 1977, p.229.
20   Grunfeld, C., *Trade Unions and the Individual in English Law*, Institute of Personnel Management 1963, p.7.
21   (1892) A.C. 25.
22   (1898) A.C. 1.
23   (1901) A.C. 495.
24   Citrine, N.A., op.cit., p.16.
25   (1901) A.C. 426.
26   Webb, S. and B., op.cit., p.606.
27   (1921) 1. Ch.1.
28   *Reynolds* v *the Shipping Federation* (1924) 1. Ch.28.
29   Especially *Crofter Hand Woven Harris Tweed* v *Veitch* (1942) A.C. 435.
30   McCarthy, W.E.J., op.cit., p.214.
31   (1964) A.C. 1129.
32   Wedderburn, K.W., *The Worker and the Law*, Penguin Books 1965, p.261.
33   Ibid., p.263.
34   Ibid., p.273.

3 The Donovan Commission and the Industrial Relations Act 1971

The primacy of voluntary action, or the abstention by the state from direct interference, is often regarded as the cardinal feature of British labour relations. But by the early 1960s, partly as a consequence of the country's poor economic performance and an increase in the number of unofficial strikes, voluntarism in labour relations was increasingly being called into question. It was in these circumstances that in 1965 the Labour government established a Royal Commission, with Lord Donovan as chairman, to investigate trade unions and employers' associations. The Commission reported in 1968 and its comments and recommendations on the closed shop were included in the chapter in the report entitled 'Safeguards for Individuals in Relation to Trade Unions'.[1]

Here the arguments for and against the closed shop were briefly considered and it was stated that

> the closed shop as it operates at present is not always in the best interests either of workers or of the community as a whole. It is liable from time to time to cause substantial injustice to individuals from which they have no effective means of redress. It also contributes to a system of training which is out of date and inadequate to the country's needs.[2]

The report went on to say that 'it might be argued on these grounds that the closed shop should be prohibited', but in the next four paragraphs this policy was rejected for a variety of reasons. It was first argued that to prohibit the closed shop would frustrate the public policy of promoting the development of collective bargaining. Then it was said that a ban would be ineffective because less than a fifth of the workers in closed shops were covered by formal agreements and in any case many of these would continue on an informal basis. Finally, questions were raised about how non-unionists would be compensated for loss of their jobs where a majority refused to work with them and how legal action could be taken against such a majority. In this way the Commission came to the conclusion that it would be wrong to ban the closed shop. Instead they argued that 'it is better to recognise that under proper safeguards a closed shop can serve a useful purpose and to devise alternative means of overcoming the disadvantages which accompany it';[3] and they went on to make the astonishingly naive claim that because their other proposals would enable more trade unions to organise and bargain without need for the closed shop 'we believe, therefore, that in many cases unions should in time feel able to dispense with its aid'.[4]

The Ministry of Labour (now the Department of Employment) had recommended in its written evidence to the Commission against the banning of the closed shop and had also emphasised the importance of safeguards for individual workers. Four specific cases were mentioned:

1   where workers have conscientious reasons for not belonging to trade unions;

2   where workers, though willing to belong to a trade union, are refused admission or expelled unreasonably;

3   where there are irregularities in the conduct of the affairs of a union operating a closed shop and individual members are adversely affected;

4   where a closed shop is introduced in an establishment where 100 per cent membership does not already exist.[5]

The members of the Donovan Commission accepted that in situations of this kind remedies should be available for individuals who suffered from the operation of a closed shop. They took cases (1) and (4) together and recommended that where a closed shop was introduced the position of those employees who had conscientious or other reasonable grounds for refusing to join the union should be protected. This recommendation was linked with the proposal that in future employees should be given a statutory remedy, through the existing system of industrial tribunals, against unfair dismissal and that the normal remedy should be financial compensation. The Commission thought that an employee who was dismissed for refusing to join a trade union following the introduction of a closed shop

> should be able to succeed against the employer as long as he can show that he has reasonable grounds for refusing to join the union. It is the responsibility of the employer in concluding a closed shop agreement to bear in mind the interests of existing employees who are not in the union and ensure that they are adequately safe-guarded.[6]

As far as refusal to admit an applicant to membership or unreasonable expulsion was concerned (case 2), the Commission accepted that injustice could occur and proposed the establishment of a new, independent review body, consisting of a legally qualified chairman and two trade unionists appointed by the Secretary of State after consultation with the TUC. This body would have the power to declare that an individual whose application for union membership had been unreasonably refused 'should become and remain a member'[7] of that union. And it would have the power to award compensation, payable by the union, to an individual whom the union had unjustifiably expelled. These proposals would also have covered case (3), as those who faced expulsion and possible loss of their jobs for protesting against union malpractices would have been protected by them.

The Commission also looked for a general improvement in the position of individuals through a reform of trade union rule books. As they pointed out,

> It is obviously important that these rules should be clear and unambiguous so that the individual member is able to ascertain without undue difficulty what his rights and obligations are. Trade union rule-books generally fall far short of reaching a satisfactory standard in this respect. In many unions they have been altered piecemeal over the years and have become confused, self-contradictory and obscure.[8]

To remedy this situation the Commission made detailed proposals about desirable changes in trade union rule books, including proper procedures to deal with the admission of new members and the disciplining, and possibly expulsion, of existing members. These proposals would have become effective through the Commission's further recommendation that registration should become obligatory instead of voluntary, giving the Registrar of Trade Unions a measure of control over the content of trade union rules.

McCarthy had written in 1964 that the closed shop should be accepted 'as a growing and justifiable feature of British industrial relations which needs to be subjected to a greater measure of public control to eliminate its abuses and unnecessary use'.[9] The evidence of the Ministry of Labour to the Donovan Commission indicated that the Ministry shared McCarthy's view. It is, then, not surprising that the Commission was persuaded that, despite its disadvantages, it was sensible to allow closed shops to continue provided that individuals were safeguarded against their rigours. But it is one thing for a Royal Commission to make proposals and quite another for a government to turn those proposals into law. In fact the report of the Donovan Commission was rapidly overtaken by political events.

The Industrial Relations Act 1971

As the principle of 'voluntarism' in British labour relations came increasingly under attack in the 1960s a political battle developed about the future course of labour law. On the one side the Conservative Party was calling for a more interventionist policy involving an elaborate legal framework within which trade unions could operate and a greater degree of control over them. These views were published in 1968, just before the Donovan Commission reported, in the policy document 'Fair Deal at Work'. On the other side the Labour government was committed by its establishment of the Donovan Commission to some reform of labour law. But when proposals were published as the White Paper 'In Place of Strife'[10] in 1969 it became clear that reforms which were unacceptable to the unions were out of the question, and the Prime Minister and the Secretary of State for Employment were publicly rebuffed.[11] In the following year the electorate returned a Conservative government. The way was now open for legislation based on the 'Fair Deal at Work' proposals and despite vigorous opposition in Parliament and peaceful demonstrations outside by the TUC the Industrial Relations (IR) Act received the royal assent in August 1971.

One writer described the new Act as 'revolutionary'.[12] Elsewhere it was said to be 'a major philosophical break from the past with regard to the role of law in industrial relations'.[13] It is difficult to disagree with either of these comments, especially if they are applied to that part of the Act which was concerned with the right of the worker to join or not to join a union.

The agency shop

Because the protection of the right not to join a trade union, even when balanced by a statutory right to join, is seen by British trade unionists as a fundamental assault on the ability of employees to organise, it was inevitable that section 5 of the IR Act, which provided these rights, would come under heavy attack. The critics insisted that the section was prompted by an excessively individualistic philosophy which had no place in British industrial relations and was not even welcomed by employers.[14] They also argued that the right not to join a registered or unregistered union was not equally balanced by the right to join because this latter right applied only to registered unions. And yet section 6 and sections 11-16 of the IR Act provided for registered unions to negotiate 'agency shops', very similar to those permitted by the American Taft-Hartley Act of 1947, which meant that the right not to join might, in practice, be seriously qualified. The hope of the government was that formal agency shops, approved either by a majority of the workers eligible to vote or by two-thirds of those actually voting, would replace the largely informal closed shop arrangements which covered several million workers. And as one writer observed, 'For many units of employment outside the two or three million jobs where there is a closed shop now, either by practice or agreement, the agency shop would be a distinct step forward for the unions'.[15]

But the agency shop, like most of the legal immunities and other benefits which the Act provided, was only available to registered unions. Registration was the cornerstone of the Act and the ultimately successful policy of the unions was to destroy the Act by refusing to register. As the TUC Handbook on the Act put it:

> Registration of trade unions has existed since 1871 but the Act incorporates a new system of registration which means surveillance of unions by the state. This registration lies at the heart of the Act. Because of this, Congress has decided that unions affiliated to the TUC should be instructed not to register.

However, the success of the unions' policy does not alter the fact that the intention of the government was to encourage the agency shop, and under an agency shop agreement it was no longer an unfair industrial practice to 'dismiss, penalise or otherwise discriminate' against a worker who refused either to join the union or to pay appropriate contributions to it in lieu of membership or to pay contributions to a charity where he could satisfy the union or an industrial tribunal that he 'genuinely objected on grounds of conscience' to paying contributions to a trade union. As section 6(1) put it:

> Where an agency shop agreement is for the time being in force, a worker to whom the agreement applies shall not have the right, as between himself and the employer to whom the agreement

applies, to refuse to be a member of the trade union with which the agreement was made unless he agrees to pay appropriate contributions to the trade union in lieu of membership of it.

Of course the agency shop was criticised on the grounds that friction would develop between full members and contributing non-members and that it was not an adequate substitute for an existing, comprehensive closed shop. It was also attacked as 'a victory for the individual over the majority since it takes for granted as paramount the right to *dissociate*'.[16] But would those employees who had not previously been trade union members but, following a ballot about the agency shop which had gone in favour of it, were faced with the options described above have agreed with this sentiment? It is perhaps more likely that they would have asked whether the Act provided a genuine right not to join a union, especially after experience showed that the conscience clause would be strictly interpreted by the tribunals, in that there had to be a religious basis for objection to trade unionism. This view was upheld by the National Industrial Relations Court in the first case of its kind which reached it — *Hynds* v *Spillers French Baking Ltd. and S.U.B.A.W.*[17] — when the court stated that grounds of conscience involved a 'belief or conviction based on religion in the broadest sense' rather than personal feeling.

The de-registration policy of the TUC naturally meant that very few agency shops were negotiated. Only two unions of any size — the National Union of Bank Employees and the Bakers' Union — decided that the benefits of the agency shop outweighed the disadvantages of expulsion from the TUC and the consequent risk of poaching of their members by TUC unions. NUBE signed agency shop agreements with the Yorkshire Bank and the Trustee Savings Bank, both of which led to significant increases in membership. The Bakers' Union signed agreements with the two major employers' federations and several smaller non-federated bakeries and the increase in membership was dramatic. 'In 1971, membership fell by 2,313; in 1972, after the agency shop agreements were signed and activated, membership rose by 4,002 to 50,473.'[18] What about the charge that the provision for contributing non-members and conscientious objectors would undermine the ability of trade unions to organise properly and to negotiate from a position of strength? The figures speak for themselves. Out of 13,600 members covered by NUBE's agreements with the Yorkshire Bank and the Trustee Savings Bank there were 26 contributing non-members and around 50 conscientious objectors. And it was reported that 'throughout the baking industry, all employees in agency shops appear to be full members of the union'.[19] These figures led to the conclusion that 'there is no evidence that the existence of contributing non-members or conscientious objectors undermined their authority *vis-à-vis* either the employers or their members'.[20] Thus the limited experience of NUBE and the Bakers' Union suggested that agency shops could have provided a significant boost to trade union membership and organising ability.

The provision for agency shops significantly modified the right not to join a union. Sections 17-18 and Schedule 1 of the Act, which allowed 'approved closed shops' in certain circumstances, extinguished that right altogether apart from those who could prove conscientious objection. But this was an exceptional arrangement which also applied only to registered trade unions. First, an application for an approved closed shop had to be supported jointly by the union and the employer. Then the Commission on Industrial Relations had to investigate the application and report in favour of it on the basis of criteria laid down in Schedule 1,5. Finally the National Industrial Relations Court had to give its approval. Parlaiment had made this concession as a result of intensive lobbying by the actors' union, Equity, and the National Union of Seamen. These two unions felt the need for this kind of union security so strongly that they chose to remain registered in defiance of the TUC's instructions and their applications to organise closed shops had both been approved by 1973.

The attitude of employers to section 5

Given that the policy of non co-operation by the unions rendered much of the IR Act inoperative, the question of employer attitudes to section 5 must now be explored. How did employers react to the right not to join a trade union and how effective was that right in practice?

Two major surveys of management attitudes were carried out after the Act had been in operation for nearly two years. Weekes et al. surveyed 77 of *The Times* top 1,000 companies, 14 nationalised industries and 13 employers' associations;[21] and the Department of Employment surveyed some 300 organisations, generally the larger and more progressive companies in Britain.[22] Admittedly the Department warned that the data coming out of their survey were 'impressionistic and not easily subject to precise quantitative analysis', but the fact that its results were very similar to those of the other survey suggests that they contained a good deal of the truth.

Two of the main findings of the Department of Employment report were (a) that the main preoccupation of managements has been to avoid the consequences of the Act rather than put it to positive use and (b) that the Act's provisions on closed shops have had little effect. And in the body of the report it was stated that 'by all accounts the closed shop situation remains very much as it was before the Act, with management and unions generally sharing in a tacit understanding that the status quo should be maintained'. However, that is not to say that management made no response at all to the introduction of the right not to join a union. Two-thirds (i.e. about 200) of the organisations surveyed by the Department had previously developed either formal closed shops or informal 100 per cent shops covering some of their employees and 40 per cent of these organisations claimed to have abandoned the closed shop. But this abandonment

> usually meant written evidence pertaining to it (the closed shop) rather than the institution itself. The others admitted to actively trying to preserve the closed shop where it already existed. Although a few managers mentioned that they would agree with the principle behind section 5 of the Act, they usually added that it was simply not operational. In fact, most managers who had previously entered into closed shop arrangements saw positive advantages in maintaining them. These included the elimination of union rivalry, greater union discipline and the ensured implementation of agreements.[23]

Weekes et al. were even more confident about the determination of employers to circumvent the new right not to join a union:

> Every manager whom we interviewed, who had a direct responsibility for collective bargaining, whether in the private or in the public sector, wanted to preserve the status quo where there were closed shops. No company at any level issued direct instructions to the contrary.[24]

The evidence from the two surveys that a large majority of employers who had previously operated closed shops found the new section 5 right an embarrassment and did their utmost to circumvent it is overwhelming. Most of them preferred to evade the law, accepting that their attempts to maintain closed shops would sometimes cause them difficulties and expense.

The difficulties could be caused either by new recruits who refused to join the union or by existing employees who might either deliberately resign from their union as a matter of principle or simply let their membership lapse and were then unwilling to make up the arrears. Before the Act new recruits could have been informed bluntly that union membership was a condition of employment. This was now illegal. A policy of 'active encouragement' had to be substituted for one of 'explicit insistence', but it was relatively easy to weed out, at the interview stage, applicants who showed any reluctance to join a union after their appointment to a job. There were plenty of other grounds on which they could be rejected.

Section 20 of the IR Act obliged employers to give all employees a written note about their new right to join or not to join a union. This might have been expected to cause a number of resignations, but in the event fears on this score proved groundless. The unions responded by pressing more employers to introduce the check-off, and as a result of this pressure there was a development of a trend which had originated in the early 1960s.

Cases arising under section 5 and related sections

The joint efforts of unions and employers to frustrate the implementation of the right not to join a union was one of the reasons why the number of section 5 applications to industrial tribunals was very small during 1972 and 1973 (the only two full years in which the Act was supposed to have the force of law) and the number of successful applications even smaller. Table 3.1 illustrates the position.

Table 3.1
Section 5 Applications to industrial tribunals 1972-73

	Section 5(1)(a) Right to be a union member	Section 5(1)(b) Right not to be a union member	Section 5(1)(c) Right to take part in union activities
Conciliated and non-conciliated withdrawals	83	58	86
Conciliated agreement or compensation	20	16	15
Tribunal dismissal of application	59	22	52
Tribunal declaration of rights or compensation	12	25	11
Other or not known	2	–	–
Total	176	121	164

Source: Table compiled by the Department of Employment and reprinted in Industrial Relations Review and Report no.84, July 1974, p.10.

The table shows that altogether 121 employees made formal use of the right not to join a union. Of that number 16 achieved agreement or compensation at the conciliation stage and 25 received a declaration of rights or compensation from a tribunal decision. The tiny number of section 5(1)(b) applications indicates not that there were few infringements of this right, but that it was very rarely exercised. This was in marked contrast to the use of the new right not to be unfairly dismissed, which was exercised by 14,547 applicants in the period 1972-73.

In those few cases which were taken to the tribunals and the courts, and in which it was decided that an individual's right not to join a union had been infringed, the immediate question which arose was 'what could the law do for a worker whose colleagues refused to work with him?' Certain statements by the chairmen of the tribunals and the National Industrial Relations Court (the appeal court from the tribunals) indicated that these lawyers understood the difficult realities of industrial life. For example in *Jones* v *Vauxhall Motors Ltd.*[25] the applicant, a non-unionist, sought only a declaration of his right to be offered overtime like other employees. The employer's reason for not offering Jones overtime was simply that his colleagues had refused to work overtime with him. In granting the declaration the tribunal expressed relief that Jones had sought only a declaration because it felt that an order directing the company to offer him work could lead only to the situation of his working alone.

However, the other cases concerned with the right not to be a union member pale into insignificance in comparison with the Langston case, which was the longest running of any under the IR Act.[26] Joseph Langston was a welder who had worked for Rootes Ltd. and their successors, Chrysler U.K. Ltd., for many years at the Ryton car assembly plant in Coventry. He had been a member of the AEU, later the AUEW, since 1927, but had had several skirmishes with shop stewards before he finally resigned from his union in September 1972, insisting that he was protected by the IR Act. His workmates thought otherwise, and Langston was sent home on full pay following the threat of strike action. Langston's case went first to an industrial tribunal in Birmingham, then to the National Industrial Relations Court, from there to the Appeal Court and finally arrived back at the NIRC after Chrysler had dismissed Langston and compensation for unfair dismissal had been agreed.

During this final stage of the case Sir John Donaldson, president of the NIRC, had to face the fundamental question of whether or not he could recommend or order Chrysler to take Langston back. In the end he gave section 1 of the Act, which stated that it should 'have effect for the purpose of promoting good industrial relations', precedence over the right not to be a trade union member contained in section 5(1)(b), arguing that 'the plain fact is that no industrial tribunal could possibly, in the general climate which exists, recommend that Chrysler, as good employers, ought to take you back'. Weekes et al. remarked that this decision of Sir John Donaldson 'confirmed what employers had told us — that as a last resort some managements were willing to pay unfair dismissal compensation rather than break up long-established closed shops'.[27]

The consequences of the IR Act

In the face of determined collusion between employers and trade unions to preserve closed shops where they already existed, the law on its own proved incapable of providing an effective right to refuse to be a trade union member. Naturally after 1971 employers had to be wary of forming new closed shops which could have involved them in numerous claims for compensation. But a survey conducted in 1978 indicated that 10 per cent of closed shops for manual workers and 15 per cent for non-manual workers actually started in the period 1971-73 when the IR Act supposedly safeguarded the right not to join a union.[28] It is known that the closed shop was increasing its coverage between 1968 and 1971 in some industries, for example engineering,[29] and it is, therefore, possible that the passage of the IR Act slowed down the rate of increase. But the evidence indicates that the IR Act neither broke up existing closed shops nor prevented the introduction of new ones.

The IR Act and other safeguards for individuals

The section 5 right not to join a union was at the heart of the attempt by those who drafted the IR Act to safeguard individuals. If an individual has an effective right not to join a trade union he has complete protection against undesirable trade union coercion. But the Donovan Commission had suggested that other kinds of safeguards were necessary. Their criticism of trade union rule books and their proposals for improvements have already been mentioned. But little has yet been said about another proposal by the Commission which was incorporated into the IR Act and was to be of considerable significance for the individual who wished to contract out of a closed shop once the Act had been repealed in 1974. This was the recommendation that statutory machinery should be introduced so that all employees would have an effective remedy — normally compensation — against 'unfair dismissal'. Cases of unfair dismissal should be speedily dealt with by the industrial tribunals, which had been established in 1964 and already dealt with cases under the Redundancy Payments Act 1965. This proposal was accepted by the Labour government in 1969 and also incorporated into the IR Act. It was then, a bi-partisan policy and the only major innovation of the IR Act which remained in force when the Act was repealed. What exactly did the Act provide as far as unfair dismissal and the improvement of trade union rules was concerned?

Unfair dismissal

Sections 22-32 of the Act dealt specifically with the matter of unfair dismissal. It was provided that 'in every employment to which this section applies every employee shall have the right not to be unfairly dismissed by his employer; and accordingly, in any such employment, it shall be an unfair industrial practice for an employer to dismiss an employee unfairly' (section 22(1)). Section 24 laid down the reasons which could justify dismissal and placed the onus on the employer to prove that his reason was a good one, for example misconduct, redundancy or refusal to contribute to a union if an agency shop was in force. But the sections which followed excluded a large number of employees from the new right. For example there was a two-year qualification period of continuous employment for most dismissals and over 80 per cent of all dismissals occurred in the first two years of service.[30] Thus in practice only a small minority of those actually dismissed were given the right to complain of unfair dismissal. However, when the IR Act was repealed but this right was maintained and extended, questions were bound to arise about the fairness of the dismissal of an employee for non-membership of a trade union.

Rights for trade union members

The TUC is reluctant to take any notice of criticism from outside the trade union movement. But the fact that there were two leading trade unionists on the Donovan Commission perhaps helped to provoke a response by the General Council to the comments of the Commission about the inadequacy of trade union rule books. A detailed questionnaire about their existing rules and practice was sent to all TUC affiliated unions late in 1968 and after the completed questionnaires had been analysed the General Council recommended to the 1969 Congress that union rules should observe certain principles in relation to the admission and disciplining of members.[31] It was left to individual unions to implement these recommendations in their own time. This voluntary process was rudely overtaken by section 65 and schedules 4 and 5 of the IR Act which together would, it was hoped, establish certain basic standards for trade union rules, especially those concerning the admission, disciplining and expulsion of members, the election of officers and the holding of ballots. But schedule 4 also contained certain requirements for unions to spell out in their rules their organisational structure and pattern of authority. For example paragraph 10 stated that 'the rules must specify any body by which, and any official by whom, instructions may be given to members of the organisation on its behalf for any kind of industrial action, and the circumstances in which any such instructions may be so given'. Obligations of this kind meant that the unions were just as unremittingly hostile to section 65 and schedules 4 and 5 as they were to other parts of the Act. The trigger mechanism for introducing these new standards was the process of registration, and the Registrar had to be satisfied that the rules met the new standards laid down in the Act. But because most trade unions declined to register these provisions were as ineffective as the Act as a whole.

The Donovan Commission had made some modest proposals about the rights of trade union members in 1968. The attempt by a Labour government to implement those proposals through legislation was destroyed by the unions in 1969 and the repeal of the IR Act in 1974 meant that the more ambitious scheme of a Conservative government had suffered the same fate. Would the government now accept that it was impossible to impose reforms of this kind on the trade unions from outside? In the chapters which follow an attempt will be made to answer this question and to describe the closed shop policies which followed the repeal of the IR Act.

References

1   Report of the Royal Commission on Trade Unions and Employers' Associations 1968, Cmnd. 3623, HMSO, chapter X, pp. 160-76.
2   Ibid., p.162.
3   Ibid., p.163.
4   Ibid., p.164.
5   Ibid.
6   Ibid., p.152.
7   Ibid., p.166.
8   Ibid., p.169.
9   McCarthy, W.E.J., op.cit., p.279.
10   Cmnd. 3888, HMSO, 1969.
11   This episode was fully documented by Peter Jenkins in *The Battle of Downing Street*, Charles Knight 1970.

12   Paterson, P., *An Employer's Guide to the Industrial Relations Act*, Kogan Page 1971, p.13.

13   Thomson, A.W.J. and Engleman, S.R., *The Industrial Relations Act, A Review and Analysis*, Martin Robertson 1975, p.2.

14   See especially Wedderburn, K.W., 'Labour Law and Labour Relations in Britain', *British Journal of Industrial Relations*, July 1972, p.270.

15   Macbeath, I., *The Times Guide to the Industrial Relations Act*, Times Newspapers, p.63.

16   Wedderburn, K.W., op.cit., p.283.

17   (1974) S.L.T. 191.

18   Weekes, B., Mellish, M., Dickens, L. and Lloyd, J., *Industrial Relations and the Limits of the Law*, Blackwell 1975, p.52.

19   Ibid., p.54.

20   Ibid.

21   Attitudes towards the closed shop from this survey were reported in Weekes, B. et al., op.cit., pp 41-50.

22   The report of this survey was printed in full in *Industrial Relations Review and Report*, nos 83 and 84, July 1974.

23   *Industrial Relations Review and Report*, no.83, July 1974, p.11.

24   Weekes, B. et al., op.cit., p.42.

25   (1972) ITR 250.

26   *Langston v AUEW* (1973) ICR 211; (1974) ICR 180; *Langston v AUEW* (No.2) ICR (1974) 510. This case has been discussed at length by various commentators. See especially Weekes, B. et al., op.cit., pp. 58-61; Thomson, A.W.J. and Engleman, S.R., op.cit., pp. 59-60; Kahn-Freund, O., 'The Industrial Relations Act 1971 — Some Retrospective Reflections', *Industrial Law Journal*, 1974, pp. 194-9; and Hepple, B.A., 'The Right to Work at One's Job', *Modern Law Review*, November 1974, pp. 681-4.

27   Weekes, B. et al., op.cit., p.61.

28   Hart, M., 'Why Bosses Love the Closed Shop', *New Society*, 15 February 1979, p.352.

29   Weekes, B. et al., op.cit., p.39.

30   Ibid., p.26.

31   TUC Report 1969, pp 141-4.

4 The Trade Union and Labour Relations Acts 1974 and 1976

Mr Heath's Conservative government was brought down by a combination of economic and labour relations problems in February 1974. It was replaced by a Labour administration which did not have an over-all majority in the House of Commons and was not, therefore, in a position to dictate entirely the shape of new legislation. Thus the Act which repealed the 1971 Industrial Relations Act — the Trade Union and Labour Relations Act 1974 — contained amendments of which the government and the unions strongly disapproved. The government found this situation intolerable. Mr Wilson, the Prime Minister, called another general election in October 1974 and emerged with an overall majority of three seats in the House of Commons. The new government was, therefore, in a position to reshape TULRA 1974 and it immediately presented an amending Bill — the Trade Union and Labour Relations (Amendment) Bill — to achieve this end. Despite its modest size of only five pages, the Bill took 17 months to make its stormy way through Parliament, reflecting the fact that, in the opinion of one commentator, 'it treated us to yet another dose of ideological asseveration reminiscent of the post-Donovan period, reviving arguments which might otherwise have been quietly interred'.[1] Much of the parliamentary opposition was centred on that part of the Bill which made it more difficult for non-members to resist union membership when a closed shop was being introduced. It was widely thought that this sub-clause contained a serious threat to the freedom of the press.[2] But eventually, after the need for a voluntary charter about the freedom of the press had been conceded, the government had its way. The Act came into force in 1976 and for four years the law which governed the closed shop in Britain was the TULRA 1974 as amended by the TULR(A)A 1976 (hereafter simply referred to as TULRA).[3]

The 1976 Amendment Act was of some importance, but the foundation of the new law relating to the closed shop was laid by the 1974 TULRA. What did it provide? Section 1 of the Act repealed the 1971 Act and then re-enacted certain parts of it, including those sections which contained the right not to be unfairly dismissed. Thus the statutory right not to be a trade union member disappeared, but the right to join a union and take part in its activities, first introduced in 1971, was maintained, in that dismissal for exercising this right was (and still is) automatically unfair (technically 'an inadmissible reason').[4] Where it is alleged that these rights have been infringed, it is for the employer to prove why he dismissed an employee and especially that none of the main reasons was 'inadmissible'.

This right for employees to join a union and take part in its activities applies to all unions, whether an employer recognises them or not. As Kahn-Freund has indicated it can create 'at least potentially, an explosive situation'.[5] It can also place the employer in an impossible position, in that he 'may find himself threatened by a strike or other industrial action on the part of one group if he tolerates organising activities of the other and by that other group if he refuses to do so'.[6] And the fact that the law specifically prevents the employer from having a right of recourse against those exercising the pressure on him can only add to his misery.[7] These circumstances obviously acted as an incentive to the employer to eliminate the possibility of an inter-union dispute by negotiating a 'union membership agreement' (closed shop) with the recognised union or unions; especially when the 1974 Act specifically provided that where a UMA existed dismissal for non-membership of a specified union was fair, subject only to protection for certain objectors. Exactly how did TULRA 1974 provide for closed shops?

The right not to be unfairly dismissed, first introduced in 1971, was re-enacted. That immediately raised the question: could an employee be fairly dismissed for leaving his union where a closed shop existed? This question was answered in schedule 1 para. 6(5) of the Act which had to be read together with the definition of a 'union membership agreement' contained in section 30. The purport of these provisions was reasonably clear. Where an employer could show that a union membership agreement, i.e. a formal or informal closed shop, existed between himself and one or more independent trade unions, non-membership of a union was to be a good reason for dismissal without compensation unless the employee could prove a religious objection to joining any trade union or provide 'any reasonable grounds' for objecting to membership of a particular trade union. This last exception was one of the amendments inserted against the wishes of the minority Labour government.

Thus the 1974 Act permitted, but did not of course compel, every kind of closed shop subject only to the two exceptions already mentioned. There is little doubt that the new legislation positively encouraged employers to negotiate union membership agreements and to ensure that they conformed to the law. As Weekes put it, 'It would seem that many managements, particularly in the public sector, are determined to avoid the loss of unfair dismissal cases and in consequence intend to firmly enforce the categories of membership negotiated as part of union membership agreements'.[8] However, as soon as the Labour government had an adequate majority, it took steps to alter the 1974 TULRA. What was the effect of the 1976 Amendment Act?

It made two significant changes, the second of which was highly controversial. First, the definition of a union membership agreement was altered to ensure that agreements or arrangements which tolerated a few non-unionists would still be valid. Instead of having to have 'the effect of requiring the terms and conditions of employment of every employee of that class to include a condition that he must be or become a member of the union . . . ' a UMA now had to have 'the effect *in practice* of requiring the employees for the time being of the class to which it relates (whether or not there is a condition to that effect in their contract of employment) to be or become a member of the union . . . '. At the same time the definition was widened so that instead of having to be 'a member of the union or one of the unions which is or are parties to the agreement or arrangement or of another *appropriate* independent trade union' an employee could be a member of 'another *specified* independent trade union' and the word 'specified' was extended to include a union accepted by the parties as equivalent to the specified union. In addition, the parties could identify employees of a class 'by reference to any circumstances or characteristics whatsoever', so that particular groups (e.g. newspaper editors) might be omitted from the relevant class.

Complementary to the first of these changes to the definition of a UMA was the elimination of the word 'all' from para. 6(5) of Schedule 1 of TULRA 1974. It was this sub-paragraph which made dismissal for non-membership of a union fair where a UMA existed. Instead of an employer having to show that it was the practice, in accordance with a UMA, for 'all the employees of that employer or all employees of the same class as the dismissed employee to belong to a specified independent trade union or to one of a number of specified independent trade unions', he now only had to show that it was the practice, in accordance with a UMA, for 'employees for the time being' of the same class to be members of a specified trade union. It seems clear that the changes in the definition of a UMA, together with the elimination of the word 'all' from para. 6(5) of Schedule 1 of TULRA 1974, meant that Parliament intended that closed shops could be operated more flexibly in future; in other words, it would be possible for a small minority of employees to remain outside the union where a UMA existed without making dismissal for non-membership unfair. But how large could such a small minority be? In its attempt to reintroduce a measure of flexibility into the closed shop, Parliament had also introduced a considerable element of uncertainty which presumably the tribunals were expected to resolve. Inevitably this would lead to a good deal of confusion and argument about the extent of organisation required to establish a valid closed shop.

It seems likely that the principal aim of these changes in the definition of a closed shop was to ensure that it covered the wide variety of British closed shops, which included a rapidly growing number of written agreements as well as unwritten, informal arrangements. But an important effect of the changes was that UMAs could be operated somewhat more flexibly without jeopardising their validity.

The second change was seen by those who opposed the Act as a fundamental threat to individual liberty, so that one writer described the new Act as 'the greatest disaster which has befallen liberty in my lifetime, a defeat for freedom comparable to those the Stuart Kings attempted to inflict — and failed'.[9] Section 1(e) of the Act repealed the words 'or on any reasonable grounds to being a member of a particular trade union' from the TULRA 1974. The consequence of this change was that the non-unionist who was unwilling to join the union after a closed shop had been introduced could find himself faced with fair dismissal unless he could prove that he genuinely objected 'on grounds of religious belief to being a member of any trade union whatsoever'. As one commentator remarked:

> It is clear that the restriction of non-membership to those who can adduce religious belief virtually rules out objection to the closed shop under the Act for the great mass of workers, for even amongst the diminishing numbers of the 'religious' in a secularist society there are very few who can found an objection to trade union membership upon scriptural or other canonical sources.[10]

Thus, to alter the 1974 Act in this way was to remove all statutory protection from those who objected to trade union membership on conscientious or other 'reasonable' grounds. It is perfectly true that employers were still free to insist that the rights of those who objected to trade union membership on grounds other than those of religious belief (e.g. conscientious objectors who were atheists or agnostics) should be protected. And a majority of written agreements which were negotiated between 1974 and 1980 included a protection clause for non-unionists wider than the statutory minimum of religious belief. Nevertheless, few would deny that the extent of the protection for individual objectors to the closed shop which Parliament deems to be necessary is of fundamental importance. Nor would it be denied that there is a difference in principle between Parliament laying down an adequate degree of protection by statute against the infringement of individual liberties and providing an extremely narrow statutory protection, i.e. religious belief, and permitting employers to be more generous to objectors. But was it totally unreasonable of the Labour government to wish to repeal the somewhat vague phrase which allowed an individual to remain a non-unionist if he objected 'on any reasonable grounds to being a member of a particular union'?

Statutory protection for the objector to trade union membership

Where the closed shop is a legal arrangement there is general agreement that some protection must be provided for the employee who has genuine moral or conscientious reasons for not joining a union, especially when the introduction of a closed shop might lead to the dismissal of a long-service employee. Even the trade unions in Britain have publicly recognised this need and in 1979 the TUC claimed that 'for many years unions, voluntarily and without any legal requirement, have made provision for conscientious objectors to be excluded from the closed shop provisions, but in some cases on the understanding that they make an equivalent payment to charity'.[11] But there is no agreement about how broad the statutory protection for the individual ought to be and it seems likely that the courts will usually have considerable difficulty in interpreting those words in a statute which attempts to provide a degree of protection.

The wording of that part of the 1974 TULRA which performed this function (already quoted above) was criticised by the chairman of an industrial tribunal when he gave his decision in the case of *Sarvent* v *Central Electricity Generating Board*.[12] In this case the six applicants had been dismissed from their employment at Ferrybridge C power station for not being members of one of the four unions signatory to the NJIC agreement for electricity supply manual workers. Instead they all belonged to the Electricity Supply Union, a small organisation not recognised by the employer. The tribunal decided that the applicants had been unfairly dismissed on the ground that the UMA had not been properly enforced, i.e. the employer had failed to establish that it was the practice for all the employees of the same class as the applicants to belong to one of the NJIC unions party to the agreement. Thus the decision did not hinge on the question of whether the applicants could show that they genuinely objected 'on any reasonable grounds to being a member of a particular union' (there was no objection on grounds of religious belief). However, because this phrase was used by the applicants to assist their case the respondents pressed the tribunal to say something about it and the chairman acceded to this request. He referred to 'the extremely difficult problem' of what constituted an objection 'on any reasonable grounds' and went on to say that:

> there is no guidance whatsoever from Parliament on what constitute such grounds and we all three strongly resent being given the task of deciding this question . . . Parliament should say what are reasonable grounds (e.g. religion, conscience or any other specified reason) and then a Tribunal after hearing evidence can make their findings of fact and say whether the statutory grounds exist.[13]

The decision in the *Sarvent* case was published in January 1976. Within two months the 1976 TULR(A)A had become law and the exemption which had caused the Leeds Tribunal some difficulty had been repealed.

Proving the 'practice' of the closed shop under TULRA

TULRA 1974, together with the decision in the *Sarvent* (Ferrybridge) case, encouraged employers to enforce the closed shop much more strictly. They had to establish 'the practice' of the closed shop 'for all the employees of that employer or all employees of the same class as the dismissed employee' if they were to avoid paying compensation for unfair dismissal where employees were dismissed for non-membership of a union. How would this be interpreted in the courts? In the *Sarvent* case the tribunal scrutinised in detail the level of union membership among industrial staff at electricity generating stations. They stated that of the 39,000 and more industrial staff 'our impression is that under the system at present employed there could well be 1,000 or more persons who should be members of one of the NJIC unions under their terms of employment and are not members for one reason or another';[14] and they therefore concluded that 'the respondents have not shown that it was the practice in accordance with the union membership agreement for all employees of the same class as the applicants to belong to one of the NJIC unions'.[15] But the rules for establishing the practice were quite deliberately relaxed in TULR(A)A 1976. How would the tribunals interpret the new rules?

This question was temporarily answered by the Employment Appeal Tribunal in January 1978 in the case of *Himpfen* v *Allied Records*.[16] At the critical date 33 out of 42 employees were members of the specified union. Was this a sufficient proportion to establish the practice? In coming to its decision the tribunal quoted the unamended text of para. 6(5) of Schedule 1 of TULRA 1974. Not only that, but they actually emphasised the word 'all', where TULRA had provided that it had to be the practice, in accordance with a UMA, 'for *all* the employees of that employer, that is to say, for *all* employees of the same class as a dismissed employee, to belong to the specified union, or one of the specified unions'.[17] As mentioned earlier, the word 'all' was removed by TULR(A)A 1976, but it seems that the tribunal was unaware of this amendment to the statute. In the same way the EAT went on to consider the statement of the industrial tribunal in the case of *Strover* v *Chrysler (UK) Ltd.*[18] that 'we find the practice is established only if the employer can show that all or almost all employees of the relevant class are members and that the necessary steps are taken to compel any employee to join the relevant trade union if and when it is discovered he is not a member'. They also quoted the judgement of the EAT in the case of *Home Counties Dairies Ltd.* v *Wood*[19] which contained the passage: 'We think that there is sufficient elasticity in the expression "It is the practice for all employees" to allow for the situation where there was one odd man out when the statute came into force and when its provisions fall to be applied', and inferred that the actual number of employees who had become union members was relevant to the question of whether the practice existed. This was a reasonable inference. But both of the cases quoted by the EAT had been decided by reference to TULRA 1974. It was strange that no reference whatever was made to the important amendments contained in TULR(A)A 1976, which had come into effect before the date of dismissal. The considered view of the EAT in the *Himpfen* case was that it was necessary for 'almost all the employees of the relevant class' to be union members on the critical day and that it should be the policy of the company to require the others to join. The tribunal thought that what was 'almost all' of a workforce would depend upon the facts in each case, but in their view 33 out of 44 was not a sufficient proportion. Thus the dismissal in the *Himpfen* case had been unfair.

Decisions of this kind laid a severe obligation on employers to see that UMAs were rigidly enforced, in marked contrast to the 'informal, relaxed closed shop which commonly existed before 1971'[20] and, it would seem, in contrast to the intention of TULR(A)A 1976. It was, then, not very surprising that in a later case an industrial tribunal insisted that TULRA 1974 had been deliberately amended by TULR(A)A 1976 so that closed shops could be operated more flexibly. In the case of *Taylor* v *Co-operative Retail Services Ltd.*[21] a tribunal at Birmingham had to decide whether or not the practice of the closed shop had been maintained when 10 out of 90 milk roundsmen were not members of the specified union (USDAW) on the critical date (the day when notices of dismissal for non-membership were issued). In coming to the decision that the practice was being observed the tribunal pointed out that insofar as the facts in this case were indistinguishable from *Himpfen*, *Himpfen* was binding on them 'save insofar as we may consider that the decision depends upon the misapprehension of the Employment Appeal Tribunal as to the language of section 6(5) as it was in force on the date of dismissal, the 3 September 1976'.[22] They went on to say that they would have reached a different decision on this part of the case if they had had to decide it under the unamended TULRA 1974, and accepted that 10 non-members could not come within the 'one odd man out' principle. But they argued that they had to take into account the important 1976 amendment 'and we think that the amendment does cover just the sort of situation that has arisen in this case. It seems to us that the question that we have to decide is really a question of fact and degree'.[23]

The decision in the *Taylor* case was confirmed by the Employment Appeal Tribunal in October 1980, but leave to appeal was granted and it seems likely that the case will be heard by the Court of Appeal in 1981. It may be, then, that the case will provide a definitive ruling on the meaning of the 'practice' of the closed shop as relaxed by TULR(A)A 1976. But it would seem that by removing the word 'all' from TULRA 1974 Parliament has introduced a considerable element of uncertainty into what exactly constitutes the practice. The EAT argued in the *Taylor* case that it was a question of fact for the industrial tribunal to decide whether a practice of joining a union was established in any particular case. The problem with this approach is that it would lead to a diversity of decisions with the possibility of injustice as between some dismissed non-members and others, according to the view of the tribunal hearing the case. But the only way to avoid the case by case approach is for the tribunals or the courts to provide guidance on what is to be understood by 'the practice'. Such guidance would have to be based on factors which were common to each case, and the most important factor is, perhaps, the ratio of non-members to members on the critical date, the day of dismissal. Before the *Taylor* case the tribunals were clear that 'all or nearly all' of the employees of the same class as the dismissed employee had to be union members. In other words an occasional 'odd man out' who had slipped through the net could be overlooked, although perhaps 99 per cent had to be members. But how far did Parliament extend that flexibility by removing the word 'all'? To 98 per cent or 95 per cent or 90 per cent membership? If justice is to be dispensed in an even-handed way, surely that question will have to be answered sooner or later. And if the courts attempt to answer that question it should be remembered that a percentage minority seems less significant when small numbers are being considered. For example it might be thought that 5 non-members out of a group of 50 employees, or 10 per cent, would not invalidate a closed shop. But in the *Sarvent* case the UMA covered about 40,000 industrial staff. Is it likely that a tribunal would consider that 'the practice' had been established if 4,000 out of a group of 40,000 employees were outside the union, although in percentage terms the number of non-unionists would be the same as in the group of 50?

Another element which the tribunals will now have to take into account is the requirement in para. 37 of the Code of Practice on the Closed Shop that 'closed shop agreements should be operated flexibly and tolerantly and with due regard to the interests of the individuals as well as unions and employers'. It could (and no doubt will) be argued that whatever the intention of Parliament in 1976 the emphasis has now been changed by the Employment Act 1980 and even where the practice has been established dismissal of non-members is unnecessary and unfair.

Where employers, as in the *Taylor* case, quite deliberately determined to establish the practice there was naturally an impact on the minority who preferred not to join a union for conscientious or other reasons. Also the consequence of a disagreement between a member and his union, which could conceivably lead to expulsion from the union, became more serious and the way in which TULRA attempted to deal with this particular problem must now be considered.

Trade union disciplinary rules and the establishment of the independent review committee

The Donovan Commission had been concerned about the unsatisfactory state of the rule books of many trade unions. The Commission pointed out that because technically trade unions were voluntary associations, if the rules were not unlawful and if the body set up to adjudicate upon offences acted within the rules and observed the rules of natural justice 'courts of law . . . have no jurisdiction to review its findings or to mitigate the penalty imposed'.[24] Because expulsion from a trade union could have a serious effect on a member's livelihood, especially where a closed shop existed, and because a trade union disciplinary committee was in effect acting as judge and jury in its own cause, Donovan recommended that trade union members who thought that they had been unfairly penalised 'should have a right of complaint, in the last resort, to an independent review body'.[25] The Commission envisaged a statutory body consisting of three members 'of whom two would be chosen from a panel of trade unionists appointed by the Secretary of State for Employment and Productivity after consultation with the TUC, and one would be a lawyer who would act as chairman'.[26]

This proposal of the Commission, like most of its recommendations, was overtaken by the 1971 IR Act. But the encouragement given by the 1974 TULRA to the development of closed shops meant that it was even more important in 1974 than it had been in 1968. How did the 1974 TULRA attempt to improve trade union rules and prevent the unreasonable exclusion of a would-be member or the unreasonable expulsion of a member?

Sections 5 and 6 of the 1974 TULRA were concerned with these related issues, but it must be remembered that these sections were among those parts of the Act forced upon the unions and a minority Labour government by the opposition in Parliament and that the unions were determined that these provisions should be repealed at the earliest possible moment. Section 5 gave a worker aggrieved by his exclusion or expulsion from a trade union the right to apply to an industrial tribunal for a declaration that he was entitled to be a member of that union. Section 6 specified various conditions which union rules had to meet before the Registrar could enter a union on his list. It was made obligatory for the rules to include a procedure to be followed in cases of expulsion and to provide for an appeals procedure against such a decision. It was also laid down that the rules should not depart from the rules of natural justice.[27]

Trade union officials naturally defend their rules, including their disciplinary rules, as meeting proper standards. They also argue, quite logically, that their aim is to build up the union by attracting new members and that expulsion is only used as a last resort. Thus the opposition of the TUC to these sections of the 1974 TULRA is better explained by its deep-rooted antipathy to outside control over trade union rules and to its conviction that lawyers and the courts tend to side with the individual against the union than by its objection to these particular provisions of the Act in themselves. However, following the general election of October 1974 the TUC view prevailed. TULR(A)A 1976 repealed sections 5 and 6 of TULRA 1974 and the statutory control over trade union rules and protection for the excluded or expelled worker disappeared.

But the Labour government would not accept that the problem of unions expelling members where a closed shop existed, and thereby forcing them out of employment, could be ignored. As a *quid pro quo* for that part of TULR(A)A 1976 which repealed sections 5 and 6 of TULRA 1974 the government exacted a promise from the TUC that it would establish an 'Independent Review Committee' (IRC) and this committee duly came into existence in April 1976, one month after the Amendment Act became law. The nature of this committee and the work which it has done will be considered in some detail in the next chapter.

References

1   Drake, C.D., 'The Trade Union and Labour Relations (Amendment) Bill', *Industrial Law Journal*, 1976, p.2.
2   On this Parliamentary battle see Beloff, N., *Freedom under Foot*, Temple Smith 1976.
3   Most of the provisions of these two Acts relating to the closed shop were consolidated in the Employment Protection (Consolidation) Act 1978, section 58(3). However, the definitions of 'union membership agreement' and 'class' are still to be found in TULRA section 30(1) and (5A).
4   Schedule 1, para. 6(4)(5) and (6) and para. 11(1) of the 1974 TULRA. The current equivalent provisions are to be found in section 58(1) and section 77 of the Employment Protection (Consolidation) Act 1978. The right not to be unfairly dismissed for trade union membership and activities was strengthened by section 53(1) of the Employment Protection Act 1975 which forbade employers to discriminate against employees who were would-be or actual trade unionists.
5   Kahn-Freund, O., *Labour and the Law*, Stevens 1977, p.176.
6   Ibid.
7   Employment Protection (Consolidation) Act 1978, section 25(2). Originally Employment Protection Act 1975, section 55(2).
8   Weekes, B., 'Law and the Practice of the Closed Shop', *Industrial Law Journal*, December 1976, p.222.
9   Johnson, P., 'Towards the Parasite State', *New Statesman*, 3 September 1976, p.299.
10   Drake, C.D., op.cit., p.9.
11   TUC Guides to Negotiating Procedures, Conduct of Disputes, Union Organisation, February 1979, p.20.
12   (1976) IRLR 66.
13   Ibid., para. 62.
14   Ibid., para. 48.

15   Ibid., para. 55.
16   (1978) IRLR 154.
17   Ibid., para. 11.
18   (1975) IRLR 68.
19   (1976) IRLR 380.
20   Weekes, B., op.cit., p.219.
21   Case No. 34231/77. This case has not yet been officially reported, but a report of the decision of the EAT, which heard the case on appeal, was printed in *The Times* on 24 October 1980.
22   Case No. 34231/77, para. 39.
23   Ibid., para. 43.
24   Donovan Report, p.170.
25   Ibid., p.171.
26   Ibid., p.176.
27   For a thorough discussion of the rules of natural justice see Rideout, R., *Principles of Labour Law*, 3rd ed., Sweet and Maxwell 1979, pp. 275-80. Rideout states (p.275) that 'essentially there is only one rule of natural justice. Until a few years ago this might be stated thus "that where a matter is properly required to be subject to a judicial or quasi-judicial process the persons concerned are entitled to a fair hearing before an impartial tribunal"'. See also Kahn-Freund, O., *Labour and the Law*, 2nd ed., Stevens 1977, pp 180-93.

5 Conscientious and religious objection to union membership under TULRA and the work of the Independent Review Committee

The members of the Donovan Commission had been of the view that when an employer dismisses an existing employee who refuses to join a trade union following the introduction of a closed shop 'the employee should be able to succeed against the employer' (in a claim for unfair dismissal) 'so long as he can show that he has reasonable grounds for refusing to join the union'.[1] The Labour government of 1974-79 rejected that recommendation. Once TULR(A)A 1976 had become law the objector's only statutory avenue of escape was convincing evidence that he genuinely objected 'on grounds of religious belief to being a member of any trade union whatsoever'. But it must be remembered that employers could insist on a broader conscience clause in a UMA, and many did so. How then, did the tribunals deal with those applicants who based their appeal on grounds of religious and conscientious objection?

The problem of conscientious objection had first arisen under the IR Act, in which it was provided that where an agency shop had been negotiated those who objected 'on grounds of conscience' to joining a union or paying contributions in lieu could pay equivalent contributions to a charity instead. Few agency shops were implemented, but nevertheless a handful of employees claimed exemption on these grounds. One of them was a Mr Drury, who had been a member of the Bakers' Union from 1964 to 1970 but had then let his membership lapse. The union signed an agency shop agreement with his employer in 1972 and Drury claimed the right, as a conscientious objector, to pay contributions to a charity. The industrial tribunal held that 'where a worker has once been a union member and does not base his claim on religious grounds, his objections to joining a union or paying contributions to it cannot be considered genuine objections on grounds of conscience within the meaning of S.10(2) of the IR Act'.[2]

A somewhat similar case involving an agency shop agreement was heard before the Scottish division of the National Industrial Relations Court.[3] Mr Hynds, who had been a shop steward in the Scottish Union of Bakers, had a disagreement with other union officials and left the union in early 1972. Hynds claimed that from that time onwards he was a 'conscientious objector' as regards union membership, but three witnesses gave evidence that Hynds had stated on more than one occasion that he would rejoin the union if he was reinstated as shop steward. Not only that, but he had attempted to form a rival union in the company after he had left the Bakers' Union. It was, then, not surprising that the court decided that Hynds did not qualify as a conscientious objector to trade unionism. What was most significant about this particular decision was the remark that 'in our opinion "grounds of conscience" necessarily points to and involves a belief or conviction based on religion in the broadest sense as contrasted with personal feeling, however strongly held, or intellectual creed'; and the court went on to cite the decisions in the *Drury* and *Newell*[4] cases as justification for the view that a true conscientious objector is one who objects on religious grounds.

The decisions in the *Drury* and *Hynds* cases suggested that it was difficult, if not impossible, to distinguish between a genuine conscientious objection and a genuine religious objection. If this was a correct view it might be thought that the change made by the 1976 Act — the restriction for exemption from membership to grounds of religious belief — was not a change of any major significance. But what exactly did the words of the statute mean? It was not long before a tribunal was asked to decide that question.

Following the enactment of the 1974 TULRA British Rail negotiated a union membership agreement with three trade unions — the National Union of Railwaymen, the Associated Society of Locomotive Engineers and Firemen and the Transport Salaried Staffs Association. The agreement laid it down that any employee who was in breach of it could be dismissed after 1 November 1975 when the agreement came into effect. At this time the Amendment Act was well on its tortuous way through Parliament and the only exemption which the agreement allowed was the new statutory one of genuine objection on grounds of religious belief to being a member of any trade union whatsoever. Messrs Cave and Cave (father and son), both members of a religious sect called the Christadelphians, claimed that they qualified for exemption on grounds of religious belief. British Rail disagreed and the two men were dismissed. They took their case to a tribunal which unanimously recommended reinstatement.[5] On what grounds was the recommendation based?

Mr Cave senior had worked for British Rail for 26 years. For the first 20 of those years he remained outside a union and non-membership was no bar to his employment. Then in 1970 British Rail decided to implement a closed shop. Mr Cave and his son were both granted exemption from membership on grounds of conscience provided they paid a weekly donation to a charity and this condition was accepted. But in 1975 they were told that they had to prove their objection to membership on grounds of religious belief and they were summoned before an Appeal Panel which consisted of the Industrial Relations Manager of the London Midland Region and one representative from each of the three trade unions. The appeals failed, and as the industrial tribunal pointed out they were foredoomed to fail because British Rail and the unions agreed in advance that exemption on grounds of religious belief would only be granted to those employees who belonged to a religious sect or denomination having a written rule which prohibited trade union membership and made expulsion the penalty for breach of that rule. The Christadelphians had no such written rule, although the tribunal was satisfied that they 'believe it to be their duty as part of their religious belief to hold themselves aloof as far as possible from many of the combinations of men and from some of the institutions which exercise power and compulsion in temporal affairs'. However, the tribunal was unable to accept the interpretation which British Rail had placed on the exemption clause:

> In our opinion the Act quite simply does not exclude any employee from enjoying the right not to belong to a trade union merely because he cannot support his convictions by means of rules whether or not reduced in writing. To bring himself within the exemption an employee need do no more than show that he genuinely objects on grounds of religious belief to being a member of any trade union whatsoever.

Of Cave senior the tribunal was 'satisfied that it is his genuine belief founded in his religion that he ought not to join any trade union'. His son was in the same category and it followed that both dismissals were unfair.

In the light of the decision in the Cave and Cave case British Rail slightly modified its attitude. Three months later, Mr Goodbody, who had 16 years' service with British Rail and had never been a member of a trade union, appealed against unfair dismissal to an industrial tribunal in Exeter on the grounds that his personal interpretation of the scriptures was that God was forbidding him to join a union and to strike for higher wages.[6] The respondents did not challenge the genuineness of Goodbody's claims or that he was a sincerely religious man, but they submitted that a religious belief must be a belief of a religious body as opposed to a purely personal conscience. They claimed that an individual's personal belief was no more than conscience. The tribunal disagreed, holding that the words of the statute imported:

> a subjective or personal test. It is the employee, not the religious community to which he belongs, who must object to union membership on religious grounds; it is the individual's own belief that has to constitute a valid ground for such objection. Had Parliament intended that it is the religious beliefs of the community of which the employee is a member that have to be considered, then they could readily have said so.

The tribunal went on to say that if the above view was wrong, and they had to consider the beliefs of the community, the test imposed by British Rail — that the community must forbid trade union membership — was 'altogether too high'. In Goodbody's case they had not the slightest doubt that 'trade union membership would be a source of acute, deep-seated and continuing disapproval and grave embarrassment to both Mr Goodbody personally and to his fellow members within the Brethren'. Thus on these grounds, too, the tribunal held that Goodbody could object to being a trade union member.

The *Saggers* case, in which British Rail was once again involved, also raised the question of whether it was the religious belief of the individual employee or the sect to which he belonged which had to be taken into consideration.[7] Saggers was a Jehovah's Witness and this sect did not forbid its members to join a union. But the EAT accepted that the belief of an individual could differ from that of his sect and they argued that:

> In such a case if an Industrial Tribunal is convinced that, in spite of the differences between the two, the employee does really and truly believe what he says he believes, then there is no conceptual impossibility about accepting that that is his religious belief.

Thus the EAT rejected the notion that 'belief' had to refer to the religious sect of which the employee was a member.

But in the *Saggers* case the relationship between religious and conscientious objection also had to be considered by the EAT because the industrial tribunal had attached importance to the fact that instead of allowing objection on grounds of conscience, as in the IR Act, TULRA had substituted grounds of religious belief. In giving the decision of the EAT Arnold J. dealt with this matter at some length. He suggested that in 'perhaps the overwhelming majority of cases' there would be no distinction between an objection on grounds of conscience or religious belief; but he insisted that in some cases — for example an acknowledged atheist of strong moral principle or a religious man who 'forms a moral objection to a particular course of action for reasons other than those which inform his religious life' — conscience could direct or forbid a certain course of action 'having been brought to that point of conviction by moral or ethical considerations which do not possess a religious content'. Presumably Parliament also held this view, because if conscientious objection could not be distinguished from objection on grounds of religious belief, there would have been no point in excluding conscientious objection from the 1976 TULR(A)A. That Act was deliberately drafted to allow even the strongest conscientious objector to trade union membership to be dismissed unless he could also prove a religious basis for his objection. It indicated that whatever the trade unions might say about the desirability of protecting the rights of conscientious objectors, they were unwilling in practice to use their influence with a Labour government to achieve this end.

However, where the basic rights of individuals were infringed, as in the British Rail cases, it would be wrong to pin the whole blame on to the government, although the primary responsibility must be theirs. TULRA as amended specifically allowed UMAs to exempt particular classes of employees, and research has shown that a majority of agreements permitted existing non-members to remain outside the union.[8] Even where an agreement, like the British Rail UMA, was rigid in respect of existing non-members it could have incorporated flexibility in other ways, for example by exempting genuine conscientious objectors as well as objectors on grounds of religious belief. Thus where employers like British Rail found themselves in difficulties at the tribunals over religious objectors, those difficulties were largely of their own making. In contrast to the majority of employers, British Rail had negotiated a rigid UMA, containing only the minimum statutory exemption, and had even attempted to define that exemption in an unduly restrictive way.

Perhaps the most surprising feature of the government's determination to remove statutory protection from conscientious objectors was the fact that a comparatively small number of employees were adversely affected. In order to enable a few dozen, or at the most a few hundred, employees to be forced into union membership, the government was willing to provoke a wave of indignation and resentment against its policies. Why is it likely that the number of conscientious objectors would have been small?

The problem of the conscientious objector

The problem of the conscientious objector normally arose only at the time a closed shop was introduced, and it only arose from that minority of UMAs which were rigid, i.e. did not permit existing non-members to remain outside the union.[9] The usual practice under TULRA was for a notice to be posted stating that from a certain date — perhaps four or six weeks later — union membership would be compulsory unless employees could prove a valid objection. Even those who had a deep-rooted objection to membership might understandably have been reluctant to attempt to contract out. It is one thing to have a sincere objection to trade unionism and quite another thing to turn that objection into a coherent case which would stand the scrutiny of an appeal panel or an industrial tribunal. The applicant would probably need evidence from friends or colleagues that he did indeed have a genuine conscientious objection to trade union membership. Remarks made in the *Saggers* case suggested that it would be difficult for an employee who was not a practising member of a religious body to prove that he was a conscientious objector, and the decision in the *Drury* case showed that a conscientious objection would not normally be acceptable unless the employee had never been a trade unionist. In other words, a tribunal would be reluctant to concede that conscience could change or develop. Close consideration of the appeal system, which was usually created and sometimes operated by the managers and trade unionists who negotiated the UMA, would probably suggest that the chances of winning an appeal were slim. The industrial tribunals were intended to provide a quick, impartial and inexpensive way of resolving disputes, but it was two years and nine months from the time Saggers first applied for exemption from the closed shop until the final decision in his case, and many applicants would be helpless without expert legal advice and representation by a lawyer at the hearing.[10]

There were, then formidable obstacles in the way of proving an objection to union membership on grounds of conscience (if the UMA provided for it). Where rigid UMAs were introduced which provided only the minimum statutory exemption, like those negotiated by British Rail or Strathclyde Regional Council, the number of objectors on grounds of religious belief was very small[11] and if the law had also allowed for conscientious objectors it is unlikely that their number would have been much greater.

It could, of course, be argued that the small number of religious objectors indicated that there were very few who objected in principle to trade union membership and that the whole question of extending the statutory protection from religious to conscientious objectors, or to all non-members, was a storm in a teacup. But even those who, like McCarthy and the members of the Donovan Commission, accept the justifiability of the closed shop usually also accept that the non-union employee who feels threatened by the introduction of a closed shop should be protected by the law.[12] And as Baroness Seear pointed out in the debate on the Employment Bill, 'It cannot be said too often that an injustice done to one person is serious and an offence, just as much as an injustice done to 1,000 people. To say that there are not many people who suffer is to show a total misunderstanding of the nature of justice and injustice'.[13]

If Parliament decrees that the closed shop is not unlawful and that an employee may be fairly dismissed for not joining a union when the practice has been established, clearly the extent of the statutory protection given to a non-member at the time a UMA is negotiated becomes an issue of public policy. The narrowing down of that exemption under TULRA to those who objected on grounds of religious belief was seen by many as a scandal which infringed basic human rights and liberties. It led to three dismissed employees of British Rail — Messrs Young, James and Webster — taking the UK government before the European Commission of Human Rights and successfully arguing that their dismissal contravened the European Convention on Human Rights.[14] But by the time the Commission gave their decision in June 1980 a new government had been elected in Britain and a new bill to make fundamental amendments to this part of TULRA[15] was well on its way through Parliament.

The work of the Independent Review Committee

The reasons for the establishment of the IRC were discussed at the end of the last chapter. Something more must now be said about the nature of the committee and its achievements.

The committee's terms of reference are narrow. It exists only 'to consider appeals from individuals who have been dismissed, or given notice of dismissal, from their jobs as a result of being expelled from, or of having been refused admission to, a union in a situation where trade union membership is a condition of employment'.[16] Thus it is specifically concerned with disputes between individuals and trade unions in closed shop cases and has no general jurisdiction over the question of exclusion or expulsion from a trade union.

Another important feature of the IRC is that it has no statutory basis, in contrast to the review body recommended by Donovan. The members[17] were appointed by the TUC, acting in consultation with the Secretary of State for Employment and the chairman of ACAS (the official arbitration and conciliation service). The committee meets in Congress House, the headquarters of the TUC, and its secretariat is drawn from the staff of the TUC. Kahn-Freund has suggested that 'if one tries to look at it with the eyes of a worker rightly or wrongly believing himself to have been unjustly excluded or expelled from a union, one wonders whether he will believe in the impartiality of a body set up by the TUC'.[18]

In a critical review of the committee's work after the IRC had been in existence for nearly two years and had dealt with eleven cases it was pointed out that 'in no case have the complainants been re-employed, although this is not surprising as the employer is beyond the scope of the Committee'.[19] The IRC reacted swiftly to this criticism.[20] They did not refer directly to the problems of re-employment, but they did say that they had developed a process which they called 'post-hearing conciliation'. The object of this process was to explore further the possibility of finding an agreed solution to the dispute and to try to ensure that the complainant did not remain unemployed if he was at the time of the hearing. In their 1978 report the committee commented briefly on six cases in which there had been post-hearing conciliation sessions, and mentioned in particular 'that in all three cases where they were asked to do so the unions involved tried to secure the re-engagement of the complainants. One attempt failed, but negotiations are still in progress in the other two cases with employers who have so far refused to re-engage the complainants.[21]

The total failure of successful applicants to the IRC to achieve re-employment was stressed again in a 1979 review of the work of the committee.[22] This time the comment was followed by a suggestion that the committee should change its terms of reference to consider exclusions or expulsions from trade unions *before* employees were dismissed or given notice of dismissal. There would seem to be much sense in this suggestion. However, such a change would not be effective unless those unions which operate closed shops altered their rules to make a reference to the IRC a prerequisite of expulsion. Such an alteration is certainly desirable; whether it is likely is another matter.

In its 1980 report to the General Council of the TUC the IRC summarised its work since its inception.[23] It had received complaints in 47 cases of which 17 fell outside its term of reference. In some other cases the complainants either did not proceed or reached a settlement, with the committee's help, without a formal hearing. Thus the committee held a formal hearing in 19 cases, of which the results were as follows:

> In eleven cases involving sixteen complainants, the Committee made a recommendation in one form or another that the union should admit or re-admit the complainants. In three cases involving five complainants, the Committee recommended that the union should, under the conditions stated by the Committee, give sympathetic consideration to admit or re-admit. In five cases involving twenty-one complainants no recommendation was made.[24]

Perhaps the most significant statement made by the committee in its 1980 report was that 'in no case where the Committee has made a recommendation for action have the union or unions involved failed to comply'.[25] In 1978 the TUC wrote to all affiliated unions reminding them to ensure that individuals were aware of their membership rights where a closed shop existed 'both within the union and in respect of the Independent Review Committee'.[26] It seems that unions had already developed a respect for the decisions of the IRC or that they took the 1978 reminder to heart.

Given that the committee made no recommendation for admission or re-admission to the union in only five out of nineteen cases, it is difficult to justify the suggestion that its affinity with the TUC inevitably makes the IRC partial towards the unions. Its decisions show that the committee is not afraid to find that unions have acted wrongly, and that expulsions have been invalid, where there is evidence that this has been the case.[27]

Table 5.1 shows the trend of complaints received during the period of the committee's operation.

Table 5.1

Period	Number of complaints received by the IRC
April 1976–July 1976	4
July 1976–July 1977	16
July 1977–June 1978	12
July 1978–June 1979	13
July 1979–June 1980	2
Total	47

There is, then, no indication from these figures that the problem of exclusion or expulsion from a trade union where a closed shop exists is a growing one. On the contrary, it seems either that individuals are meekly accepting the authority of the union, or that unions are dealing more carefully with applicants or members who commit serious offences. The experience of the IRC suggests that sections 4 and 5 of the Employment Act 1980, which provide a statutory remedy of compensation for individuals who have been unreasonably excluded or expelled from a union where a closed shop exists, will not be widely used. But to say that is not to suggest that these provisions are not desirable as a back-up to the IRC.

References

1   Donovan Report, p.152. But three members of the Commission thought that where pressure from the union had forced the dismissal the compensation should be paid by the relevant union.
2   *Drury* v *Bakers' Union* (1973) IRLR 171.
3   *Hynds* v *Spillers-French Baking Ltd.* (1974) SLT 191.
4   *Newell* v *Gillingham Corporation* (1941) 1 All E.R.552. This case was about conscientious objection to military service.
5   *Cave and Cave* v *British Railways Board* (1976) IRLR 400.
6   *Goodbody* v *British Railways Board* (1977) IRLR 84.
7   *Saggers* v *British Railways Board* (1977) IRLR 266 and (1978) IRLR 435.
8   See table 6 in Gennard J., Dunn, S. and Wright M., 'The Content of British Closed Shop Agreements', *Department of Employment Gazette*, November 1979, p.1091.
9   Ibid.
10   Applicants would, of course, normally be in a financial plight. Legal aid may be available for *advice* from a solicitor, but not for *representation* at a hearing. The cost of representation could easily amount to hundreds or, in a lengthy case, thousands of pounds. One of the reasons for the formation of the Freedom Association in 1975 was to give advice to those who thought they had been unjustly victimised by the introduction or operation of a closed shop. In some cases the Association has assisted applicants with the cost of representation at an industrial tribunal.
11   When Strathclyde Regional Council introduced a closed shop in 1978 the main trade union concerned (NALGO) estimated that its membership would increase by 6,000. Only 43 of these appealed to the Joint Review Panel which was established to hear claims from religious objectors, and 34 of these succeeded.

12   McCarthy, W.E.J., op.cit., p.263.
13   House of Lords *Hansard*, vol.409, no.133, May 1980, col.872.
14   This case is discussed in some detail in Appendix A to chapter 7.
15   Which had become section 58(3) of the Employment Protection (Consolidation) Act 1978.
16   From a leaflet setting out the committee's terms of reference, procedure and membership. However, in at least one case the committee has taken evidence and given a decision *before* the employees were dismissed. An appeal to the IRC is a procedural stage in certain UMAs.
17   From its inception until the present time (1981) the members were Professor Lord Wedderburn (Chairman), Lord McCarthy and Mr G.H. Doughty.
18   Kahn-Freund, O., op.cit., p.192.
19   *Industrial Relations Review and Report*, April 1978, pp. 10-12.
20   Report of the IRC to the TUC, TUC Report 1978, pp. 390-1;
21   Ibid.
22   'The Independent Review Committee: The Success of Voluntarism?' *Industrial Relations Review and Report*, no.208, September 1979, pp. 2-6.
23   Appendix 1 to the General Council's Report to the 1980 Congress, p.344.
24   Ibid.
25   Ibid.
26   TUC Guides to Negotiating Procedures, Conduct of Disputes and Union Organisation (the closed shop). Reprinted in the 1979 TUC Report, pp. 398-405.
27   See, for example, the decision in the case of Mr Collins et al. and the National Union of Funeral Service Operatives, TUC Report 1979, pp. 364-70. This was one of the cases in which the union accepted the recommendation to re-admit the complainants, but the employer refused to re-engage them (letter from Mr B. Ward, secretary to the IRC, dated 16 September 1980). Printed reports of decisions by the IRC are made available to the press and are also published in the Annual Report of the TUC.

6 The extent of the closed shop and the nature of union membership agreements 1964-80

The extent of the closed shop

(a) McCarthy's survey of 1962-64

Before 1964 it was possible to say that the closed shop existed among certain groups of workers in some industries or in some areas of the country. But there was no information about the spread of the practice among the labour force as a whole. McCarthy's pioneering research, published in 1964,[1] was the first attempt to dispel this ignorance by providing estimates of the number of employees in various industries and services, and in the economy as a whole, covered by the closed shop in all its varieties.

McCarthy concluded that the closed shop affected about 3.75 million workers, i.e. roughly 16 per cent of the 22,800,000 employees in Great Britain or 1 worker in 6. This meant that about 39 per cent, or 2 out of every 5, of the 9.5 million trade unionists were covered by the closed shop. He also stated that his estimates erred on the side of caution. Wherever there was a serious doubt about the right figure 'the one chosen was well on the low side of the estimates'. Nevertheless, these figures are significant because they provide a benchmark against which the subsequent extent of the closed shop can be measured. Without them it would be impossible to say whether the closed shop was growing or declining in certain industries and in the economy as a whole. As it is, although these and later figures are unlikely to be completely accurate, recent research of a similar kind makes it possible to be reasonably confident about trends in the extent of the closed shop in Britain.

McCarthy's breakdown, by industry, of the workers covered is given in table 6.1.

Table 6.1

Manufacturing and extractive industry	
Engineering	1,200,000
Mining and quarrying	630,000
Printing	275,000
Iron and steel manufacture	210,000
Shipbuilding and ship-repair	150,000
Textiles	110,000
Small scale metal manufacture	45,000
Timber and furniture	40,000
Clothing	40,000
Food, drink and tobacco	35,000
Chemicals and oil refinery	35,000
Paper, box and carton manufacture	20,000
Fishing	10,000
Other manufacturing	10,000
	2,810,000
Transport	
Sea transport	80,000
Docks and inland waterways	90,000
Railways	80,000
Passenger transport and car hire	100,000
Road haulage	30,000
Air transport	10,000
	390,000
Building and civil engineering	100,000
Distribution	
The co-operative movement	300,000[1]
Other distribution	20,000
	320,000
The services	
Local government	45,000
Entertainment	45,000
Public utilities	30,000
Other services	20,000
	140,000
TOTAL	3,760,000

1 Including productive workers employed by co-operative wholesale societies.

Source: McCarthy, W.E.J., *The Closed Shop in Britain*, p.29.

In addition to the above breakdown, McCarthy classified workers 'according to how far particular occupations, or clearly defined working groups are dominated by the closed shop'.[2] He distinguished four different situations in which the closed shop is prevalent to a greater or lesser degree and divided the various trades into the categories of (a) comprehensively closed, (b) mainly closed, (c) mainly open and (d) comprehensively open. Of the workers covered by the closed shop, 1.47 million were in comprehensively closed and 1.38 million in mainly closed trades, and over 98 per cent of these workers were engaged on manual work. When the remaining workers covered by the closed shop were included, i.e. those employed in mainly open trades, the proportion of manual workers fell to 92 per cent. In fact, McCarthy thought that the total number of non-manual workers in closed shops was not more than 300,000 and of these 210,000 were covered by the closed shop in co-operative distribution.

Three conclusions, more or less related to the findings mentioned above, may be drawn from McCarthy's analysis of the closed shop. First, it was heavily concentrated in certain sectors of the economy. Second, non-manual workers, apart from those in co-operative distribution, were hardly affected by it. And third, there was often a correlation between the level of unionisation and the extent to which employees were 'closed shop prone', although such a correlation was not universal. McCarthy listed eight trades which were over 90 per cent organised without becoming in any sense closed shop prone. They were as follows:[3]

1   Non-industrial civil servants
2   Teachers and other non-manual groups employed by local authorities
3   Sections of the industrial civil service
4   Firemen
5   Footplate workers on the railways
6   Clerical and administrative workers in nationalised industries
7   Electricity workers employed by nationalised undertakings
8   Boot and shoe operatives.

Later in his study McCarthy explored the reasons why these groups of workers exhibited such 'untypical tolerance' towards the few non-unionists who worked with them.[4]

(b)   The LSE survey of 1978-80

In the years which followed McCarthy's survey it was known that the coverage of the closed shop was growing. But there was widespread ignorance about the extent and nature of that growth. Elliott suggested in 1975 that 'closed shops are now being introduced, negotiated or claimed for something like 3 million workers. This is in addition to some 4 million workers who it is estimated are already covered'.[5] Wigham, writing in 1976, was unwilling to be so specific. He simply stated that 'no-one knows how fast closed shops are spreading . . . . One guess is that the proportion of workers covered by a union membership agreement has risen from some 15 per cent in the early 1960s to between 20 and 25 per cent (of the workforce)'.[6] It was in these circumstances that in 1978 a research team at the London School of Economics, led by John Gennard, undertook a major survey into the extent and nature of the closed shop, and the main results of their work were published in two articles in late 1979 and early 1980.[7] In the second of these articles Gennard stated that he had obtained 'reliable information about the extent of the closed shop among 19 million of the estimated 22 million in employment thus giving a coverage rate of 84 per cent'.[8] What should be said about this claim?

First, it was qualified by the statement that 'in certain industries, notably construction, it proved difficult to obtain reliable quantitative information, although closed shops were known to exist'.[9] Gennard admitted that his figure of 89,000 workers covered by closed shops out of 1,219,000 workers in that industry was 'likely to be a substantial underestimate'.[10]

Secondly, it seems that Gennard had difficulty in tracing written UMAs, which have spread rapidly in recent years especially in the public sector and among local authority employees.

Thirdly, as stated (but easily forgotten) more than 3 million employees were not covered by Gennard's survey. Even if only 10 per cent of these were in closed shops, compared with 28 per cent of the 19 million employees surveyed, Gennard's total would be increased by 300,000.

It must be remembered that Gennard, like McCarthy, produced a *minimum* total and that the actual total may be considerably higher.

The most important parts of Gennard's research are summarised in table 6.2. The table shows that at least 5.2 million of the 22.2 million employees in Great Britain were covered by the closed shop in 1978-79. In other words, since 1963 at least 1.4 million additional employees had become subject to compulsory unionism during a period when the total number of employees was declining by 600,000, so that the proportion covered rose from 16 to at least 23 per cent. The growth was even more vigorous than the figures suggest because in this period the workforce in some of the industries with a closed shop tradition shrank significantly. Thus in coalmining the number covered by the closed shop fell from 630,000 to 296,000 and in shipbuilding from 150,000 to 90,000. It follows that the closed shop must have been

Table 6.2

The extent of the closed shop: coverage

	No. of employees June 1978 (thou.)	No. of workers covered (thou.)	No. known to be in closed shop (thou.)	No. in pre-entry closed shops (thou.)	No. in post-entry closed shops (thou.)
Agriculture, forestry and fishing	377	360	3	1	2
Mining and quarrying	341	296	296	—	296
Food, drink and tobacco	696	500	266	12	254
Coal and petroleum products	36	30	20	1	19
Chemical and allied industries	429	325	137	62	75
Metal manufacture	459	370	228	33	195
Mechanical engineering	925	786	412	79	333
Instrument engineering	147	118	16	2	14
Electrical engineering	740	629	220	53	167
Shipbuilding and marine engineering	175	145	99	64	35
Vehicles	764	650	369	65	304
Metal goods nes*	537	460	178	11	167
Textiles	464	330	100	33	67
Leather, leather goods and fur	40	36	6	2	4
Clothing and footwear	365	300	83	6	77
Bricks, pottery, glass, cement	263	190	88	5	83
Timber and furniture	259	195	76	21	55
Paper, printing and publishing	537	445	354	176	178
Other manufacturing	328	270	137	28	109
Construction	1,219	1,086	89	5	84
Gas, water, electricity	340	335	273	—	273**
Transport and communications	1,426	1,150	798	91	707
Distributive trades	2,683	2,200	397	20	377
Insurance, banking and business finance	1,134	920	52	—	52
Professional and scientific services	3,575	3,200	126	3	123
Miscellaneous services	2,364	2,140	132	44	88
Public administration and defence	1,586	1,300	226	20	206
All	22,209	18,766	5,181	837	4,344

*nes — not elsewhere specified.   **some of these probably operate as pre-entry.

Source: Gennard, J., Dunn, S. and Wright, M., 'The Extent of Closed Shop Arrangements in British Industry', *Employment Gazette*, January 1980 pp. 17 and 19.

spreading rapidly in some industries and services, and Gennard's figures indicate where much of this growth took place:

> In food, drink and tobacco the number of workers affected by such arrangements has grown from 35,000 (four per cent) to 266,000 (about 40 per cent); in clothing and footwear from 40,000 (seven per cent) to 83,000 (23 per cent) despite a shrinkage in employment in this SIC; in public utilities from 30,000 (eight per cent) to 273,000 (80 per cent); and in transport and communications from 390,000 (23 per cent) to 798,000 (56 per cent).[11]

There was especially rapid expansion in the service sector, where employment had grown by 42 per cent since 1962, and among non-manual (white-collar) employees. Gennard estimated that by 1979 at least 1.1 million white-collar workers were covered, compared with 300,000 in the early 1960s. But it was still true that a very large majority (78 per cent) of the closed shop population were manual workers.

Following McCarthy, who had suggested that the number of workers covered by pre-entry closed shops in 1964 was 'unlikely to be more than three-quarters of a million',[12] in comparison with 3 million covered by post-entry closed shops, the LSE team also distinguished between the two main varieties. Their research showed that the number covered by pre-entry closed shops had risen hardly at all to 837,000, and that most of the growth had taken place in post-entry closed shops, where the number covered had risen from about 3 million to 4.3 million.

Thus the general pattern of growth between 1964 and 1979 became clear. By the end of this period the closed shop was still found more commonly among manual workers, but it had spread significantly into white-collar areas of employment. Much of this growth took the form of formal, written agreements which introduced post-entry closed shops. And at the same time, as several of the older closed shop industries contracted for economic reasons, the practice had spread rapidly in the food, drink and tobacco, and clothing and footwear industries, in public utilities and in the transport and communications sectors, so that overall there was a very substantial increase in the total number of employees covered by the closed shop.

(c) Helen Jackson's research into written union membership agreements, 1975-81[13]

The scope of Helen Jackson's research has been narrower than that of McCarthy or the LSE team. Her concern has been solely with the extent and nature of formal, written UMAs which only became widespread after TULRA 1974. Jackson's research has shown that written agreements are far more numerous and cover more employees than was previous realised. And because her figures for some categories of employees covered by written UMAs are greater than Gennard's figures for the same categories of employees covered by *all* closed shops, it is clear that Gennard's estimate for the minimum closed shop population in 1979 is too low.

At the time of writing (May 1981) Jackson's research is still incomplete, but a brief article containing some preliminary results has shown that her work will add considerably to our knowledge of the nature of the closed shop and its coverage in 1977-78 and 1980-81.[14] Jackson has details of over 1,000 written UMAs which indicate that 'about 5 million workers are or have been covered by those alone',[15] and she admits that her collection is by no means exhaustive. According to her figures in 1978, nearly 2 million workers in the public sector alone were covered by formal agreements — these included 1.34 million in the main nationalised industries, like the railways and the post office, and in other public utilities, and 643,000 local authority employees. This last figure is in marked contrast to that of the LSE team which found 66 local authority agreements covering 'fewer than 200,000 workers'.[16]

These early results have led Jackson to conclude that when Gennard's figures for informal UMAs are taken into account 'the total closed shop population in Great Britain in 1978 must have been above 7 million workers'.[17] It follows that the growth of the closed shop between 1964 and 1978 was more rapid than has hitherto been supposed. But it is not true to say that the coverage in 1981 is even greater. On the contrary, Jackson's latest figures indicate that the coverage has actually been declining in recent years, largely as a result of rising unemployment. Her preliminary estimates suggest that the closed shop population covered by her agreements has fallen by about 300,000 and that the recent decline in the total closed shop population 'may well be in excess of half a million'.[18]

The registration of written UMAs

The nature and extent of the closed shop in Britain is clearly a matter of public interest, and the recent research by Gennard and Jackson has indicated the difficulty of arriving at an accurate figure for its coverage. Because many British closed shops are unwritten, informal arrangements this difficulty cannot be completely overcome, but it would certainly be possible to produce regular, accurate figures for the number and coverage of written UMAs. This could be done by requiring written UMAs to be registered and for the employers concerned to report annually the numbers covered by them; either the Certification Officer for Trade Unions or the Director General of Fair Trading could conveniently discharge such a function. If the closed shop is to remain legal in the UK it is desirable that such a register should be established, thus avoiding difficult and expensive research which may be based upon confidential information. Until an official, public register is kept, uncertainty about the extent even of written agreements is bound to remain.

The nature of union membership agreements

It would be wrong to suppose that the term 'union membership agreement' is a comprehensive one which includes every kind of agreement made between employers and unions about union membership. In 1977 BP Chemicals negotiated an agreement with the Association of Scientific, Technical and Managerial Staffs (ASTMS) which established a centralised bargaining system covering foremen and staff at a number of sites and included the following statement:

> The company and the union recognise the right of an employee to join a union or not, as the individual employee decides. However, in order to promote and assist in the development of constructive relationships, the company and the union undertake to inform employees recruited into the common interest groups concerned of the existence of this agreement. The company will refer such new employees to the appropriate union representative.
>
> The union undertakes that its members employed by the company will respect the rights of, will not object to working with, and will co-operate with, employees who are not members of their union.[19]

Clearly this agreement is about union membership. But it is not a UMA as the law has defined that term since 1974. As Hawkins has emphasised:

> The key characteristic of a UMA under the law as it stands is a *requirement* that employees who fall within its scope must join one of the specified unions. An agreement which simply *encourages* 100 per cent union membership does not satisfy the legal definition of a UMA and cannot therefore be used by management to justify the dismissal of non-members.[20]

Thus, strictly speaking, a UMA is a *compulsory* union membership agreement and only those agreements which make union membership a normal condition of employment should come under the definition of a UMA. However, the dividing line between voluntarism and compulsion may, in practice, be a very narrow one. A written agreement may 'encourage' all employees of a particular class to join the appropriate union and make no mention of the right not to join; and those who do not respond to this 'encouragement' may be aware that opportunities for overtime are denied them or that they will not be considered for promotion. 'Encouragement' of this kind may lead to 99.9 per cent, or even 100 per cent, trade unionism in practice, but when discussing written UMAs it is better to restrict the term to those agreements which make it plain that union membership is a condition of employment. For example, paragraph 1 of the agreement between the British Railways Board and the Transport Salaried Staffs Association provided that:

> As from 1 August 1975, it shall be a condition of employment of each member of the staff of the Board, subject to the following clauses and points of interpretation, that he shall be a member of the Transport Salaried Staffs' Association.[21]

A clause of this kind lies at the heart of every formal UMA. Other matters which the negotiators will have to consider are:

1 The class of employees covered by the agreement and exemptions to its coverage, e.g. part-time employees

2 The form of the conscience clause

3 The time limits for joining the union

4 The specification of unions

5 Procedures for resolving disputes arising from the agreement

6 Provisions for maintaining or revising the agreement, e.g. the introduction of the check-off.

Some of these matters will be considered in more detail later in this chapter, but it must now be emphasised that the term UMA is in no way restricted to formal, written agreements, however widely these may have spread in recent years. Traditions in British industrial relations die very hard and the statutory definition of a UMA was deliberately designed to include closed shops ranging from 'arrangements', often derived from custom and practice and nowhere mentioned in a written agreement, to those which are the subject of formal, written agreements from two to seven pages in length. Because the latter variety has recently become much more common, they tend to be more readily associated with the term 'UMA'. But the law knows no distinction between the written and the unwritten agreement; it is only concerned with the degree of enforcement *in practice* of the closed shop, and it is likely that the unwritten arrangement, or the agreement which is contained in a single sentence, will be just as closely enforced as the formal agreement covering several pages. A classic example of the former is to be found in the shipbuilding industry where the agreement about a 'Procedure for the Avoidance of Disputes' between British shipbuilders and the Confederation of Shipbuilding and Engineering Unions which came into force on 1 August 1977 included the following statement in respect of manual employees:

Union Membership

1.1 In order that negotiations can be conducted on a fully representative and authoritative basis it is accepted that all manual employees should be members of an appropriate signatory union.

Among no group of employees is the closed shop more strictly enforced that among manual workers in shipbuilding.[22] Thus it is clear that the length and nature of the agreement is in no way related to its effectiveness. However, in most cases there is a relationship between the type of UMA and the nature of the closed shop, in that short or unwritten agreements or arrangements are normally connected with pre-entry closed shops of skilled craftsmen, while longer, written agreements are almost exclusively post-entry in character. As has already been mentioned, the LSE team analysed 136 written UMAs in the course of their research. All of these were post-entry, and as the team pointed out, '"pre-entry" practices, which are found in parts of the printing, dock-working, ship-building, steel making, merchant shipping and entertainment industries, are relatively in decline mainly because of dwindling employment in those sectors'.[23] They went on to say that pre-entry practices rarely become the subject of formal, written agreements and that 'in the same factory it is not unusual to find the semi and unskilled workers covered by a formal post-entry agreement and the skilled grades covered by an unwritten, de facto pre-entry closed shop'.[24] The present position is, therefore, that a dwindling minority of the closed shop population are covered by pre-entry closed shops which are either entirely a matter of custom and practice or the subject of a brief reference in an agreement about working practices and procedures, as in shipbuilding; but formal, written post-entry closed shop agreements have spread rapidly in recent years. Because research into UMAs is naturally concentrated on formal agreements, there is a danger that the importance and effectiveness of unwritten *de facto* agreements will be overlooked.

The LSE team analysed 136 written UMAs in terms of the date of signing; the results are given in table 6.4.

Table 6.4
Year of signing of 136 written union membership agreements

		Manual	Non-manual	All UMAs
Before	1971	8	1	9
	1971	—	—	—
	1972	1	—	1
	1973	—	—	—
	1974	1	1	2
	1975	3	4	7
	1976	31	22	53
	1977	30	15	45
	1978	5	10	15
	1979	3	1	4
Total		82	54	136

Source: Gennard, J. et al., 'The Content of British Closed Shop Agreements', *Department of Employment Gazette*, November 1979, p.1089.

Not surprisingly the table shows a flurry of closed shop activity after the passing of TULRA. Some of these agreements were simply the formalising of previously informal closed shop arrangements. Nevertheless, it is clear that TULRA encouraged the spread of formal, written agreements as well as the spread of the closed shop. It would appear that the growth in written agreements reached a high peak in 1976-77 and declined thereafter, but some of the agreements of these two years are later editions of earlier agreements which were redrafted in the light of TULR(A)A 1976, so the peak is somewhat exaggerated.

UMA exemptions

Commentators on UMAs have focused attention on the exemptions contained in them.[25] TULRA simply provided a floor for exemptions by making unfair the dismissal of any employee who genuinely objected 'on grounds of religious belief to being a member of any trade union whatsoever'. There was nothing to prevent employers and unions agreeing on wider exemptions and the evidence indicates that many of them did so. It is useful to distinguish between those exemptions which apply to existing employees and those which apply to new employees, because normally existing employees have been more generously treated than new employees.

(a) Exemptions for existing employees

For the reasons discussed in the previous chapter very few existing employees were in a position to make use of the narrow, statutory religious objection clause. Thus, unless the agreement contained additional exemptions they were faced with the choice of joining the union or being dismissed. Presenting long-service employees with this choice was hardly calculated to enhance public esteem for employers and unions who negotiated rigid UMAs of this kind. As Wigham put it, 'The spectacle of workers inviting the sacking of colleagues from undertakings where they have been employed for years is distasteful. It suggests a vindictiveness which reflects discredit on the movement and it is unnecessary'.[26] A majority of negotiators agreed with this view and drew up agreements which exempted all existing non-unionists from membership. Of the 136 UMAs studied by Gennard, 86 contained an exemption of this kind (although 12 of these provided for payment of a sum equivalent to union dues to a charity in lieu of membership); while the remaining 50 made membership compulsory for all employees with certain exceptions, of which objection on grounds of religious belief — the minimum statutory exemption — was much the most common.[27] However, according to Gennard, over half of these 50 agreements simply formalised previous 100 per cent closed shop practices and exemption for non-members was, therefore, irrelevant. Benedictus found that, out of 78 agreements studied, existing non-members were exempted in 29 and all existing employees were exempted in 16; in other words 45 out of 78, or nearly three-fifths of the UMAs studied, exempted existing non-members. Thus it seems that while a majority of all UMAs were flexible in respect of existing non-members a substantial minority conformed rigidly with TULRA in that the vast majority of these employees were faced with the choice of joining the union or being dismissed.

(b) Exemptions for new employees

In marked contrast to the exemption provided by a majority of UMAs for existing non-members it is quite exceptional for a UMA to allow new employees exemption from membership except on the statutory grounds of religious objection or, in a minority of cases, on those grounds slightly widened by a conscience clause. Thus there is a clear obligation on all new entrants who cannot take advantage of conscientious and religious objection clauses to join the union. In Gennard's sample of 136 UMAs 84, or 65 per cent, acknowledged the rights of new entrant religious objectors and 23, or 18 per cent, contained a conscience clause.[28] Where no exemptions are mentioned, the minimum statutory exemption should be understood. Only a very small number of new entrants could make a case for non-membership under these exemptions. But do they really mean anything at all?

These exemptions apply to *new employees*, not to *would-be employees*. The position of the objector to trade union membership on religious, conscientious or any other grounds who is applying for a job in a firm or an industry covered by a UMA is a very weak one. The experience of the 1971 IR Act showed that where employers and unions are determined to enforce a closed shop, 'awkward' characters will usually be screened out at the interview stage. Where a UMA exists employers will take care to inform applicants for employment that union membership is a condition of work and will ask them directly whether they are willing to join the appropriate union; and most applicants will understand that a negative, or perhaps even a hesitant, answer to this question will automatically disqualify them from employment. Some employers may be reluctant to admit that the conscientious or religious objector to trade unionism is debarred from employment in their firm, but one UMA states categorically that non-unionists on grounds of conscience or for any other reason will not be employed, and this policy does not contravene the unfair dismissals legislation provided it is applied prior to an individual's engagement.[29]

Some organisations will have laid down a procedure for dealing with appointments, where UMAs exist. In the case of one Area Health Authority[30] application forms are sent out by post and on an additional form the applicant is told that a UMA exists and asked whether he or she would be willing to join the appropriate trade union. The procedure then states that:

> With regard to the process of shortlisting (in cases where this is necessary) the factors revealed by the above form will obviously be taken into account and any statement of objections will be balanced against the ability and potential which the objector seems to possess

and goes on to lay down the process to be followed 'in the unlikely event of the Authority wishing to appoint a candidate who expresses specific objections to joining a trade union in the context of a Union Membership Agreement'. An appeal panel would be established, consisting of an equal number of management and trade union representatives, chaired by an officer of ACAS. Responsibility for producing evidence and references would rest with the applicant and no objection would be heard unless he had 'two referees (not relatives) who have known the applicant for some time and will state, in writing, the reasons why the applicant holds these objections, and can give an assessment of the validity of these views'; the applicant would also be partially responsible for the costs of the panel hearing. In order for the application to succeed the agreement of both sides of the panel would be necessary, and if it did succeed the applicant would have to pay a sum equivalent to the trade union subscription to a charity approved by the panel. If the application failed, the conditional offer of employment would be withdrawn.

Reference in the above appeals procedure to a *conditional* offer of employment indicates that this employer operates a two-stage screening process in the case of all new appointments to areas of work covered by UMAs. In the first place all applicants are asked if they would be willing to join a union and at this stage those who express unwillingness are likely to be ruled out as suitable employees. Secondly, as a check on the fact that their willingness to join is genuine, their appointment is not confirmed until they have actually joined the union, and the procedure agreement provides that successful candidates '*will be given a maximum of four weeks after taking up appointment to take out union membership*'. A contract of employment is only issued after this has been done.

It is unlikely that many employers have such a detailed procedure as the one quoted above for dealing with new appointments where UMAs exist. Nevertheless their method of appointment will probably be designed to ensure (a) that new employees are willing to join the union and (b) that they do in fact join within a few weeks of starting work;[31] and there is no reason to believe that this aim will not be achieved.

*(c)   The effect of exemptions for
      existing and new employees*

In practice exemptions for new employees will have very little effect. The same has not been true of exemptions for existing employees, especially where they allowed non-members to retain their status after the introduction of a UMA. But given that all new entrants will have to join the union whether the UMA is rigid (i.e. does not allow existing non-members to stay outside the union) or flexible (it does permit such an arrangement) the ultimate effect of both rigid and flexible UMAs will be the same — all the employees covered by the agreements will eventually become union members. Of course in the case of a flexible UMA this may take some time, even forty years if there are young employees who are determined to take advantage of the exemption and to soldier on with the same employer until retirement. Nevertheless, in every case the union will ultimately achieve its aim of a completely closed shop and the possibility of exemptions will disappear.

Reasons for the recent growth of the closed shop

Economic change has brought about the decline of many industries, for example shipbuilding, in which the closed shop was a normal practice. Meanwhile it has spread into new areas and its coverage has continued to grow. Thus contemporary, not traditional, reasons must be sought for this growth. They may be found in changing attitudes of employers and new legislation which has encouraged the development of written agreements and their strict enforcement.

Management attitudes

Weekes[32] and Hart[33] have discussed the reasons why some managers have accepted, or perhaps even welcomed, the maintenance or introduction of a closed shop. Thus it can no longer be assumed that the closed shop is always imposed on reluctant employers by trade unionists under the threat of industrial action. The two reasons usually given for management support for the practice are (a) that it helps to stabilise relationships by avoiding fragmented multi-union bargaining and (b) that it enables the union to exercise control over potential dissidents and thus ensure that sometimes unpopular collective agreements are kept. For example the Central Electricity Generating Board defended the closed shop in the *Ferrybridge* case on the grounds that 'the Board are convinced that these arrangements have brought peaceful industrial relations within the industry coupled with dramatic improvements in efficiency and mobility'.[34] Weekes has stated that 'the avoidance of further multi-unionism was by far the most powerful argument advanced by managers for protecting the closed shop',[35] but a recent survey showed that while managers in firms with closed shops agreed that their two most important advantages were that they helped to stabilise relationships and that they ensured that the union represented all workers, there was some disagreement about which of these two advantages was more important.[36]

Changing management attitudes may be partly a cause and partly an effect of the legislation, notably TULRA, which made dismissal fair for non-membership of a union where a closed shop exists *and directed the legal sanction against the employer, not the trade union*. The consequence of this statute and the way in which the tribunals interpreted it, at least in the period 1976-80 (see chapter 4 of this book), was that employers had a direct interest in ensuring that if a closed shop existed it was operated strictly, even if initially non-union employees were exempt.

It is sometimes argued that the voluntarist tradition of British industrial relations means that changes in labour law will be largely ineffective, and certainly the experience of the IR Act showed that the introduction of totally new rights, like the right not to join a union, placed a burden on the law which it could not sustain. But the sharp increase in the number of written UMAs in the years following TULRA surely indicates that legislation may have some effect on the development and the nature of the closed shop. The favourable legal climate which TULRA created must be a major reason for the spread of written UMAs and the growth of the closed shop in the period 1975-80.

The check-off

One of the consequences of the expansion of the closed shop has been the growth of the check-off, or the deduction of union dues from pay by the employer. The TUC recently reported that about 50 per cent of all union members were now covered by the check-off, in comparison with some 20 per cent in 1968.[37] There are various administrative advantages for employers who introduce the check-off instead of allowing shop stewards to wander through the establishment collecting small sums of money each week, but the change in the law relating to the closed shop has made it increasingly important as a device by which management can enforce a closed shop and thus alleviate the problems of the *Ferrybridge* case. Use of the check-off also alleviates the problem of employees allowing their membership to lapse. These problems are alleviated, and not eliminated, because the Truck Acts provide that the check-off must be optional and in practice a small minority of employees may insist on paying their union dues directly to the union.

Public opinion and the change in policy 1979-80

At the time of a general election voters are presented with a basketful of policies by each political party. Changes in voting patterns do not, therefore, indicate changes in the degree of support or distaste for a particular policy; changes of this kind can only be tested by specialist opinion polls. The appendix to this chapter contains the results of such a poll about the closed shop carried out in 1979. Attitudes at that time may be compared to those revealed by the 1959 answers to a single question on the same topic. The comparison suggests that opinion against the closed shop may have hardened between 1959 and 1979, and that the Conservative pledge partially to undo TULRA by protecting individual employee rights in several ways, without providing a general right not to associate, quite closely reflected public opinion including opinion among trade unionists. The way in which that pledge was translated into law, following the return of a Conservative government in 1979, will be examined in the next chapter.

References

1   McCarthy, W.E.J., op.cit., *passim*. But the estimates of the extent of the closed shop are to be found on pp. 27-38.
2   Ibid., p.30.
3   Ibid., p.36.
4   Ibid., pp 161-75.
5   Elliott, J., *The Financial Times*, 18 December 1975.
6   Wigham, E., *The Times*, 4 June 1976.
7   Gennard, J., Dunn, S. and Wright, M., '(a) The Content of British Closed Shop Agreements' and '(b) The Extent of Closed Shop Arrangements in British Industry', *Department of Employment Gazette*, November 1979, pp. 1088-92 and January 1980, pp. 16-22.
8   Ibid. (b), p.16.
9   Ibid., p.17.
10   Ibid.
11   Ibid., p.18.
12   McCarthy, W.E.J., op.cit., p.52.
13   The research is being carried out as part of a PhD degree at University College, London, under the supervision of Professor R. Rideout.
14   H. Jackson, 'The Extent of the Closed Shop in Britain Today', *Free Nation* (newspaper of the Freedom Association), April 1981, p.5.
15   Ibid.
16   In a letter to the *New Statesman*, 20 June 1980.
17   H. Jackson, op.cit.

18   Ibid.
19   Quoted in *Industrial Relations Review and Report*, no.169, February 1978, p.17.
20   Hawkins, K., *Handbook of Industrial Relations Practice*, Kogan Page 1979, p.84.
21   For the full text of this and six other UMAs see *Closed Shop Agreements* published by the Institute of Personnel Management, 1976. The details of more than fifty UMAs were described in *Industrial Relations Review and Report* between 1975 and 1979.
22   Although in some yards occasional non-members who have experienced a religious conversion may be informally tolerated by their workmates.
23   Gennard, J. et al., op.cit. (a), p.1088.
24   Ibid.
25   Gennard, J. et al., op.cit. (a) and Benedictus, R., 'Closed Shop Exemptions and Their Wording', *Industrial Law Journal*, September 1979, pp. 160-71.
26   Wigham, E., *The Times*, 4 June 1976.
27   Gennard, J. et al., op.cit. (a), pp. 1091-2.
28   Ibid., p.1090.
29   See Benedictus, R., op.cit. (note 25), footnote 8, p.161.
30   This information was provided in confidence and the Authority must, therefore, remain anonymous.
31   In the LSE sample of 136 UMAs, 80 per cent insisted on membership within four weeks or less. Of the remaining 20 per cent 2 per cent stipulated a period of two months, 4 per cent over two months and in the remaining 14 per cent the period was unspecified. Gennard, J. et al., op.cit. (a), p.1090.
32   Weekes, B., 'Law and the Practice of the Closed Shop', *Industrial Law Journal*, December 1976, pp. 215-6.
33   Hart, M., 'Why Bosses Love the Closed Shop', *New Society*, 15 February 1979, pp. 352-4.
34   (1976) IRLR 68.
35   Weekes, B., op.cit., p.216.
36   Hart, M., op.cit., p.353.
37   See the article 'The Check-off System: A Review of Some Recent Agreements', *Industrial Relations Review and Report*, no.196, March 1979, pp. 2-6.

Appendix

(a)   Results of the 1959 Gallup poll

A representative sample of the population was asked the following question:

> If the majority of workers in a trade or works are union members, and find that the existence of a minority of non-members weakens the union in wage and other negotiations, do you think the union members are or are not justified in putting pressure on the non-members to join the union by refusing to work with them?

That question was answered as follows:

(The figures are percentages)

Working population

	Total	Trade union member	Non-member	Wives of members	Others
Are justified	33	70	23	36	20
Are not justified	55	23	68	42	61
Don't know	12	7	9	22	19

Source: McCarthy, W.E.J., op.cit., p.3.

(b)   Results of the 1979 opinion poll

A survey on attitudes towards industrial relations and trade union power carried out by Opinion Research Centre in April 1979 contained five questions relating to the closed shop. The questions and the answers to them were as follows:

1   Some people believe a man or woman has the right to belong or not to belong to a trade union, whichever they choose. Others believe that all employees in large companies should belong to a union because non-union workers get the benefit of union bargaining without paying their dues. Which view do you take?

(The following figures are all percentages)

	All	Trade union members	Active trade union members	Non-members
People have a right to join or not to join a union	73	58	52	78
All employees should join the union	23	39	46	17
Don't know	4	3	2	5

2   Do you agree or disagree with the following: all people working for large companies should be made to join the union if a vote is taken and a majority of workers want an all-union or closed shop arrangement?

	All	Trade union members	Active trade union members	Non-members
Agree	36	54	60	29
Disagree	55	42	37	60
Don't know	9	4	3	11

3 Do you agree or disagree with the following: those people who refuse to join a union for political, moral or other strong reasons should be allowed to stay out, but should pay their union dues?

	All	Trade union members	Active trade union members	Non-members
Agree	47	52	53	44
Disagree	39	38	40	39
Don't know	14	10	7	7

4 Do you agree or disagree with the following: those people who refuse to join a union for moral, political or other strong reasons should be sacked?

	All	Trade union members	Active trade union members	Non-members
Agree	8	12	17	7
Disagree	85	81	75	87
Don't know	7	7	8	6

5 Do you agree or disagree with the following: no union should have the power to force an employer to sack someone who refuses to join the union?

	All	Trade union members	Active trade union members	Non-members
Agree	75	67	61	78
Disagree	19	26	33	16
Don't know	6	7	6	6

7 The Employment Act 1980

By the winter of 1978-79 — the 'winter of discontent' — Mr Callaghan's Labour government was becoming increasingly unpopular with its allies, the trade unions, and also with some other sections of the electorate. The Conservative victory in the 1979 general election was, therefore, no great surprise and the victory was naturally followed by legislation to fulfil the party's pledge to change the law on the closed shop.

That pledge had been spelt out in the 1979 manifesto.[1] Its three main elements were first, that those arbitrarily excluded or expelled from a union should be given the right of appeal to a court of law; second, that 'existing employees and those with personal conviction' should be adequately protected against the closed shop and amply compensated (not reinstated) if they lost their jobs as a result of it; and third, that new closed shops should accord with 'the best practice' and should only be introduced after an 'overwhelming majority' of the workers concerned had voted in favour by secret ballot. The third proposal was to be supported by the publication of 'a statutory code under Section 6 of the 1975 Employment Protection Act'. In other words, the government envisaged that ACAS, the tripartite arbitration body, would draw up a Code of Practice for the introduction of UMAs which industrial tribunals would be bound to take into account. The second and third elements, together with the Code of Practice, formed the heart of the new policy, which was to impose severe controls on the introduction of new closed shops without providing a general right not to associate or in any way attempting to break up existing UMAs.

These proposals sprang out of the desire to give individual employees some protection against compulsory unionism, but the desire was tempered by an unwillingness to place too great a burden on the law or to antagonise the unions. Mr Prior, Secretary of State for Employment and chief architect of the new policy, had been a member of the cabinet which had approved the IR Act in 1971. He was determined that his legislation should be more effective and longer lasting than that ill-fated measure. Consequently, as soon as the new government's proposals were published he found himself caught in a cross-fire between the Labour opposition, who deplored any change in the law, and a significant minority of his own party who saw the proposals as thoroughly inadequate. However, the Employment Bill was given high priority in Parliament, few amendments were accepted and it received the royal assent in August 1980. How did it translate closed shop policy into law?

Six of the 21 sections of the Employment Act are concerned with various aspects of the closed shop but five of these deal with rather special cases and will be rarely used. Section 7 of the Act, together with the Code of Practice,[2] is the section which changes the ground rules for the renegotiation or introduction of UMAs and is much the most important part of the new closed shop law. The purpose and likely effect of the other five sections (4, 5, 10, 15 and 18) will, therefore, be briefly discussed before section 7 and the Code of Practice are considered in some detail.[3]

Writing about the problem of individuals being excluded or expelled from a trade union Kahn-Freund has argued that 'the absence of any statutory provision is almost as deplorable as the absence, until recently, of a law against unfair dismissal'.[4] Sections 4 and 5 remedy this defect by providing that individuals who are unreasonably excluded from, or expelled by, a specified trade union where a UMA exists may make a complaint to an industrial tribunal (not a court, as suggested in the manifesto) and may be awarded compensation if the tribunal declares that the complaint is well-founded. Sub-section 5 of section 4 specifically allows the tribunal to find that the union has acted unreasonably even when it has acted strictly in accordance with its rules. In other words it suggests that trade union rules for admission and discipline (especially expulsion) may not meet proper standards. Is this likely to be the case and how often are individuals unreasonably excluded or expelled from unions?

The LSE research team which investigated the extent of the closed shop and the nature of UMAs in 1978-79 has also looked closely at the rules on admission, discipline and expulsion of 79 TUC unions with just under 12 million members.[5] They found that 'With certain exceptions, the admission and disciplinary rules of most of the unions

87

studied do not reach the standards of procedural elaboration required by the 1971 Industrial Relations Act or recommended by the TUC's 1969 proposals',[6] but they also stated that 'There are probably few instances of injustice to individual members'.[7] These statements are not necessarily inconsistent. The absence of an appeals procedure against expulsion does not necessarily mean that members' rights are being infringed. Nevertheless it is clearly desirable, as the TUC agreed in 1969, that union rules should include proper procedures for disciplining members and for appeals against exclusion or expulsion, and the possibility of having to pay compensation may encourage some unions to bring their rules up to a proper standard and to ensure that they are observed. The relevant part of the Code of Practice (paras 47-53) largely overlaps the 1969 TUC recommendations and is not, in itself, controversial.

This new statutory right is in addition to existing common law remedies based upon the constitution and rules of the union as a contract of association, supplemented by the rules of natural justice, and also to the domestic appeals machinery within unions as well as the Independent Review Committee. Thus the aggrieved applicant or expelled member will have to decide which remedy it is in his or her best interest to pursue. If an expelled member who has been dismissed, or is under notice of dismissal, wishes to be readmitted to his union so that he can continue to pursue his trade, he may do better to take his case to the IRC, and the small number of cases heard by the IRC in the period 1974-80 hardly suggests that there will be a rush of applicants to take advantage of this new right.

Section 10 gives an employer who has a liability to pay compensation for an unfair dismissal a right to seek an indemnity from a third party, normally a trade union, in certain circumstances. These circumstances will arise if the inducement takes the form of actual or threatened industrial action and the pressure was exercised because the employee was dismissed for not being a trade union member. The section may be seen as an attempt to prevent a union from forcing an employer to introduce a UMA through the back door, by compelling a minority of non-members to join the union where a UMA does not already exist. Dismissal for non-membership remains presumptively fair where there already is a UMA. If the employer requires the union 'to be joined' and the tribunal finds that the dismissal was unfair it may order the union to indemnify the employer as is 'just and equitable in the circumstances' and this may amount to complete indemnity.

Two sub-sections to this clause attempt to protect the non-unionist employed on a 'union-only' sub-contract and thereby to deter contracts of this kind. In the first case the employer who has become liable for unfair dismissal as the result of a 'union-only' contract can shift the whole cost of the compensation payable on to the contractor or client by a joinder similar to that already described. The second sub-section, by a process which Lord Wedderburn has described as 'triple joinder', allows the contractor in his turn to join the union or other person which or who threatened or took strike action against him to ensure that the 'union-only' condition of the contract was observed. It is difficult to estimate the effectiveness of section 10, but it seems rather unlikely that sub-contractors will put much faith in it.

Section 15 complements sections 7 and 10 of the Act, which are concerned with dismissal on grounds of non-membership of a union, by providing a right against action short of dismissal, and in particular against compulsion to join a union. If a non-member believes that he is being unfairly treated in any way because of his unwillingness to join a union, he may complain to a tribunal and receive compensation if the tribunal finds his complaint well-founded. An employer may still recommend or encourage his employees to join a union, but if the encouragement is over-enthusiastic he could find himself liable for compensation. As in the case of section 10, joinder is available for employers who have been forced to take action by virtue of an actual or threatened strike; but it is difficult to see how an employer could use this provision when a group of employees were making life unpleasant for a particular non-member.

Section 18, known as the SLADE clause, was introduced specifically to counter the recruiting tactics of that union, which were strongly criticised in the Leggatt Report.[8] This recruitment was directed at artists and designers who supplied artwork to fully organised printing firms. The section operates by removing these recruiting tactics from the protection of section 13 of TULRA 1974; it may be important in the context of this particular industry, but it is not unreasonable to think of this section as dealing with a special case.

It is time to turn away from the subsidiary closed shop clauses of the Act to consider the main clause — section 7. Section 7 operates by amending the law on unfair dismissal and the closed shop, which was previously contained in section 58(3) of the Employment Protection (Consolidation) Act 1978. Under that sub-section, where a closed shop is being effectively enforced dismissal for non-membership of a union is presumptively fair unless the employee can sustain a genuine religious objection to membership. Section 7 inserts three new exemptions into section 58(3) of the EPCA, two of which affect *all* UMAs while the third applies only to UMAs coming into effect after August 1980. These three exemptions will now be considered in turn.

New sub-section (3A) contains a conscience clause which broadens and swallows up the previous religious objection clause. Dismissal of an employee for non-membership of a union where a UMA is in effect will now be unfair 'if he genuinely objects on grounds of conscience or other deeply-held personal conviction to being a member of any trade union whatsoever or of a particular trade union'. What kind of objections to union membership are likely to be held valid under this new clause?

On the axiom that the greater includes the lesser it is clear that the kind of religious objections which were held to be valid under the previous exemption will retain their validity. But the exemption has been widened to include 'grounds of conscience or other deeply-held personal conviction' and fears have been expressed that these widened grounds will be abused by those with shallow objections to union membership, such as meanness in relation to union dues.[9] It is difficult to predict exactly how the tribunals will interpret these words, but the decisions in the *Drury* and *Hynds* cases suggest that they will look very carefully at the history of the applicant for exemption and that they will certainly want to know if he has ever been a trade union member in the past. If he has, then he will have to provide a very good reason why he now objects to joining a union. This reason could presumably be of two kinds. It could be connected with a change of heart on the part of the applicant, perhaps through a religious conversion, or it could be connected with a change of policy on the part of the union. If a previously peaceful union, possibly one whose members provided a vital public service, suddenly changed its policy and engaged in strikes or other disruptive action, there might be those who would want to argue that membership of such a newly militant body was incompatible with their conscience. And if tribunals were willing to accept arguments of this kind the wider conscience clause might prove to be a check on the more militant elements of closed shop unions.

A specific question which arose during the debates in Parliament on the Act was whether the words 'deeply held personal conviction' covered the employee who refused to join a trade union on the ground that it was affiliated to a political party with which he disagreed. When a group of Conservative and cross-bench peers pressed Lord Hailsham, the Lord Chancellor, to give his opinion on this particular issue, he suggested that the words were 'intended to exclude the trivial, the frivolous, the self-interested, the prejudiced or the spiteful, but the words are not intended either to restrict the deeply-held personal convictions of the individual or the legitimate rights of trade unions'[10] and he went on to say that 'of course they are wide enough to include political beliefs . . . ; if they are deeply held and personal, political beliefs are, of course included'.[11]

Because most large British unions are affiliated to the Labour party while a substantial proportion of union members support other parties[12] it might appear that this ruling opens the door for a mass defection from their unions by non-Labour supporters in existing closed shops. But this is not so. These members have been living with their consciences for some time and have had a statutory right to abstain from paying the political levy.[13] It would need a change of policy on the part of their unions, for example the frequent use of overtly political strikes, to enable these members to make use of the exemption. It must be appreciated that a conscience clause is normally used *only when a closed shop is introduced*. Its main purpose is *to protect existing employees who are non-members* and believe that they have good grounds for staying outside the union.[14] Because the other parts of section 7 make it extremely difficult to implement new closed shops, and in any case provide complete protection to all existing non-members against compulsory membership, it seems that in practice the new, wider conscience clause will be rarely used.

New clause (3B) of section 7 fulfils the manifesto promise that existing employees must be adequately protected against the closed shop, by making their dismissal unfair, provided they have not been a member of a specified union since the agreement came into effect. In other words it makes obligatory what the negotiators of most UMAs have agreed voluntarily and in so doing makes the recurrence of fair dismissal for existing non-members impossible when a closed shop is being introduced. But will any more new closed shops be negotiated? New clause (3C), together with sub-section (3) of section 7, lays down the very strict conditions which have to be met before a new UMA comes into that category which makes dismissal for non-membership fair.

The manifesto pledge was that a new closed shop agreement would only be valid 'if an overwhelming majority of the workers involved vote for it by secret ballot'. The Act fulfils this promise by laying it down that dismissal for non-membership shall be regarded as unfair unless the UMA has been approved in a secret ballot by *'not less than 80 per cent of those entitled to vote'*. Even where there is considerable enthusiasm for the closed shop among that part of the workforce concerned and the employer co-operates to the extent of allowing the ballot to be held at the workplace or by post (as recommended in the code of practice) it seems unlikely that more than a very few UMAs will be approved by the required statutory majority. Trade unions have been busy negotiating closed shops since TULRA 1974 and recent research suggests that union membership is already a condition of employment for most of those groups of workers who are reasonably amenable to such an arrangement.

Most post-1974 UMAs have been introduced without any indication from the employees concerned whether or not they approve of the change from voluntary to compulsory unionism. It is, of course, true that many employers would not negotiate a UMA until a large majority of the particular employees had voluntarily joined the union, but the slender evidence which exists suggests that a significant proportion of these *voluntary* union members may be opposed to *compulsory* unionism. Despite the absence of a statutory requirement for a pre-UMA ballot in the period 1974-80 a few unions, or union branches, did in fact hold a ballot about the closed shop, usually in response to a body in the membership which was opposed to the idea. In 1979 a UMA was proposed for approximately 2,500 white-collar employees of Sandwell Council, of whom just over 2,000 were members of NALGO. In the ballot which was held (among union members only) 1,480 ballot papers were returned of which 746 were against the closed shop and 734 in favour. Following the ballot, which was decided on a straight majority of members voting, the UMA proposal was abandoned.[15]

A body of members of the same union, employed by the Strathclyde Regional Council, forced a somewhat similar ballot, also in 1979. In this case the ballot followed the introduction of a strict UMA which did not provide exemption for existing members (apart from religious objectors) and as a consequence of which 11 employees were dismissed. In a 68 per cent poll the result was 5,214 in favour of continuing the closed shop and 5,028 against.[16]

It would be wrong to argue that these results are in any way 'typical', and that if pre-UMA ballots had been required by TULRA they would have followed this pattern. In particular it is probable that a higher proportion of manual than non-manual employees would have voted in favour of the closed shop. But the results suggest that a significant proportion of voluntary trade unionists may be opposed to the closed shop and that it is going to be extremely difficult for trade unions to meet the conditions for new effective UMAs laid down in section 7. Lord McCarthy has suggested that 'one of the aims of the Government in introducing the ballot provisions is to make the negotiation of new closed shops impossible'.[17] The government has been rather coy about its aim, but there are those who will conclude that section 7 will make it almost as difficult to negotiate a new closed shop as to get a camel through the eye of a needle.

As has already been made clear, clause (3B) of section 7 protects all existing *non-member* employees against dismissal in the unlikely event of the introduction of a new UMA. Sub-section (3C)(b) goes further and protects the existing *members* who are opposed to compulsory unionism but have been outvoted by the 'overwhelming majority'. An employee is protected against unfair dismissal if 'he has not at any time since the day on which the ballot was held been a member of a trade union in accordance with the agreement'. The implication of this sub-section is that all members who are opposed to compulsory unionism should cast their vote against the closed shop and then resign from the union on the day of the ballot. Even if the 80 per cent majority is achieved, they receive the right to continue to work as non-members. It is, therefore, possible that where a union with, say, 95 per cent membership holds a ballot for a UMA, it will lose a significant proportion of its membership through resignation on the day of the ballot. The existence of this right, together with the very great difficulty of achieving the necessary majority, could convince trade unionists that it is pointless to attempt to negotiate new UMAs.

The code of practice on the closed shop

The manifesto proposals included the issuing of a code of practice, but at that stage it was suggested that the code should be issued by ACAS, to stand alongside the Codes on Disciplinary Practice and Procedures, Disclosure of Information and Time Off for Trade Union Duties and Activities. ACAS Codes are respected because of the employer and trade union elements of ACAS. They are necessarily cautious, but the fact that they have been agreed by employers and unions means first that they are readily accepted and second that they present no major problems for the tripartite industrial tribunals and the Central Arbitration Committee which are obliged to take them into account in determining questions to which they are relevant.[18] When the new government realised that ACAS would be unwilling to issue a code on such a contentious issue as the closed shop, it provided, in section 3 of the Employment Act, for the Secretary of State for Employment to issue codes of practice 'as he thinks fit for the purpose of promoting the improvement of industrial relations'. These codes are to be admissible in evidence and taken into account by *courts* as well as industrial tribunals and the CAC,[19] and they may, therefore, be described as quasi-law. It could be argued that the code of practice on the closed shop contains an important part of the new law on that subject. How far does it supplement the relevant sections of the Act iself?

A considerable part of the code is simply a guide to the law on the closed shop and an explanation of the changes introduced by the Employment Act. Because the Employment Act is a complex measure and the closed shop elements in statutory labour law are now scattered between the 1980 Act, the Employment Protection (Consolidation) Act 1978 and TULRA 1974 (as amended) it is certainly desirable that some guidance should be given to managers, trade unionists and others who may be mystified by the tergiversations of the parliamentary draftsmen. But as soon as the code goes further than guidance, it could cause acute embarrassment to the tribunals and courts which have to take it into account.

For example para. 42 of the code calls for the 'periodic review' of existing UMAs. Para. 45 further suggests that where the employer and union concerned favour continuing the UMA (this is very likely in most cases) 'they should ensure that it has continued support among the current employees to whom it applies. Where no secret ballot has previously been held — or where one has not been held for a long time — it would be appropriate to use one to test opinion'. This recommendation must be considered in relation to the parliamentary debates on the Employment Bill. A group of Conservative MPs, who thought that the Bill was too weak, supported an amendment which would have made ballots obligatory for *all* UMAs.[20] Thus the government had an opportunity to write this provision into the Bill, but the amendment was rejected.[21] Given the unwillingness of the government to legislate on this matter it is difficult to believe that they intend to implement paras 42-46 of the code. It would, of course, be absurd for the recommendations to be enforced on private employers until action has been taken over the UMAs which cover a large number of employees in the public sector.

The likely effectiveness of the Act and the code

The 1971 IR Act failed to protect the right to dissociate. Are the closed shop provisions of the Employment Act likely to be any more effective?

It must be emphasised that the aims of the Employment Act are much more modest than those of its predecessor in two particular respects. First, the new Act does not provide a general right not to join a union or attempt in any way to ban the pre-entry or post-entry closed shop; it simply seeks to prevent the spread of the closed shop unless an overwhelming majority of employees favour its introduction. Secondly, where the new Act attempts to prevent the infringement of individual rights, it does so not by providing a 'right to work' without union membership conditions (whatever that concept may mean in British law) but by providing for compensation for dismissal. Thus the employer who dismisses an 'awkward' employee may find it costly to do so, although the Act allows him to pass the cost of the compensation on to the union in those cases where trade union pressure has forced the dismissal.

Because of the relative modesty of the aims of the Employment Act, it seems probable that their central intention — to prevent the spread of UMAs — will be achieved. Certainly the determination of some employers and unions, for example, Rochdale, Sandwell and Walsall

Councils, to negotiate a UMA in the weeks before the Act became law indicates that in their view section 7 will be effective. If experience shows this expectation to be correct, it will be clear that the failure of the closed shop provisions of the IR Act did not prove that the law cannot in any way affect the behaviour of British employers and unions with regard to union security. The question is rather one of the kind of changes which the law attempts to bring about in practice, how large a change it attempts to achieve at any one time and how far it works with, rather than against, public opinion and especially the opinion of employers and unions.

It should perhaps be added that even if the provisions of the Employment Act bring the negotiation of UMAs to a complete standstill, it is not going to be easy to establish exactly what it has achieved because there is no complete information about the number of UMAs signed in each of the years 1975-80. Gennard's analysis of 136 written agreements (chapter 6, p.75) shows that numbers reached a peak in 1976 and 1977, with 53 and 45 new agreements being signed respectively; the figure for 1978 was 15 and only 4 of the agreements had been signed in 1979. This research suggests, therefore, that the number of new UMAs declined rapidly after 1977. Thus it could be that the 1980 Act practically shut the stable door after most of the horses had already bolted.

Future possibilities

For several decades now the law on the closed shop in the USA and West Germany has been static and agitation for change has been ineffective. This was also true of the law in Britain from the passing of the Trade Disputes Act 1906 until 1971. In marked contrast to this pattern, over the past ten years British public policy has been extremely fluid. Since 1970 it seems that both major political parties have determined to use labour law, including the law on the closed shop, as a political football to be kicked with the greatest possible vigour immediately one or the other was returned to power.

Because of the unusually close links between the trade unions and the Labour Party and because political power regularly changes hands in Britain as a body of floating voters becomes discontented with the government of the day, it is difficult to see an end to this game unless there is a radical change in the British political scene. The formation of the Social Democratic Party might herald such a change. Meanwhile a vigorous debate continues within the Conservative Party about the adequacy of the Employment Act, and as this book was going to press (August 1981) it had become clear that a growing number of employers and Conservative members of parliament wanted stronger measures to protect individual rights. For example, the Confederation of British Industry, the main spokesman for British employers, reported 'a strong and increasing dislike among its members for the practice of the closed shop'[22] and stated that the majority view of its members was that 'the Government should, as a matter of urgency, initiate further steps towards the elimination of the closed shop'.[23] Representations of this kind led the Secretary of State for Employment to promise, in the House of Commons on 30 June 1981, that further changes in the law would soon be made. But he carefully refrained from making any specific commitments.

In this next legislative step the main question which the government will have to answer is whether it intends to take some positive action about existing closed shops in addition to curbing new ones. Paragraphs 42-45 of the Code of Practice, which recommend a periodic review of existing closed shops (and a ballot in most cases) have proved to be a dead letter. Will the government, therefore, provide by statute, rather than by Code of Practice, that unless existing agreements are approved by ballot, dismissal for non-membership of a union will become unfair and subject to penal compensation? Such a measure would clearly make some impact on the extent of the closed shop. At the same time it must be acknowledged that attempting to break up existing closed shops is distinctly more difficult than preventing the development of new ones. If ballots are made compulsory for *existing* closed shops, as reason and justice demand,[24] it would, then, be advisable to provide for a fall-back position for cases where the normally required majority (80 per cent of those eligible to vote) was narrowly missed.

The 1971 Industrial Relations Act allowed for closed shops to be approved after careful consideration in cases where a majority of the workers eligible to vote, or not less than two-thirds of those who actually voted, favoured such an arrangement.[25] These less stringent conditions could be made available once again. Where the normal 80 per cent majority had not been achieved, but the above conditions had been met, it would be for the employers and/or unions concerned to put their case for the continuation of the closed shop to a special committee, which would adjudicate on it in accordance with certain criteria. A fall-back provision of this kind would indicate the government's intention to deal reasonably with existing arrangements and could prevent some existing closed shops simply going underground.

Thus the immediate future of public policy on the closed shop in Britain depends on the course of the debate within the Conservative Party. Meanwhile there is little doubt that a future Labour government would once again facilitate the negotiation of closed shops as far as possible, although this would depend on changes in political opinion among the electorate as a whole. The outcome of events of this kind is notoriously unpredictable.

References

1   The Conservative Manifesto 1979, p.10.
2   The Codes of Practice on Picketing and the Closed Shop were approved by Parliament in November 1980.
3   A more detailed commentary on those sections of the Act by Drake, C.D., is to be found in Current Law Statutes, 1980, Part 7, chapter 42.
4   Kahn-Freund, O., *Labour and the Law*, Stevens 1977, p.193.
5   Gennard, J., Gregory, M. and Dunn, S., 'Throwing the Book — Trade Union Rules on Admission, Discipline and Expulsion', *Employment Gazette*, June 1980, pp. 591-601.
6   Ibid., p.599.
7   Ibid., p.600.
8   HMSO, Cmnd. 7706, 1979.
9   By Lord McCarthy, for example. See House of Lords, *Hansard*, vol.410, no.143, 11 June 1980, col.325.
10   House of Lords, *Hansard*, vol.411, no.160, 7 July 1980, col.934.
11   Ibid.
12   In the 1979 general election an extensive survey of the voting pattern among trade unionists produced the following result: Labour — 50 per cent; Conservative — 35 per cent; Liberal — 12 per cent. *New Statesman*, 18 May 1979, p.704.
13   Under the Trade Union Act, 1913.
14   Mr Alan Rook was an interesting exception to this general rule. In August 1980 an industrial tribunal at Newcastle upon Tyne decided that he had been unfairly dismissed for resigning from his union (NALGO), that he was a genuine conscientious objector and that he should be reinstated by his employer, the North Eastern Electricity Board. Mr Rook had consistently campaigned against the closed shop. When a UMA was introduced in 1977 he decided to continue his campaign from within the union, and he only resigned in 1978 when it became clear that his campaign was hopeless. The UMA included a conscience clause, and the tribunal, in a majority decision, decided that Mr Rook deserved to have the benefit of this clause. The case number was 23558/79.
15   Report in the *Sandwell Evening Mail*, 3 September, 1979. However, in 1980 Sandwell was one of several councils which decided to introduce UMAs before the Employment Act came into force,

regardless of the wishes of its employees. Agreements for manual and white-collar employees were introduced in March and August 1980 respectively. Those who initially declined the 'invitation' to join the union were threatened with dismissal and it was, therefore, not surprising that there was a large increase in union density among Sandwell council employees.

16   Report in the *Glasgow Herald*, 6 June 1979.

17   House of Lords, *Hansard*, vol.411, no.160, 7 July 1980, col.954.

18   Employment Protection Act 1975, Section 6(11).

19   Employment Act 1980, Section 3(8). The Codes of Practice on Picketing and the Closed Shop were the subject of a report by the House of Commons Employment Committee on 3 November 1981. The all-party committee took evidence from various bodies, including the CBI and the TUC, some of whom suggested that the Codes were 'constitutionally undesirable' (Report, para. 22). The report stated that 'This view is shared by a majority of this Committee' (ibid.). The Secretary of State for Employment commented on the report in a written statement to the House of Commons dated 13 November 1980.

20   House of Commons, *Hansard*, vols 983-4, nos 160-1, 23-24 April 1980, cols 581-640. See also the Green Paper on Trade Union Immunities, Cmnd. 8128, January 1981, pp. 66-75.

21   At the end of the debate referred to in note 20, 46 Conservative and three Liberal MPs voted in favour of the amendment extending the ballot to existing UMAs, against the wishes of the government which was supported by the Labour opposition. Backbench MPs are naturally very reluctant to embarrass their own party in this way.

22   Response from the Confederation of British Industry to the Green Paper on Trade Union Immunities, June 1981, p.14.

23   Ibid.

24   Because a large majority of the employees concerned have not had an opportunity to express an opinion about a major change in their contract of employment.

25   See p.34 of this book.

Appendix A : TULRA and the European Convention for the Protection of Human Rights and Fundamental Freedoms

Young, James and Webster *v* United Kingdom

(Application nos 7601/76 and 7806/77 to the European Commission of Human Rights)

The UMA negotiated by British Rail in 1975 had considerable repercussions. First it led to disagreement between British Rail and certain employees about the meaning of the statutory religious objection. As described in chapter 5 this disagreement was resolved by the tribunals in favour of the employees. But TULRA gave no protection to existing employees who were unwilling to join a union but had no religious objection to doing so. Forty-three British Rail employees found themselves in this position and were dismissed. They had no redress under UK law but in 1966 the United Kingdom had agreed that individuals should be allowed to petition the European Commission of Human Rights, established to make the European Convention of Human Rights effective. That Convention, which has now been ratified by all of the 21 member states of the Council of Europe, was signed by the British government in 1950 and became operative in 1953. A few determined UK citizens had already taken their case to the Commission and the Court at Strasbourg by 1975. In 1976, Messrs. Young and James, who had been dismissed by British Rail for non-membership of a union, decided to follow this example, and in 1977 Mr Webster, another dismissed railwayman, also claimed that his rights had been infringed. Because the applications were very similar, the Commission decided to join them in 1978. At the end of 1979 the Commission found, by a majority of 14 to 3, that the applicants' rights had indeed been infringed. What were the issues with which the case was concerned?

The basis of the complaint was that by allowing the applicants to be placed in a position where they had to choose between joining a trade union or being dismissed, the UK government had infringed their rights under Articles 9, 10, 11 and 13 of the European Convention on Human Rights.[1]

Article 9 protects 'the right to freedom of thought, conscience and religion'. Article 10 protects 'the right to freedom of expression'. Article 13 states that 'Everyone whose rights and freedoms as set forth in this Convention are violated shall have an effective remedy before a national authority notwithstanding that the violation has been committed by persons acting in an official capacity'. Article 11 is clearly the most relevant to closed shop cases. Part 1 of that Article protects 'the right to freedom of peaceful assembly and to freedom of association with others, including the right to form and to join trade unions for the protection of his interests', while Part 2 states that these rights shall not be unnecessarily restricted. Central to the railwaymen's case was the question of whether Article 11 (1) also protected the right *not* to join a trade union, an issue which had not previously been directly considered by the Commission. Counsel for the applicants argued that the right to associate and the right not to associate were two sides of the same coin, the freedom to associate. If there was no freedom to refuse to associate, there could not be a right to choose to associate. The UK government naturally disputed this contention. They pointed out that an early draft of the European Convention had made an explicit reference to the right not to associate but that this reference had been removed because of the difficulties which it would cause in relation to the closed shop in some countries.

In their decision the Commission decided that because Article 11 contained elements which were generally part of the rights guaranteed by Articles 9 and 10, it was unnecessary to deal with the complaints under these latter Articles separately. The Commission also decided that Article 13 could not be extended to provide the remedy which the applicants had requested. But on the central issue of the case — the rights protected by Article 11 — the Commission found in favour of the applicants. How did they reach their decision?

The Commission emphasised the importance of the right to join trade *unions* (plural) in Article 11 and argued that this excluded a trade union monopoly. 'There must be room for more than one union. Accordingly, everyone must be free to choose which of the existing unions he wants to join if he does not intend to form a new one'.[2] In the Commission's view Article 11 gave an employee who considered that none of the existing unions effectively protected his interests the right to form a new one. 'This is particularly important since unions, as these cases show, may have political affiliations. It is not in dispute that the applicants joining the particular unions available would have had to sign declarations which they could consider to have clear political implications'.[3] They went on to say that the specific problem of the railwaymen meant that 'the Commission does not have to discuss the more general question whether or not the positive freedom guaranteed by Art. 11(1) implies also a negative freedom, a question which was argued by the parties'.[4] They were concerned with a case in which the closed shop agreement which had led to the dismissal of the applicants had been concluded after they had taken up their work. 'In such a case it seems clear that there is an interference in respect of each applicant's right to form or join the trade unions for the protection of his interests in the way already explained.'[5]

In their conclusion the Commission remarked that certain Articles of the Convention obliged the state to protect individual rights even against the action of others and that, in their opinion, Article 11 was such a provision as far as dismissal on the basis of union activity *or as a sanction for not joining a specific union* is concerned (italics provided). Then they placed the blame for infringing human rights fairly and squarely on the UK government:

> In the present cases it was the legal system that made it possible that the right to join trade unions was interfered with in the cases of the applicants. After having found that Art. 11 protects against this kind of compulsion, it follows that the State is responsible under the Convention if its legal system makes such dismissal lawful (cf. Application No. 4125/69 X v. Ireland, Yearbook 14, p.222). On this basis the responsibility of the United Kingdom is engaged in the present cases,[6]

and the discussion of the issues raised by Article 11 ended with the statement that 'The Commission therefore concludes by fourteen votes against three[7] that there has been in these cases a violation of Art. 11 of the Convention'.[8]

The implications of this case are of far-reaching constitutional importance. The Commission did *not* decide that Article 11 provided a general right not to associate. But they did decide that TULRA had infringed the European Convention on Human Rights by providing too narrow a protection against the closed shop for existing non-union employees.

The decision was not only a blow to the Labour party, which had been responsible for TULRA and had also agreed to accept the decisions of the European Court as binding;[9] it was also an acute embarrassment to the Conservative government which, despite its commitment to reform of the law, had decided to resist the application of the railwaymen and had, in 1979, declined to participate in a 'friendly settlement' which is provided for in the rules of the Commission. Thus the case has now gone to the European Court, and a panel of 21 judges will give their decision in 1981. It would be very surprising if the Court came to a decision which differed widely from that of the Commission.

In November 1980 the UK government announced that the right of individual citizens to petition the European Court will be extended for a period of five years from January 1981. Thus it would appear that the present government is as ambivalent about the European Convention as it is about the closed shop issue as a whole. Meanwhile those who feel that the time is ripe for the UK to have its own Bill of Rights to protect certain individual liberties would like to incorporate the

Articles of the European Convention into UK domestic law.[10] This important debate will not be settled in the near future, but its outcome could have a significant influence on the way in which closed shop law develops in the UK.

Postscript

The 21 judges of the full European Court, one from each member state of the Council of Europe, duly gave their verdict on 13 August 1981. By a majority of 18 to 3 they ruled that the dismissal of the 3 railwaymen violated Article 11 of the European Convention on Human Rights. The Court followed the Commission in holding that it was not necessary to decide whether Article 11 guaranteed a right not to associate (although 6 of the judges in a concurring opinion argued that freedom of association also included 'a negative aspect, necessarily complementary to, a cor- relative of and inseparable from its positive aspect'[11]); but the majority accepted that Article 11 gave some protection of the right not to asso- ciate and they stated that 'To construe Article 11 as permitting every kind of compulsion in the field of trade union membership would strike at the very substance of the freedom it is designed to guarantee'.[12]

Considering the particular case of the 3 railwaymen, who had been engaged by British Rail before the introduction of the closed shop and had been threatened with dismissal unless they joined the stipulated union, the majority stated that 'such a form of compulsion . . . strikes at the very substance of the freedom guaranteed by Article 11. For this reason alone there has been an interference with that freedom as regards each of the three applicants'.[13]

The Court also considered the absence of choice of trade union membership and held that 'it strikes at the very substance of this article (Article 11) to exert pressure of the kind applied to the applicants in order to compel someone to join an association contrary to his convictions'.[14]

Finally the judges asked whether the interference in human rights was justified, and concluded that the closed shop agreement which forced the dismissal of the applicants was unnecessary and incompatible with a democratic society of which 'pluralism, tolerance and broad- mindedness'[15] were the hallmarks.

In the light of their decision, the majority referred back the question of legal costs and compensation for the applicants, but it seemed likely that these costs would have to be borne in full by the British government.

What should be said about this judgement? First, it is a total vindica- tion of the applicants, who had been dismissed without compensation from their employment in a monopoly state industry. And second, it is an indictment of TULR(A)A 1976, which is condemned as contrary to the fundamental premises of a free and democratic society. It is, in short, an indication that by 1976 the mother of Parliaments had lost her way.

Rightly regarded as the bastion of European freedom for much of the twentieth century, Britain has had to be reminded by the judges of other nations that 'democracy does not simply mean that the views of a majority must always prevail: a balance must be achieved which ensures the fair and proper treatment of minorities and avoids any abuse of a dominant position'.[16] It is to be hoped that the lesson has been thoroughly relearnt.

References

1   The full text of the Convention is printed in the appendix to Campbell, C. (ed.), *Do we Need a Bill of Rights?*, Temple Smith 1980, pp. 142-66. For an authoritative study of the Convention see Jacobs, F.G. *The European Convention on Human Rights,* Clarendon Press, Oxford 1975.
2   Report of the Commission on Applications Nos 7601/76 and 7806/77, p.34. I am indebted to Mr Norris McWhirter, deputy chairman of the Freedom Association, for a transcript of the Commission's report and the appendices to the report. The railwaymen's application to the Commission and the court was supported by the Freedom Association and had cost £75,000 by August 1981. C.G.H.
3   Ibid., p.24. One of the unions concerned with this case was the National Union of Railwaymen. New entrants must sign a pledge that they will obey the union rules, and Rule 1 says 'The objects of the union shall be . . . to work for the supersession of the capitalist system by a Socialistic order of society'. Rules 4, 5 and 6 explain that only individual members of the Labour party can become president, general secretary or assistant general secretaries of the union.
4   Ibid., p.35.
5   Ibid.
6   Ibid., p.36.
7   The Commission is an eighteen-member body. One member who was absent when the vote was taken took advantage of a special rule which allowed him to state his opinion separately. He concurred with the majority.
8   Ibid., p.37.
9   Initially in 1966 for ten years. This was extended for another five years in 1976.
10   The first book mentioned in note 1 above provides a good summary of the current state of the debate, which has generated a considerable literature in the past ten years.
11   Judgment of the European Court of Human Rights in the case of Young, James and Webster, Strasbourg, 13 August 1981, p.24.
12   Ibid., p.17.
13   Ibid., p.18.
14   Ibid., p.19.
15   Ibid., p.21.
16   Ibid.

Much the most important statute law on the closed shop — which inter-mingles with the law on unfair dismissal — is to be found in section 58(3) of the Employment Protection (Consolidation) Act 1978 as amended by section 7 of the Employment Act 1980. The amended section 58(3) and the new section 58A are printed in full below, but because they cannot be properly understood without an understanding of the statutory definition of a UMA or a 'class' of employees, these definitions are also reproduced.

(a) *Trade Union and Labour Relations Act 1974*
as amended by the Trade Union and Labour
Relations (Amendment) Act 1976

Part of Section 30(1)

'union membership agreement' means an agreement or arrange-ment which —

(a) is made by or on behalf of, or otherwise exists between, one or more independent trade unions and one or more employers or employers' associations; and (b) relates to employees of an identifiable class; and (c) has the effect in practice of requiring the employees for the time being of the class to which it relates (whether or not there is a condition to that effect in their contract of employment) to be or become a member of the union or one of the unions which is or are parties to the agreement or arrangement or of another specified independent trade union;
and references in this definition to a trade union include references to a branch or section of a trade union; and a trade union is specified for the purposes of, or in relation to, a union member-ship agreement if it is specified in the agreement or is accepted by the parties to the agreement as being the equivalent of a union so specified.

Section 30(5A)

For the purposes of this Act employees are to be treated, in relation to a union membership agreement, as belonging to the same class if they have been identified as such by the parties to the agreement, and employees may be so identified by reference to any characteristics or circumstances whatsoever.

(b)   Employment Protection (Consolidation) Act 1978 as amended by section 7 of the Employment Act 1980

Section 58(3), (5) and (6) and Section 58A.

(3) Dismissal of an employee by an employer shall be regarded as fair for the purposes of this Part if —

(a) it is the practice, in accordance with a union membership agreement, for employees for the time being of the same class as the dismissed employee to belong to a specified independent trade union, or to one of a number of specified independent trade unions; and

(b) the reason for the dismissal was that the employee was not a member of the specified union or one of the specified unions, or had refused or proposed to refuse to become or remain a member of that union or one of those unions;

but subject to subsections (3A) to (3C)

(3A) The dismissal of an employee in the circumstances set out in subsection (3) shall be regarded as unfair if he genuinely objects on grounds of conscience or other deeply-held personal conviction to being a member of any trade union whatsoever or of a particular trade union.

(3B) The dismissal of an employee by an employer in the circumstances set out in subsection (3) shall be regarded as unfair if the

Dismissal relating to trade union membership

employee —

(a) has been among those employees of the employer who belong to the class to which the union membership agreement relates since before the agreement had the effect of requiring them to be or become members of a trade union, and

(b) has not at any time while the agreement had that effect been a member of a trade union in accordance with the agreement.

(3C) Where a union membership agreement takes effect after the commencement of section 7 of the Employment Act 1980 in relation to the employees of any class of an employer, and an employee of that class is dismissed by the employer in the circumstances set out in subsection (3), the dismissal shall be regarded as unfair if —

(a) the agreement has not been approved in relation to those employees in accordance with section 58A, or

(b) it has been so approved through a ballot in which the dismissed employee was entitled to vote, but he has not at any time since the day on which the ballot was held been a member of a trade union in accordance with the agreement.

(3D) Where the employer of any employees changes in such circumstances that the employees' period of continuous employment is not broken, this section and section 58A shall have effect as if any reference to the employees of any class of the later employer included a reference to the employees of that class of the former employer.

(3E) In determining for the purposes of subsection (3B) and of section 58A(2) whether a person belongs to a class of employees, any restriction of the class by reference to membership (or objection to membership) of a trade union shall be disregarded.

(Subsection (4) was repealed by the Employment Act)

(5) Any reason by virtue of which a dismissal is to be regarded as unfair in consequence of subsection (1) or (3) is in this Part referred to as an inadmissible reason.

(6) In this section, unless the context otherwise requires, references to a trade union include references to a branch or section of a trade union.

58A (1) A union membership agreement shall be taken for the purposes of section 58(3C) to have been approved in relation to the employees of any class of an employer if a ballot has been held on the question whether the agreement should apply in relation to them and not less than 80 per cent of those entitled to vote in the ballot voted in favour of the agreement's application.

Ballots as to union membership agreements

(2) The persons entitled to vote in a ballot under this section in relation to the application of a union membership agreement to the employees of any class of an employer shall be all those employees who belong to that class, and are in the employment of the employer, on the day on which the ballot is held.

(3) A ballot under this section shall be so conducted as to secure that, so far as reasonably practicable, all those entitled to vote have an opportunity of voting, and of doing so in secret.

Note: It should be remembered that sections 4, 5, 10, 15 and 18 of the Employment Act are also designed to alleviate the problems of the closed shop for actual and potential employees. These sections are discussed in chapter 7 above.

This Appendix is reproduced with the permission of the Controller of Her Majesty's Stationery Office.

PART III

UNION SECURITY IN THE USA

8 The development of labour organisations and labour law in the USA

The deliberate intention of trade unions in the USA to achieve a measure of union security is not a recent phenomenon. In so far as they are concerned with union security, though not perhaps in other respects, craft unions are descended from medieval guilds in which membership was restricted and only guild members were entitled to do certain work. The guilds were recognised by the state and consequently grew to be extremely powerful from the fourteenth to the sixteenth century. Although their power later diminished and the guilds had practically disappeared by the seventeenth century their method of organisation for craft workers survived and was duly exported from the old world to the new.

American craft unions followed the established mode and favoured the closed shop as the most efficient method of regulating entry to trades. A Boston court recognised the right of carpenters to refuse to work with non-union members in 1675.[1] Indeed prior to the Civil War it was not unusual for unions to negotiate union security provisions similar to that found in a union constitution of 1842:

> Every person working at the business will be required to make application to join the society within one month from the time of his commencing work at any office in the city . . . on the refusal or neglect to comply with these regulations . . . the members of this society will cease to work in any office where such person may be employed.[2]

Not surprisingly the closed shop still prevails in trades and industries where crafts requiring high levels of skill and extensive training predominate, in particular when a lengthy term of apprenticeship must be served, for example printing and construction. The fact that skilled craftsmen are difficult to replace obviously gives craft unions an organisational advantage. Other unions which place less emphasis upon skill and training are still capable of operating closed, or at least union, shops as a consequence of their strategic importance, for example some groups within the teamsters (lorry-drivers), longshoremen (dockers) and some steelworkers. Whether or not a union will attempt to enforce a closed or union shop will vary with the type of employment and the availability of labour. In general the closed shop is found in skilled and strategically located trades and in industries in which employment is casual and intermittent. In other industries, for example textiles, bargaining strength and ability to demand union security provisions depend greatly upon local conditions and thus vary from region to region.

American unions seek security for much the same reasons as their British counterparts. But because they have been given a statutory obligation to represent all the employees in a bargaining unit, they are exceptionally insistent that all employees should, at the very least, make a financial contribution and preferably join the union. This statutory obligation has meant that the argument over union security is sometimes even more intense in the USA than it is in Britain.

In some industries it is claimed that union organisation would be virtually impossible without a union security agreement. This is probably true for industries such as maritime, entertainment and construction where employment is sporadic and of short duration. Due to the special conditions in these industries, unions organise most effectively prior to the contract of employment and many also operate as employment agencies supplying labour to employers. Strong union organisation of this kind may be favoured by employers and the introduction of the hiring hall sometimes 'arose more as a convenience to employers who wanted a central hiring office than as a means of union control'.[3]

Although American unions actively sought union security they found that it was not easy to obtain. At the beginning of the twentieth century all but a few were still struggling to establish themselves and gain employer recognition (see table 8.1). It was not until the late eighteenth century that the first unions managed to survive for any length of time in the USA; all were groups of either skilled or strategically important workers such as carpenters, shoemakers, printers, tailors, bakers, longshoremen and teamsters.[4] The labour movement continued to develop gradually during the nineteenth

Table 8.1
Total trade union membership and density in the USA:
selected years 1900-78[5]

Year	Civilian labour force[6] (millions)	Total union membership[7] (millions)	Density of union membership (per cent)
1900	28.8	0.9	3.0
1910	36.1	2.1	5.8
1920	41.2	4.9	11.8
1933	51.6	2.8	5.4
1938	54.6	5.8	10.7
1945	53.9	12.1	22.4
1950	62.2	14.3	23.0
1960	69.6	17.0	24.4
1970	82.7	19.7	23.8
1978	100.4	20.0	19.9

century despite the vulnerability of the newly formed unions to economic recession. The movement remained solidly craft based, however, and this situation was not seriously challenged until the appearance of the Noble Order of the Knights of Labor, a secret society founded in 1871 and opened to all in 1878. The Knights were opposed to the idea of pure craft unionism and attempted instead to unite all workers, skilled and unskilled, in one organisation. The success of this crude form of industrial unionism was spectacular and by 1886 membership had reached 700,000. However, decline was equally swift. By 1893 membership had fallen to 75,000[8] and in 1913 the society was officially dissolved.

One of the major factors in the decline of the Knights was the appearance of the American Federation of Labor (AFL) in 1886. Craft unions had not found the 'one union' approach satisfactory and the AFL, which was concerned only with those workers who could organise themselves, took advantage of this dissatisfaction. The AFL presented a policy of business unionism, intent on improving the wages and conditions of its members rather than radically changing society. Its growth was dramatic. Between 1897 and 1904 it issued 92 charters and by 1904 85 per cent of all national unions in the USA were affiliated.[9]

If craft workers had reached a tenuous security by the early twentieth century other workers were less successful. Their attempts to organise were continually frustrated although it became increasingly difficult to ignore their efforts. This determination of the unions to achieve security, and the equal determination of the employers to prevent them, inevitably resulted in industrial conflict. It was the role of the courts, prior to the 1920s, to cope with the developing problems and produce a workable labour policy. The American courts followed the English lead and applied the criminal conspiracy doctrine to labour disputes. In early cases the judiciary held that, although combination was not in itself unlawful, a concerted refusal to work, even in an attempt to improve standards of employment, was a conspiracy in restraint of trade.

The conspiracy doctrine was gradually relaxed, however, and became less freely applied. The *Commonwealth* v *Hunt*[10] decision of 1842 firmly established a narrowing of the doctrine by asserting that more than a concerted refusal to work for an employer who hired non-union labour was necessary to constitute conspiracy. This, naturally, resulted in fewer conspiracy cases and injunctions were increasingly used as a method of resolving labour disputes, particularly in the last two decades of the nineteenth century. Whether the judiciary misused its power with regard to the granting of injunctions is debatable. The unjunctions were, nevertheless, favoured by employers, who recognised a means of frustrating union organisation, but bitterly resented by organised labour. The resentment of the unions increased and the AFL launched a campaign to gain statutory protection from what it considered to be judicial interference and employer discrimination.

Until the late 1920s there were few statutes of any particular relevance to the control of union or management practices. The government had followed a policy of non-interference and the statutes that did exist were not successful. The Sherman Anti-Trust Act of 1890 was applied by the courts to labour unions, although Congress had intended that it be used only to prevent monopolistic business combinations. The Erdman Act of 1898 outlawed the yellow-dog contract — a document which included the employee's agreement not to join a union — but was declared by the Supreme Court to be unconstitutional, since it infringed the freedom of contract protected by the fifth amendment to the Constitution.[11] Similarly, the Supreme Court held a Kansas statute which attempted the same outlawing of the yellow-dog contract to be unconstitutional.[12] In the Clayton Act[13] of 1914 Congress attempted, without much success, to narrow the applicability of the anti-trust statute and to limit the power of the federal courts with regard to injunctions. Compared to subsequent legislation these early attempts to protect the right of unions to organise were ineffective. Nevertheless, they did represent a growing awareness on the part of the government that effective collective bargaining depended upon effective labour organisation.

The Railway Labor Act 1926 marked the first important step in the changeover from judicial to legislative control of labour relations. Its provisions guaranteed that unions in the railway industry would have procedures for the resolution of labour disputes. In the Norris La Guardia Act 1932 the federal courts' power to issue injunctions against labour unions was limited, and by 1941 judicial opinion had effectively changed when the Supreme Court decided that unions were virtually exempt from anti-trust statutes.[14] While the Act gave unions a shield against judicial interference it did not actually provide any encouragement to the growth of organised labour or the establishment of collective bargaining. The growth of the labour movement had continued steadily up to and following the First World War and between 1910 and 1920 membership doubled — see table 8.1. Following the war, however, craft unionism began to lose ground as new technology increased the number of semi-skilled and unskilled jobs. The AFL, faced with the changing face of production and sudden economic depression, began to falter and membership dropped dramatically so that by 1933 it had lost over a million workers. In fact union membership altogether fell by over 2 million between 1920 and 1933 (see table 8.1).

Congress was fully aware of these problems and in section 7(a) of the National Industrial Recovery Act 1933[15] attempted to persuade industry to recognise employees' rights to organise and bargain collectively. But the Act provided no power to enforce these rights and, in the face of management's resistance to organised labour, they were virtually useless. The National Labor Relations Act of 1935 (better known as the Wagner Act) attempted to overcome this problem by incorporating a means of enforcement. The government deliberately placed federal power behind union organisation by declaring that the national labour policy was the encouragement of collective bargaining; and by setting up the means whereby collective bargaining could develop, Congress hoped to create equality of power between labour and management. The inadequacies which had characterised earlier legislation were set aside by a new step in labour relations — the establishment of an effective body, the National Labor Relations Board (NLRB), created specifically by section 9 to secure compliance with the Act's provisions. At the same time the Wagner Act effectively removed the obstacles to union security devices.

The heart of Wagner was a duplicate of section 7(a) of the NIRA and states that

Employees shall have the right to self-organization, to form, join, or assist labor organizations, to bargain collectively through representatives of their own choosing, and to engage in concerted activities, for the purpose of collective bargaining or other mutual aid or protection.

This right to be recognised was linked with a complex procedure designed to determine with which union the employer was to bargain, culminating, if necessary, in an election at the plant ordered and organised by the NLRB under section 9(c). The representation election was designed to determine if the employees in a designated bargaining unit wanted to be represented by the petitioning union. Under section 9(a) the bargaining unit is the collectivity of workers to whom the terms of the contract applied, usually defined as the plant but it could equally be a craft or a class of workers. If the majority of the votes in the election support the union then that union is to be certified by the NLRB as the exclusive statutory bargaining representative for the unit (it should be noted that the Act originally called for a majority vote of the employees which the NLRB later interpreted to be a majority of employees voting).

It was hoped that this provision would not only promote union organisation but reduce inter-union rivalry, since only one union could be certified as the bargaining agent. It was, of course, advantageous for a union to be designated as the 'sole bargaining agent' with whom the employer was obliged to negotiate. The Wagner Act took an important step further and provided that the bargaining agent should be placed under a statutory duty to represent *all* workers in the unit, irrespective of membership or non-membership of the union. In a case which arose under the Railway Labor Act the Supreme Court construed that the union's right of exclusive representation also carried with it the duty to represent every worker, union or non-union, fairly and impartially.[16] Later this 'duty of fair representation', or the right of all employees to 'equal protection', was also held to apply in respect of the Wagner and Taft-Hartley Acts.

The rights granted in the Wagner Act were further protected by the introduction of a list of employer unfair practices in section 8, the most important of which banned discrimination 'to encourage or discourage membership in any labour organisation' (section 8(a)(3)). Obviously this placed a veto upon such devices as the yellow-dog contract and the black-list. A proviso to section 8(a)(3) specifically permitted all forms of union security. It provided 'that nothing in this Act, or in any other statute of the United States, shall preclude an employer from making an agreement with a labor organisation . . . to require as a condition of employment membership therein'. The combined effect of the unfair employer practices and the above proviso concerning the formulation of union security agreements was that only a requirement that a worker should belong to the union representative of the majority of employees was permissible as a part of the contract of continued employment.

The most noticeable characteristic of the Wagner Act was its one-sided nature. The Act directed all its sanctions against employers in the belief that all the shortcomings in federal labour relations resulted from the unions' inability to organise. Of course, if Wagner had also included restrictions on union activities the attainment of the principal goal of the legislation would probably not have been accomplished. The Act certainly gave unions the power to become a real force in industrial relations and as such represents the true starting point of modern labour law in the United States. The years following Wagner were characterised by a rapid increase in union membership, probably a direct result of the Act's sanctioning of union security arrangements. By 1945 union membership had reached 12 million (table 8.1) and many argued that the NLRA had in fact eliminated the need for union security. But unions remained suspicious of employers despite the new guarantees, and with a new threat of inter-union rivalry insisted upon union security provisions.

An eventful year for American labour was 1935. Not only was the Wagner Act introduced but the dominance of the AFL was challenged by the newly formed Committee for Industrial Organization (CIO). The CIO recruited members on an industry basis, regardless of skill or occupation. It successfully filled the gap in organisation which the AFL had been unwilling, or unable, to fill. The result was that a division developed in the American labour movement. Neither group was able to dominate, but with the Wagner provisions for representation union rivalry became frequent and bitter. The AFL did, however, abandon its strict craft union policy and adapted to attract semi-skilled workers.

Meanwhile critics were calling for the repeal of the Wagner Act and hoping that the judiciary would be more open to objections than Congress had been. They insisted that the provision for majority representation in section 9(a) deprived the individual of his right to negotiate with his employer and was unconstitutional under the due process clause of the Constitution. They further suggested that Congress had no jurisdiction to legislate in such a fashion. The Supreme Court, however, held the Act to be within the scope of Congress and opponents were forced to concentrate upon amending the Act's provisions.[17]

They were aided in their efforts by the labour movement itself. A series of strikes in the coal industry in 1942 focused the attention of the public upon industrial relations. The public gradually began to consider the labour movement irresponsible as they observed coercion of employees, organisational picketing, secondary boycotts and arbitrary expulsion of union members. After the Second World War the campaign for amendment was stepped up.

> Critics of the Wagner Act blamed either the Act or its administration by the NLRB as the cause of the strife. Proponents of the Act blamed management opposition to both the Act and unions as the cause. Perhaps a more accurate analysis would place the blame mainly on the growing pains of unions and the learning pains of management.[18]

By 1947 the general opinion seemed to be that the pendulum of power had swung well and truly in the direction of the unions and the pressure for amendment increased. In that year the critics were at last successful and the Labor Management Relations Act — better known as Taft-Hartley — amended the NLRA. In fact most of the major provisions that came together in the Taft-Hartley Act had already been introduced into Congress in various Bills prior to 1947.[19]

The passage of Taft-Hartley was understandably opposed by the unions. And just as Wagner's critics had sought to repeal the Act so the unions later launched a vigorous campaign for the repeal of Taft-Hartley. They were not successful, but their efforts did eventually bring about the healing of the split in the labour movement. Both the AFL and the CIO were concerned by the passage of the Act and realised that only in combining forces could they hope effectively to oppose any further legislation. Of course there were other considerations such as the pointlessness of 'raiding' each other's members, and for the CIO its depletion of members as a result of the expulsion of eleven national unions during 1949-50. Thus in 1955 the two joined forces to become a single organisation (AFL-CIO) with a combined membership of over 16 million.[20] However, the amalgamation did not have any great effect upon the ability of individual unions to organise effectively; and the strength of the organisation was not helped by the expulsion of the Teamsters in 1957 and the withdrawal of the Auto Workers in 1968. So despite the merger of the AFL and CIO, Taft-Hartley has not been repealed and after more than three decades its provisions remain virtually intact. The provisions of that Act will be carefully considered in the chapter which follows. But first it is necessary to say a little more about the differences between labour law and labour relations in Britain and the USA.

Aspects of public policy and labour relations in the USA

(a) The significance of a written constitution

In contrast to the UK where Parliament is sovereign and may introduce any legislation whatever, government in the USA may only be carried on in terms of the Constitution, a written instrument designed to limit and control political power which includes, to this end, a Bill of Rights guaranteeing individual liberties. The Constitution possesses the authority not just of law, but of supreme law, and thus provides a legal base by which governmental actions can be judged. It is superior to law enacted by Congress and any legislation contradicting its terms is void. The Supreme Court of the United States, as the appointed guardian of these constitutional guarantees, holds the authority to declare statutes unconstitutional. Thus it plays a major part in legislative evolution.

It was through judicial action, in 1936 and 1940, that the boundaries of modern US labour law were defined. Under Article 1, section 8, of the Federal Constitution Congress has the 'power to regulate commerce with foreign nations and among the several states'. This concept of inter-state commerce has proved to be extremely elastic, enabling Congress to pass laws dealing with trade, industry, agriculture and labour relations. However, at the beginning of this century the Supreme Court adopted a policy of narrowing its scope, particularly with regard to labour and employment. In a 1918 case, *Hammer* v *Dagenhart*,[21] the Supreme Court held an Act of Congress, prohibiting inter-state commerce in the products of child labour, invalid on the grounds that it was outside the inter-state commerce clause. 'That clause of the Constitution was said to extend to the inter-state transport of goods, but not to the production of goods for inter-state commerce.'[22]

When in 1936 the application of this principle threatened to destroy President Roosevelt's New Deal legislation, a full-scale constitutional crisis erupted. Roosevelt threatened to change the numerical composition of the Court and thus save the NLRA. In a series of decisions between 1936 and 1940[23] the judges prevented this dramatic action by altering their views. By 1940 the federal government had effectively acquired the power to enact legislation both to promote collective bargaining and to lay down substantive conditions of employment.

As a result of the redefinition of the commerce clause the most important labour law has increasingly become federal law. The USA is, of course, a federal republic whose member states possess their own legislative and judicial bodies and, consequently, a certain amount of political autonomy. Thus, both the federal government and state governments produce legislation. The potential incompatibility of these is reconciled in the supremacy clause of the Federal Constitution which provides that federal law made in pursuance of the Constitution 'shall be the supreme law of the land, and the judges in every state shall be bound thereby, any thing in the Constitution or laws of any state notwithstanding'. This doctrine has been applied more rigorously in labour law than in any other area; federal law in general pre-empts the field where any state attempts to act independently. In recent years, however, there has been an increased deference to the power of states to regulate in this area. The federal legislation does relate, in general, to the private sector alone and, thus, states are free to act as they see fit with regard to the public sector. One notable exception to federal supremacy in the private sector is found in the section 14(b) amendment to the NLRA, which allows the individual state legislatures discretion to ban all forms of union security within their boundaries.

(b)   The late development of federal statute law

In the UK Parliament was legislating for (or rather against) trade combinations in the eighteenth century, and the unions received their 'charter' in the Trade Union Act of 1871. In contrast, as has been seen, Congress did not begin to intervene in American labour law until the second quarter of the twentieth century, when action was taken in response to specific labour problems. As a result the main American labour statutes are not 'the product of rational evolution but political eruption',[24] and the National Labor Relations Act 1935[25] (NLRA), the Labor Management Relations Act 1947[26] (LMRA) and the Labor-Management Reporting and Disclosure Act 1959[27] (LMRDA) were produced at twelve-year intervals like massive legislative hiccoughs. The NLRA as amended by the other two statutes represents the basis of contemporary labour law in the USA.

(c)   The relative weakness of US unions

British and American unions appear to have a good deal in common. Trade union structure in the two countries has developed very much along the same lines, evolving from narrow craft unionism to the present complex system of large national unions of craft, occupational and industrial kinds. At the centre of both structures is a central co-ordinating body, the AFL-CIO in America and the TUC in Britain.[28] Within these organisations each member union retains autonomy regarding internal structure and bargaining policies. However, despite these similarities there are significant differences. American labour was divided from 1935 to 1955 between the AFL and CIO, who respectively represented craft and industrial unionism. As a result twenty years were spent in unnecessary, and often futile, organisational rivalry. Nor did the eventual merger of the two organisations effectively unite all organised labour in America, because several recalcitrant unions were eventually expelled from the Federation. In 1957 the International Brotherhood of Teamsters, Chauffeurs, Warehousemen and Helpers of America were expelled following the McClellan Committee's disclosure of corruption.[29] In 1968 the International Union of United Automobile, Aerospace and Agricultural Implement Workers of America (UAW) was expelled for non-payment of dues, which it withheld following a dispute over Federation policy. Ironically, the Teamsters, which is the largest American union, has continued to prosper while the AFL-CIO faces membership difficulties.

Not only is the AFL-CIO less comprehensive than the TUC but some of its objectives are different. American unionism, or job unionism as it is often called, is widely held to be a workplace phenomenon concerned with wages and conditions of employment. In contrast to British unionism it is not a social movement mainly because the American unions, faced with a heterogeneous society and the national emphasis upon individual advancement, could not rely on class solidarity. The basic objective of the American labour movement is not to eliminate the capitalist system but rather to share in its benefits; to this end it has supported free enterprise and shown a readiness to compromise with management. American unions have only sought to participate in management through collective bargaining. And yet despite the positive aspects of collective bargaining, and even though it has never been under major attack by any hostile ideology promoted by labour, American management generally prefers to operate non-union. Thus American unions are usually operating in a more hostile environment than their British counterparts.

(d)   The terminology and nature of union security

In marked contrast to the relatively informal British arrangements, the typical collective agreement between a company and a union in the USA is a detailed legally binding document, lasting for two or three years and covering most, if not all, aspects of the employment relationship, perhaps including union security. Compulsory membership was made illegal by the Taft-Hartley Act in 1947 and is, therefore, not to be found in formal agreements. But it is well known that it continues to exist in practice, and there is a range of other legitimate possibilities which come under the general heading of union security and must be briefly defined.

The closed shop.   The most comprehensive form of union security is known as the pre-entry closed shop in Britain and simply the closed shop in the USA. Union membership is a pre-condition of hiring and retention of membership is a condition of continued employment. Loss of membership is clearly a serious matter.

The union shop.   The union shop (British 'post-entry' closed shop) allows non-members to be hired but obliges all employees to become union members within a specified period (usually 30-60 days) and to remain in membership. The 'modified union shop' allows certain categories of employees — for example non-members when the agreement was negotiated — exemption from membership, but they will often be required to pay the equivalent of union dues and fees either to the union, as a contribution to collective bargaining expenses, or to a charity.

The agency shop.   The agency shop, or contributory non-membership agreement, allows a non-member to be hired or retained in employment without joining the union; but he must be willing to pay to the union, or in some cases to a charity, the equivalent of initiation fees and periodic dues.

The preferential shop.   This kind of agreement provides for union members to be given precedence over other applicants for job vacancies. In some occupations such as longshore (the docks) and maritime (shipping), where job assignments are allocated through a hiring hall (a union-run job agency), preferential hiring may amount to a closed shop.

Maintenance of membership.   Employees are under no obligation to join the union. But those who were members when the agreement was negotiated, or who join subsequently, must remain members for the duration of the contract. Such agreements may be 'revocable', i.e. employees may be able to leave the union during specified periods (usually ten days at the end of each year) without losing their jobs.

Exclusive bargaining rights.   In the USA a union representing the majority of employees in a bargaining unit has a statutory right to be the sole bargaining agent for all employees in that unit. This in itself could be said to constitute a limited form of security although no employee is required to become a union member, or pay dues and fees to the union, as a condition of employment.

Check-off agreement.   Most union security clauses also include an irrevocable check-off agreement, as indeed do many contracts which contain no other form of union security except the check-off itself. This means that an individual who decides to discharge his financial obligation to the union may also authorise the employer, for a fixed term not exceeding two years, to deduct union dues directly from his wages and forward them to the union. Under an irrevocable agreement the employee is bound to continue this authorisation, and the employer is equally bound to honour it, until the end of the fixed term.

Thus, between the closed shop, with its requirement of union membership as a condition of hire and continued employment, and the introduction of a check-off provision there exists a wide range of possible union security arrangements on the basis of which agreement might be reached; a 1976 survey of 1,570 major labour agreements, covering 6.7 million workers in the private sector, showed that 80 per cent contained some form of union security clause.[30] Legislation in the USA has ostensibly limited the choice available by making the closed shop and true union shop illegal. The law does not, however, impose sanctions and is not operative unless an individual employee complains of an unfair labour practice.

References

1   Toner, J.L., *The Closed Shop*, Am. Council on Public Affairs, 1942, p.59.
2   'The Constitution of the Typographical Society' in Stockton, T., *The Closed Shop in American Unions,* John Hopkins University Studies in Social Sciences, 29th Ser., 1911.
3   Bloom, G.F. and Northrup, H.R., *Economics of Labor Relations*, 8th edn, R.D. Irwin Inc. 1977, p.185.
4   Bloom, G.F. and Northrup, H.R., op.cit., p.39.
5   Up to and including 1945 figures are taken from *Trade Union Membership 1897-1962* by Troy, L., Occasional Paper 92 of the National Bureau of Economic Research 1965, p.2 (and printed in *The Review of Economics and Statistics*, February 1965). From 1950 to 1960 the figures are taken from the *Handbook of Labor Statistics 1975*, Reference edition, Bulletin 1865, published by the US Department of Labor, BLS, pp. 26 and 389. The 1970 and 1978 figures appear in Bureau of Labor Statistics, Directory of National Unions and Employee Associations, various editions.
N.B. Troy's methodology differs from that of the Bureau of Labor Statistics and therefore the data are not strictly comparable. It does, however, provide a reasonable indication of the development of the US labour movement.
6   These figures for the civilian labour force, unlike their British equivalent, include employers and the self-employed. If these groups

were excluded the labour force would be reduced accordingly and the density of union membership would rise proportionally.

7   These figures do not include agricultural workers or members of employee associations. Their inclusion would increase the total union membership figures and, thus, the density figures.

8   Bloom, G.F. and Northrup, H.R. op.cit., p.43.

9   Estey, M., *The Unions, Structure, Development and Management*, 2nd edn., Harcourt Brace Jovanovich Inc. 1977, p.17.

10   45 Mass. (4 Met) Ill (1842).

11   *Adair* v *US* 208 US 161 (1908).

12   *Coppage* v *Kansas* 236 US 1 (1915).

13   October 15 1914 38 Stat 730.

14   *US* v *Hutcheson* 312 US 219 (1941).

15   48 Stat 198-99 (1933).

16   *Steele* v *Louisville & Nashville Railroad*, 323 US 192 (1944).

17   *NLRB* v *Jones and Laughlin Steel Corp.* 301 US 1 (1936). The court held that the NLRA — Wagner Act — was covered by the inter-state commerce clause and thus Congress was within its scope of power in enacting such legislation.

18   Bloom, G.F. and Northrup, H.R., op.cit., p.599.

19   Two hundred and thirty major bills dealing with this issue were introduced from 1936 until the passage of Taft-Hartley — excluding the Taft-Hartley proposals themselves. Millis, H.A. and Brown, E.C., *From the Wagner Act to Taft-Hartley*, University of Chicago Press 1950, n.25, p.333.

20   Estey, M., op.cit., p.32. In fact 16.1 million.

21   24 US 251.

22   Kahn-Freund, O., 'The Impact of Constitutions on Labour Law', *Cambridge Law Journal*, 35(2), November 1976, p.249.

23   *NLRB* v *Jones and Laughlin Steel Corporation*, 301 US 1 (1936); *United States* v *Darby*, 312 US 100 (1940).

24   Summers, C., 'American and European Labor Law: The Use and Usefulness of Foreign Experience', *Buff. L. Rev.*, vol.16, 1966, p.217.

25   49 Stat 449, 1935.

26   Pub. L. No.101, 80th Cong., 1947, 61 Stat 136.

27   Pub. L. No.86-257, 86th Cong., 1959, 2nd sess., 73 Stat 519.

28   American Federation of Labor-Congress of Industrial Organizations and Trades Union Congress.

29   International appears in the title of most American unions and denotes their willingness to admit to membership and represent workers in the Dominion of Canada.

30   Characteristics of Major Collective Bargaining Agreements, 7 July 1976, US Department of Labor, Bureau of Labor Statistics (BLS) 1979, Bulletin 2013. The agreements covered 1,000 or more workers in the private sector.

9 The provisions of the Taft-Hartley Act

The Wagner Act survived unaltered for twelve years during which time it effectively changed the process of collective bargaining in the USA. In 1946, aware of mounting anti-union sentiment, President Truman proposed a limited revision of the Act; Congress, however, was intent on greater reform and, despite the presidential veto which it overruled by the required two-thirds majority, pushed a more substantial Bill through both Houses. The resulting statute, the Labor Management Relations Act of 1947 (commonly referred to as the Taft-Hartley Act) amended the Wagner Act considerably and shifted the emphasis of labour law so that it became less favourable to unions. Although further amendments were adopted, chiefly the Labor-Management Reporting and Disclosure Act of 1959 (the Landrum-Griffin Act), the main source of the present system of labour relations in the USA remains the Wagner Act as amended by Taft-Hartley.

The coverage of the Taft-Hartley Act is broad but it is not applicable to all employees in the USA. In Section2(3), which is substantially the same as that in Wagner, the term 'employee' is defined so as to exclude

> . . . any individual employed as an agricultural laborer, or in the domestic service of any family or person at his home, or any individual employed by his parent or spouse, or any individual contractor, or any individual employed as a supervisor, or any individual employed by an employer subject to the Railway Labor Act[1] . . . or by any person who is not an employer as herein defined.

Under Section 14(a) supervisors are specifically entitled to become and remain members of a labour organisation, but since they are not protected against employer unfair labour practices the right has little meaning. The Act's coverage is further limited by its interpretation of the term 'employer' which does not include '. . . the United States or any wholly owned Government Corporation, or any Federal Reserve Bank, or any state or political subdivision thereof . . . ',[2] thus confining its provisions to private industry. Union security arrangements in the public sector are a different matter entirely and states and localities are free to act — or not to act — as they see fit. When the public sector was excluded in 1947 the rapid post-war growth of public employee associations could not easily have been foreseen.[3] Nevertheless, the Taft-Hartley amendments prescribe the employment rights and duties of labour organisations, employers and individual employees for a large part of US industry.

The right to refrain from union membership; and unfair labour practices

The original provision of section 7 of the Wagner Act, as noted earlier, entitled employees to organise freely and it made this right effective by permitting them to elect their own bargaining representative, with whom the employer was required to negotiate. The section was amended by Taft-Hartley to provide in addition that employees

> . . . shall also have the right to refrain from any or all of such activities except to the extent that such right may be affected by an agreement requiring membership in a labor organization as a condition of employment as authorized in section 8(a)(3).

The section 8(a)(3) exception allows the elected representative of the employees to negotiate a variety of union security agreements with the employer; although what could constitute a valid union security provision was revised so that pre-entry membership conditions are no longer permissible.

As will be recalled, section 8 of the Wagner Act listed a number of unfair practices which could be committed by an employer. Section 8(b) was added in its entirety to complement the section 7 amendment and to balance the original employer unfair practices with a similar group of unfair union practices. For example, section 8(b)(1) provides that it is an unfair labour practice for a labour organisation or its agents

> . . . to restrain or coerce (A) employees in the exercise of the rights

guaranteed in section 7: Provided, That this paragraph shall not impair the right of a labor organization to prescribe its own rules with respect to the acquisition or retention of membership therein;

Taft-Hartley seeks, albeit in a limited way, to protect the rights of individual employees in relation to labour organisations, an area which Wagner had not attempted to cover.

Various union actions have been held to violate section 8(b)(1)(A) including threats of loss of employment[4] and non-violent force such as mass picketing;[5] a union which calls a strike in order to force an employer to discriminate against an employee for exercising the right of non-association is equally guilty of an unfair labour practice.[6] It remains illegal for an employer under section 8(a)(1) 'to interfere with, restrain, or coerce employees in the exercise of the rights guaranteed in section 7', including, of course, the right to refrain from union membership. Section 8(a)(3) further provides that it is unfair for an employer 'by discrimination in regard to hire or tenure of employment or any term or condition of employment to encourage or discourage membership in any labor organization'. This condition is subject to the section 8(a)(3) proviso which allows the negotiation of a valid union security agreement.

In effect the present legislation provides under section 8(a) that the employer may not lawfully discourage or encourage union membership while the union, under section 8(b), is equally restrained from putting pressure on employees to become members, either by direct coercion or indirectly by inducing the employer to discriminate against non-members. Where a violation of an employee's section 7 right to non-membership occurs, whether initiated by an employer or a union, he is entitled to the same remedies available for a violation of the right to organise. Section 10(c) grants the NLRB power to issue cease and desist orders to implement the policies of the Act by preventing further unfair labour practices. The Board may also reinstate the complainant, with back pay if considered appropriate.

With regard to the union's section 8(b)(1) right to prescribe its own rules for the acquisition and retention of membership it should be noted that according to section 8(a)(3) a union may not discriminate, or encourage an employer to discriminate, against an employee for non-membership when it has been 'denied or terminated for reasons other than the failure of the employee to tender the periodic dues and the initiation fees uniformly required . . . '. And section 8(b)(5) limits the initiation fee, which a union may charge an employee required to become a union member as a condition of continued employment, to a reasonable and non-discriminatory amount.

The Taft-Hartley provisions and
union security agreements

The Taft-Hartley amendments significantly affect the content of union security provisions, although the principles laid down by the Wagner Act concerning the circumstances which must precede their negotiation remain unaltered. The first step towards union security is still accomplished when an employer, voluntarily or following an NLRB election, recognises the union as the exclusive bargaining agent for the workers in the unit. After recognition the employer and the union enter into collective bargaining to decide upon the terms and conditions of employment. A high priority consideration for a union during negotiations, despite the fact that it acquires a measure of security as soon as it signs a contract with the employer, is the inclusion of a union security clause. However, a security agreement may only be validly negotiated if the union concerned is the recognised bargaining agent of the employees and if, as under the original Wagner Act, an authorisation election is held among the employees. Union security is a mandatory subject of bargaining; the employer must bargain about it 'in good faith' but he is under no statutory obligation to agree to it or indeed to any substantive term negotiated.

Union security agreements were increasingly used following the passage of the Wagner Act and many included pre-entry membership of the union as a condition of employment. In 1946, prior to the enactment of the Taft-Hartley Act, it was estimated that 33 per cent of all workers under agreements were covered by closed shop provisions with a further 17 per cent subject to union shop requirements.[7] While Congress had no wish to regulate the internal procedures of unions it was disturbed by their ability to expel members, often for seemingly arbitrary reasons, and where closed or union shops existed also effect their dismissal from employment. The proviso to section 8(a)(3) of the Wagner Act which stated

> . . . nothing in this Act, or in any other statute of the United States, shall preclude an employer from making an agreement with a labor organization . . . to require as a condition of employment membership therein

placed no limitation upon the form which union security could take and it was felt that it had therefore led to abuse. Congress hoped effectively to prohibit the closed shop, in all agreements negotiated between employers and unions, by enlarging section 8(a)(3) to provide that membership could only be agreed upon

> . . . on or after the thirtieth day following the beginning of such

employment or the effective date of such agreement, whichever is
the later . . . .

Under this amendment to the proviso only the union shop, itself
subject to substantial limitations, was held to be authorised, and as
will become clear later in this chapter those limitations are so substantial that, in fact, the most the statute can be held to permit is the
agency shop. The NLRB and the courts have consistently decided that
any agreement which provides for union membership as a precondition
of employment cannot 'be valid under the amended NLRA'.[8]

In 1934, well before the Taft-Hartley provisions, the 1926 Railway
Labor Act had been amended so as to make the pre-entry closed shop
illegal within the railway industry. In fact, all forms of union security
had been prohibited in an attempt to counteract the company-
dominated unions prevalent in the industry. But by 1951 the problem
had disappeared and section 2, eleventh, was added to the Act to bring
it roughly into line with Taft-Hartley by allowing post-entry union
membership agreements. RLA agreements are unusual, however, in that
employees may belong to a union which is not the elected bargaining
agent.

Hiring halls

It was a common practice in many industries, before the enactment of
the Taft-Hartley amendments, for employers to hire through the union
or at least to give preference to union members in hiring. This was
particularly true of industries where craft unionism predominated,
employers were small and work was often intermittent, for example
the construction industry. Under such a 'hiring hall' arrangement the
union, upon an employer's request, supplied the required number of
employees usually on a priority or seniority basis but sometimes simply
first come first served. Most unions operating hiring halls maintained a
register of workers available for employment and registration was
restricted to union members.

It is not clear what the intention of the Taft-Hartley Congress was
with regard to hiring-hall arrangements. In the Senate Report it states:

> In the maritime industry and to a large extent in the construction
> industry union hiring halls now provide the only method of
> securing employment. This not only permits unions holding such
> monopolies over jobs to exact excessive fees but it deprives
> management of any real choice of the men it hires.[9]

Obviously, with the Taft-Hartley prohibition of the closed shop it is no longer permissible for any union to operate a hiring hall which benefits only union members or which binds an employer to discriminate against non-members with regard to hiring, as both amount to pre-entry membership conditions. Although such arrangements are prohibited under sections 8(a)(3) and 8(b)(2) of Taft-Hartley the actual operation of a hiring hall is not contrary to the law, provided it does not become a discriminatory closed shop.

The hiring hall, or union employment agency, may exist under present legislation provided all employees who wish to work in the industry, regardless of union membership or non-membership, are enrolled on the union register. Once on the register all prospective employees must be treated equally. In *Teamsters Local 357 v NLRB* the Supreme Court made it clear that, under the Taft-Hartley Act, hiring hall arrangements were not unlawful unless they resulted in discrimination against non-union applicants.[10]

In the *Mountain Pacific*[11] decision the NLRB presented certain safeguards, to be included in collective agreements, which would, it was held, prevent abuse of hiring hall arrangements. The Board contended that the hiring hall would be *prima facie* invalid unless three specific provisions were complied with. These criteria were:

1. that applicants should not be chosen for referral on the basis of union membership or any other discriminatory condition.

2. that the employer must retain the right to reject applicants, even when they are referred for employment by the union, and

3. it should be publicised that the hiring hall is not discriminatory.

Whether or not actual discrimination occurred, a failure on the union's part to comply with these three provisions automatically invalidated the hiring hall arrangement.

In the *Teamsters Local 357*[12] case the Supreme Court insisted that actual discrimination must be shown to exist and in consequence non-compliance with the formula presented by the Board in *Mountain Pacific* was insufficient to invalidate a hiring hall. Thus, discrimination within the meaning of sections 8(b)(2) and 8(a)(3) of the Taft-Hartley Act cannot simply be presumed; it must be shown to exist. In other words, if a hiring hall is not proved to be operating discriminatorily, the unions can legally require that an employer discharge any applicant who refuses to use the union's employment agency.

The fact that Congress did not intend to ban hiring halls indiscriminately, without regard to the circumstances producing them, seems to be borne out in the exceptions which it has subsequently allowed. Shortly after Taft-Hartley was enacted an amendment was introduced to exempt the maritime unions from the prohibitions against the closed shop.[13] Hiring halls in the maritime industry have been beneficial to both employers and employees alike and, as pointed out by the NLRB, such provisions '. . . continue to serve as a means to eliminate wasteful, time consuming, and repetitive scouting for jobs by individual workmen and haphazard uneconomic searches by employers'.[14] In 1959 a further exemption was added under section 8(f) by the Landrum-Griffin amendment which provided that it would not be an unfair labour practice for an employer and a union in the building and construction industry to base priority for hiring upon seniority and length of employment in a particular geographic area.

A union is entitled to charge a fee to all employees who use the hiring hall facilities but such a fee must be reasonable and related solely to the services provided.[15] One remedy, proposed by the NLRB, to cope with discriminatory hiring halls is that all dues collected in connection with the illegal agency, for six months prior to the claim of unfair labour practice, should be returned to the employees involved.[16] The Supreme Court found that such a proposal was beyond the power of the Board to implement.[17] The remedy which has been evolved by the Board and approved by a Court of Appeal, requires the keeping of records by the union to show the operation of the hiring hall. These accounts must be made available to the NLRB regional director on request and supposedly prevent any attempt on the part of the union to enforce excessive service fees for the use of the hiring hall.[18]

The union shop

Although Taft-Hartley banned the closed shop it did sanction the operation of the union shop in sections 8(a)(3) and 8(b)(2), subject to substantial modification. Unions and management were permitted, but not compelled, to negotiate a union security agreement which required employees to join the union, 'on or after the thirtieth day following the beginning of such employment or the effective date of such agreement, whichever is the later . . . '. This provision was drastically limited by the addition of two qualifying provisos:

> Provided further, That no employer shall justify any discrimination against an employee for non-membership in a labor organization (A) if he has reasonable grounds for believing that such membership was not available to the employee on the same terms and conditions generally applicable to other members, or

(B) if he has reasonable grounds for believing that membership was denied or terminated for reasons other than the failure of the employee to tender the periodic dues and initiation fees uniformly required as a condition of acquiring or retaining membership.

Section 8(a)(3), with its provisos, represents the Congressional attempt to reconcile the conflicting demands of individual employees for freedom to refrain from union membership and the demands of labour organisations for union security measures. Congress specifically recognised the union members' objection to working with 'free-riders' and had no intention of preventing unions from obtaining support payments from such employees. According to a Supreme Court judgement, however, the policy underlying the section 8(a)(3) provisos is a determination to divorce the conditions of the employment contract from union membership.[19] The sole duty of an employee, covered by a union security clause, to pay dues and fees to the union, has led to a reassessment of both the concept of membership and the exact nature of 'compulsory dues' (that is, what the unions can require an employee to pay in respect of collective bargaining services).

The meaning of membership: the union shop or the agency shop?

The term 'require membership' in the union which appears in section 8(a)(3) meant more under the original Wagner Act than it does now under the Taft-Hartley amendment. Where a valid union shop agreement has been negotiated between union and management, an employee's *only* obligation is to be willing to tender dues and fees as required by the union. A union cannot, under section 8(b)(2),

> . . . cause or attempt to cause an employer to discriminate against an employee in violation of subsection (a)(3) or to discriminate against an employee with respect to whom membership in such organization has been denied or terminated on some ground other than his failure to tender the periodic dues and the initiation fees uniformly required as a condition of acquiring or retaining membership;

In other words the reference to membership in the statute does not refer to 'formal' membership, which usually denotes something more than a payment of periodic dues. The individual employee, who chooses not to join the union in the 'formal' sense is not subject to full union discipline since the union's imposition of any qualification or condition, other than the payment of fees, with which he does not comply cannot legally result in his dismissal from employment. As it was stated in *NLRB* v *General Motors Corporation*:[20]

> . . . the burdens of membership upon which employment may be conditioned are expressly limited to the payment of initiation fees and monthly dues. It is permissible to condition employment upon membership, but membership insofar as it has significance to employment rights may in turn be conditioned upon payment of fees and dues. "Membership" as a condition of employment is whittled down to its financial core.

In *re Union Starch Refining Co.*[21] three workers tendered dues and fees but declined to comply with any other duties related to membership in the union. The NLRB found the union's assertion that the workers' conduct amounted to a refusal to become union members was incorrect, since a willingness to tender dues and fees was all that was required to bring them under the protection of the section 8(a)(3) provisos. A minority of the Board dissented, stating that membership should consist of more than a 'mere willingness to pay the organization's dues and fees, and certainly encompasses a willingness to comply with reasonable formalities in the process of joining'.[22] Where a valid union security agreement exists the union has in theory, then, no power to discipline or dismiss an employee for any reason other than non-payment of dues and fees. Of course, a union may expel an employee who refuses to follow union directives from formal association with the union or impose fines, but if that employee is prepared to tender dues and fees he may not be dismissed from employment. He may, however, be barred from participating in union activities such as elections.

Since the payment of fees is of paramount importance to the requirement of membership, section 8(b)(5) provides that initiation fees may not be discriminatory or excessive. Similarly, there are restrictions upon what constitute dues and the amount of dues which are required. Whether a union's initiation fee is excessive under section 8(b)(5) depends upon 'the practices and customs of labour organizations in a particular industry, and the wages currently paid to the employees affected'. Nor, under section 8(a)(3)(A), may an employer distinguish between one group of employees and another; all must be treated equally. In addition, union fines are not dues or fees and refusal to pay them cannot result in legal dismissal.

Following the *Union Starch* decision it would seem that the most Taft-Hartley authorises is the agency shop and not the union shop. It will be remembered that the agency shop does not require membership in a labour organisation as a condition of continued employment but rather the payment of a service fee to the representative union. The framers of the Taft-Hartley amendments actually worked from a model of the agency shop, as is shown in the remarks made by Senator Taft during the Senate debates on the conference Bill:

> (T)he rule adopted by the committee is substantially the rule now in effect in Canada . . . that there can be a closed shop or union shop and the union does not have to admit any employee who applies for membership, but (if) the employee pays dues, without joining the union, he has the right to be employed.[23]

Senator Taft was citing a Canadian arbitration case in which the union's request for a full union shop was denied but a regular check-off of an amount equivalent to union dues from both union and non-union employees was permitted.[24]

There is in reality little difference between the modified union shop allowed by section 8(a)(3) and the traditional agency shop. The only difference would appear to be that under a union shop provision the union, subject to uniform requirements of admission, decides whether or not to enrol an employee as a union member following the tender of dues and fees, while with an agency shop agreement the choice lies with the employee who decides whether or not to join the union. It is also possible that the amount of financial support demanded will vary between union and agency shop provisions. The theory of 'compulsory dues' payment is that each employee should pay his share of the union's expenses as bargaining agent. The section 8(a)(3) union shop payment is usually taken to be the equivalent of periodic fees and dues whereas a proportional payment in consideration of actual services may satisfy an agency shop agreement.

The courts have, in fact, been imposing general limits on the payment of money which may be required by a union. For obvious constitutional reasons the Supreme Court has held that unions cannot compel the payment of monies which are to be used for political purposes,[25] a question discussed at greater length later in the chapter. More recently the lower federal courts have expanded on the Supreme Court decision to exclude payment for *any* non-collective bargaining purposes. In a Maryland district court decision, *Beck* v *Communications Workers of America*, the Special Master presiding found the service fee in an agency shop to equal just 19 per cent of the full fees and dues charged by the union.[26]

The new meaning of 'membership' contained in Taft-Hartley can only be construed, therefore, to mean that an employee should neither be forced to become a 'formal' member of a union as a condition of employment nor to pay fees and dues for any purpose other than to cover the costs necessarily incurred by the bargaining agent properly to represent all employees. Thus, the statute uses the term 'membership' when, in fact, membership as it is generally understood is not meant and the most restrictive union security agreement that can be authorised is the agency shop.

The thirty-day grace period

A union must allow a new employee at least thirty days to become a union member, that is he must be allowed no less than thirty days within which to tender dues and fees. An agreement which requires membership 'within thirty days' is sufficient to satisfy the statutory requirements of section 8(a)(3),[27] and an employee who does not tender dues and fees within the required period may be dismissed, unless he makes a 'belated tender' before the union requests dismissal.[28] One exception to this strictly observed rule is contained in section 8(f) which was added by Landrum-Griffin. Employees in the building and construction industry may be validly required to join a labour organisation 'after the seventh day following the beginning of such employment or the effective date of the agreement, whichever is later . . . '. This partial exemption was granted because of the very short duration of some jobs in the industry.

Authorisation and deauthorisation elections

The Taft-Hartley amendments originally included a legal requirement that employees should vote to authorise the union security negotiations prior to an agreement's implementation, as a protection against arbitrary action by the union hierarchy. In the first years of voting under the provision approximately 98 per cent of the 2 million employees who voted approved union security arrangements. This cannot be taken to prove that union leaders had the wholehearted support of their members, since most employees appear to have been confused as to the exact nature of the election. Employees, in fact, endorsed their belief in unionism in general. The authorisation clause was removed by a 1951 amendment[29] although the deauthorisation election, which was its negative equivalent, was retained. Under the deauthorisation provision the employees whose union had signed a union security contract were given an opportunity to 'deauthorise' the union shop. If 30 per cent of the workers in the bargaining unit request an election the NLRB is obliged to conduct one, and if a majority vote against the union shop it will no longer be a condition of the contract of employment. The NLRB is required to conduct the deauthorisation election even though the petitioning employees are not union members and even if the petition is encouraged by a rival union or the employer.

Check-off arrangements

A check-off arrangement is not strictly speaking a union security device but it is generally allied to such an agreement. The Taft-Hartley Act prohibits the compulsory check-off, the means whereby the employer deducts union dues from his workers' wages and pays them directly to the union. Under section 302 an employer is prohibited from making any payments to the employees' representative except:

> . . . with respect to money deducted from the wages of employees in payment of membership dues in a labor organization: Provided, That the employer has received from each employee, on whose account such deductions are made, a written assignment which shall not be irrevocable for a period of more than one year, or beyond the termination date of the applicable collective agreement, whichever occurs sooner . . . .

It seems strange that the check-off provision was not included in section 8(a)(3) considering the relationship which exists between it and union security.

Political expenditure

Even the limited membership requirement of payment of dues and fees sanctioned by Taft-Hartley in section 8(a)(3) has not been acceptable to some employees. It has been argued that the section 8(a)(3) union shop provision forces employees to support ideological and political associations irrespective of their own personal beliefs. Congress supported the unions' right to eliminate the 'free-rider' but did not provide any guidelines as to what extent an employee should also contribute to the political activities of the organisation. The Federal Corrupt Practices Act of 1947, which was amended by Taft-Hartley[30] and made applicable to labour organisations, forbids unions to use dues directly in election campaigns, but the use of funds for lobbying and the publication of political articles is permissible. Under an RLA case a dissenting employee was permitted to refrain from paying any political expenditure which he objected to,[31] while in *The Brotherhood of Railway and Steamship Clerks* v *Allen* the dissenting employee was held to be entitled to refrain from all political expenditure without having to show particular objections.[32]

Religious objectors

In the past religious objectors have not been as fortunate as those who have protested at the use of their funds for political purposes. Taft-Hartley provided that unions must not discriminate against non-unionists but it made no special provisions for religious objectors except in one limited case. Section 19 of the Act was added in 1974 and specially protected employees of health care institutions who had religious and conscientious objections 'to joining or financially supporting labor organizations'. However, they might be required to make an equivalent contribution to a non-religious charitable fund. Those who did not come within the scope of section 19 might have gained some protection from the Civil Rights Act of 1964[33] which makes it an unfair labour practice for a labour organisation:

(1) to exclude or to expel from its membership, or otherwise to discriminate against any individual because of his race, color, religion, sex or national origin;

(2) to limit, segregate or classify its membership . . . in any way which would deprive an individual of employment opportunities because of . . . race, color, religion, sex or national origin;

(3) to cause, or attempt to cause an employer to discriminate against an individual in violation of this section.

These stipulations do not, however, affect the requirement that all employees covered by a union security agreement pay support fees to the union. In one case a group of workers objected to paying money into a common treasury used to support unbelievers, as they were required to do under an RLA agreement.[34] They did state a willingness to pay an equivalent sum to charity, as health-care workers are now entitled to do under section 19, but they were unsuccessful.

Seventh-Day Adventists have been a predominant group attempting to assert a right to refrain from the payment of union dues and fees, but they too have been unsuccessful.[35] The courts have been extremely strict with regard to religious objectors. Judge Learned Hand expressed the general judicial view in *Otten v Baltimore and Ohio Railroad Co.*:

. . . the First Amendment gives no one the right to insist that in pursuit of their own interests others must conform their conduct to his own religious necessities . . . . We must accommodate our idiosyncrasies, religious as well as secular, to the compromises necessary in communal life, we can hope for no reward for the sacrifices this may require beyond our satisfaction from within, or our expectations of a better world.[36]

More recently, however, attempts have been made under Title VII of the Civil Rights Act to balance the interests of religious employees who object to union security requirements with those of the employer and the union. The Civil Rights Act currently holds that an employer has an obligation to 'reasonably accommodate' the religious beliefs of an employee unless such accommodation would result in 'undue hardship' with regard to the conducting of business.[37] A reasonable accommodation would appear to be possible in most instances without undue hardship to the employer provided the employee pays the equivalent of dues and fees to a charity.

The question of reasonable accommodation may become redundant as a consequence of an Act recently passed by Congress.[38] The Act amends Taft-Hartley by expanding the section 19 health care exemption to cover all religious objectors. Thus, genuine religious objectors are now exempt from all obligations with regard to union membership and the payment of fees and dues.

The Landrum-Griffin Act

It will be recalled that Taft-Hartley specifically provided in section 8(b)(1)(A) that a union should retain the right 'to prescribe its own rules with respect to the acquisition or retention of membership. . . .'. Nevertheless, congressional concern for the rights of individual employees led to close scrutiny of the internal policies and practices of labour organisations. The 1950s were marked by a number of governmental investigations into union administration. In 1952-53, for example, the practices of the International Longshoremen's Association were reviewed by the New York State Crime Commission of Racketeering on the New York City waterfront. More important were the well publicised findings of the McClellan Committee — the Select Committee on Improper Activities in the Labor or Management Field 1957-59 — which revealed corruption in certain unions and led to the enactment of the Landrum-Griffin Act in 1959.[39] The Act was chiefly directed at the regulation of internal union procedures, but it also contained several amendments and additions to Taft-Hartley.

The law begins in Title I with what is called the Bill of Rights for union members, designed to provide certain standards of union democracy and to safeguard the rights of the individual employee in his role as a union member. The title includes, among other things, the right to attend, to participate and to vote in union meetings and elections and the right of an individual member to sue his own union, and it guarantees freedom of assembly. The union officials are placed under an obligation to provide copies of collective bargaining agreements on request. Of especial interest with regard to union security is protection from increases in dues or the imposition of special assessments, except where specified procedures are followed. These include a membership referendum conducted by secret ballot, or a vote of the national union convention. It is also provided that:

> No member of any labor organization may be fined, suspended, expelled, or otherwise disciplined except for non-payment of dues by such organization or by any officer thereof unless such member has been (A) served with written specific charges; (B) given a reasonable time to prepare his defense; (C) afforded a full and fair hearing.

Section 101(b) adds that 'Any provision of the constitution and bylaws of any labor organization which is inconsistent with the provisions of this section shall be of no force or effect'.

Unlike the Wagner and Taft-Hartley Acts a violation of one of the rights guaranteed under Title I is not remedied by an administrative agency, the NLRB. An injured party is entitled to 'bring a civil action in a district court of the United States for such relief (including injunctions) as may be appropriate'. The time and cost involved in bringing such a law suit obviously limits this section's effectiveness in protecting the individual union member.

Title II of the Act outlines reporting requirements which must be met by labour organisations, union employees and officers and employers. All reports must be filed with the Secretary of Labor, failure to do so being open to criminal sanctions. The union is required to give financial details such as yearly income, assets, expenditures, payments and loans to business and union officers. The union is further required to adopt a constitution and bylaws which must also be filed with the Secretary. The information outlined in the constitution must include, among other matters, details of initiation fees and regular membership dues or fees or other periodic payments, as well as the provision made and procedures followed with respect to qualifications for, or restrictions on, membership and the imposition of fines, suspensions and expulsions of members. These provisions complement the Taft-Hartley sections 8(a)(3) and 8(b)(1) which prohibit unions from charging discriminatory initiation fees and dues. The reporting provisions of Landrum-Griffin are not, however, innovatory; Taft-Hartley incorporated a compulsory reporting provision, although the data so required were only open to governmental or union membership scrutiny. Landrum-Griffin provides that all union reports are open to public inspection.

Section VII was included, almost as an afterthought it would seem, to amend certain provisions of the Taft-Hartley and Wagner Acts. In particular, Landrum-Griffin added the section 8(f) exemption for the construction industry with regard to the union security conditions of Taft-Hartley. Construction unions were also allowed to boycott non-union construction work or any sub-contracting work done on the construction site. Another group of unions in the clothing industry — the Amalgamated Clothing Workers of America and the International Ladies Garment Workers Union — were exempted from the Landrum-Griffin ban on secondary boycotts. The existence of unusual conditions within both the clothing and construction industries was held to make such preferential treatment necessary.

The primary concern of Landrum-Griffin was the control of internal union procedures. It attempted to do this by introducing standards of behaviour in the form of a Bill of Rights. The emphasis upon union constitutions was considered necessary to safeguard the rights of individuals, so that where an employee chooses to become a union member and is covered by a union security clause he can expect that certain standards of democracy are adhered to by the union. It is difficult, even impossible, to say whether union members are effectively better off following Landrum-Griffin. The Act may have heightened the unions' sensitivity to constitutional standards and, thus, vicariously have prevented abuse, but little evidence exists one way or another.[40]

References

1   The Railway Labor Act provides similar, though not identical, provisions to the Taft-Hartley Act and covers all railway and airline workers.
2   Section 2(2).
3   Between 1974 and 1976 the National Education Association recorded the largest growth in membership, making it the second largest labour group in the US after the Teamsters B-14 (No.172) The Bureau of National Affairs, Inc., Washington D.C. 20037,1977.
4   *Seamprufe Inc.* 82 NLRB 892, 1949, enforced 186 F.2d 671 cert. denied, 342 US 813, 1951.
5   *Longshoremen's and Warehousemen's Local 6 (Sunset Line and Twine Co.)* 79 NLRB 1487, 1948.

6   *Wyandotte Chems. Corp.*, 108 NLRB 1406, 1954.
7   Rose, T., 'Union Security Provisions in Agreements, 1954', *Monthly Labor Review of the Bureau of Labor Statistics in the United States*, vol.78, part 6, June 1955, p.654.
8   E.g. *Operating Engineers, Local 542 v NLRB*, 329 F.2d 512, 3d Circ. 1964.
9   Legislative History of the Labor Management Relations Act 1947, Report No.105, p.412.
10   *Teamsters Local 357 v NLRB* 365 US 667, 47 LRRM 2906, 1961.
11   119 NLRB 883, 41 LRRM 1460, 1950, Enforcement denied, 270 F.2d, 425, 44 LRRM 2802 (ca 9 1959).
12   (1961) 365 US 667.
13   96 Cong. Rec. 8433, A1 802, 81st Cong., 2d Sess., 1950.
14   *Mountain Pacific Chapter*, op.cit., note 11.
15   *NLRB v Local 138, Operating Engineers*, 385 F2d 874 (2d Cir 1967).
16   *Plumbers and Pipefitters (Brown-Old Plumbing and Heating Co.)* 1956, 115 NLRB 594.
17   *Local 60; United Brotherhood of Carpenters and Joiners v NLRB* 365 US 651, 1961.
18   *J.J. Hagerty* 153 NLRB 1375, 1965.
19   *Radio Officers' Union v NLRB*, 347 US 17, 1953.
20   Senate Reports No.105, 80th Cong. Quoted in *NLRB v General Motors Corp.*, 373 US 734, 83 Sup Ct., 1453, 1963.
21   186 F2d 1008, 1951.
22   Ibid., p.792.
23   93 Cong. Rec. 4887, 1947, Remarks of Senator Taft.
24   *Ford Motor Co. of Canada v UAW* Lab Arb 439, 17 LRRM 2782, 1946.
25   *The Brotherhood of Railway and Steamship Clerks v Allen* 373 US 113, 1963.
26   Civil No. M-76-839. Report filed 18 August, 1980. The 19 per cent assessment is, however, subject to modification in the event of the CWA filing a proper motion to show that amounts in excess of 19 per cent were properly chargeable to present and future agency fee payers.
27   *NLRB v Television and Radio Broadcasting Studio Employees* 315 F 2d 398,52 LRRM 2744, CA3, 1963.
28   *IAM Lodge* 508, 190 NLRB 61, 1971.
29   65 stat 601, 1951, 29 USC S159(c), 1958, amending 61 Stat 143, 1947.
30   Section 304.
31   *International Association of Machinists v Street*, 367 US 740, 1961.
32   Op.cit., note 25.

33   Act of 2 July 1964, Pub. Law, 78 Stat 241.

34   *Wicks* v *Southern Pac. R.R.* 231 F 2d 130, 1956, cert. denied, 351 US 946, 1956.

35   For example, *Gray* v *Gulf, M & O R.R.*, 429 F 2d 1064, 1066 n.4 (5th Cir 1970).

36   205 F 2d 58 (2d Cir 1953).

37   42 USC S2000e(j) (1976).

38   Bill 8HR 4774, 7 December 1980, 96th Congress.

39   It should be appreciated that the bulk of the Committee's attention was focused on just 7 out of more than 180 international unions then active. Estey, M., op.cit., p.118.

40   For further discussion of union democracy and the Landrum-Griffin Act see Ross, P. and Taft, P., 'The Effect of the LMRDA Upon Union Constitutions', *New York University Law Review*, vol.43, part 2, April 1968, p.305, and Bellace, J.R. and Berkowitz, A.D., 'The Landrum-Griffin Act, Twenty Years of Federal Protection of Union Members' Rights', Labor Relations and Public Policy Series No.19, University of Pennsylvania 1979.

10 Section 14(b) and the right to work issue

Without doubt the most controversial amendment made by Taft-Hartley, with respect to union security arrangements, has proved to be section 14(b) which provides:

> Nothing in this Act shall be construed as authorizing the execution or application of agreements requiring membership in a labor organization as a condition of employment in any State or Territory in which such execution or application is prohibited by State or Territorial law.

This clause is unusual since it runs counter to the established practice, particularly in labour relations in the private sector, that federal law pre-empts state law. Provisions enacted by the individual states in accordance with section 14(b), therefore, take precedence over the federal provisions outlined in section 8(a)(3) provided that they are more restrictive in nature and their operation is confined within state boundaries.

State laws banning or limiting union security were already in existence prior to the 1947 amendments — Florida introduced the first such legislation in 1944 — and raised the question of whether they could legally coexist with section 8(a)(3) of the original NLRA which licensed all forms of union security agreements. Congress was not unaware of the developing situation and indicated that section 14(b) was enacted to resolve the relation of the federal legislation to the individual states:

> Many states have enacted laws or adopted constitutional provisions to make all forms of compulsory unionism in those states illegal. It was never the intention of the NLRA . . . to preempt the field in this regard so as to deprive the states of their powers to prevent compulsory unionism. Neither the so-called "closed shop" proviso in section 8(3) of the existing Act nor the union shop and maintenance of membership proviso in section 8(a)(3) of the conference agreement could be said to authorize agreements of this sort in states where such arrangements were contrary to the state policy. To make certain that there should be no question about this, section 13 was included in the House Bill. The conference agreement, in section 14(b), contains a provision having the same effect.[1]

In section 14(b) Congress plainly abandoned the idea of a uniformly imposed federal labour code, with respect to union security, in order to allow the states to follow their own restrictive policies. The resulting legislative measures have become best known as right to work laws, although unions object to this term as misleading and have dubbed them 'right to wreck' and 'right to scab' laws.[2] The unions are not alone in their dislike of the phrase:

> These laws do not and were never intended to guarantee a right to work or a right to a job . . . (note 8). A careful reading of any one of the right-to-work statutes or constitutional provisions will verify the misnomer. The focal point of these statutes is membership or non-membership in a labor union as a condition of employment.[3]

Nevertheless since the principal objective of right to work laws is to outlaw compulsory unionism, by making all union security agreements illegal which require union membership or financial support as a condition of employment, proponents would argue that they do provide a right to work free from union interference. Right to work remains the term in common use, although it might be more accurate to describe such measures as 'voluntary union membership laws'.[4]

As noted earlier, some states had already introduced legislation prior to Taft-Hartley, while other states gradually took advantage of the new section 14(b). However, the validity of the new statutes was soon to be challenged. Their constitutionality was questioned in 1949 on the grounds that they violated the First Amendment — freedom of speech and assembly, the Fourteenth Amendment — due process and equal protection of the law, and Article 1 section 10 — impairment of contracts — of the Constitution. The Supreme Court, nevertheless, upheld the validity of the laws enacted in accordance with section 14(b)[5] and right to work opponents were forced to concentrate their attack upon legislative amendment. A notable attempt to repeal the offending section of Taft-Hartley was made during the 1965-66 congressional session but, although a Bill to that effect was approved in the House of Representatives, it was filibustered to death in the Senate. Right to work statutes have now been in existence for over 30 years and would appear to be a permanent feature of American labour law.

Currently 20 states have some type of right to work legislation operating with regard to the private sector. The provisions were brought into effect in the following states either by statutory enactment or by constitutional amendment or by a combination of both of these measures: Alabama, Arizona, Arkansas, Florida, Georgia, Iowa, Kansas, Louisiana, Mississippi, Nebraska, Nevada, North Carolina, North Dakota, South Carolina, South Dakota, Tennessee, Texas, Utah, Virginia and Wyoming. In five other states, Delaware, Hawaii, Indiana, Maine and New Hampshire, previously enacted legislation has been repealed. The last successful right to work campaign was waged in Louisiana in 1976 while unsuccessful campaigns were fought in such states as Idaho and New Mexico.

There is little consistency among the states in the wording or application of right to work measures. Many provisions are, however, worded similarly to the first right to work law passed by Florida in 1944:

> The right of persons to work shall not be denied or abridged on account of membership or non-membership in any labor union or labor organization, provided that this clause shall not be construed to deny or abridge the right of employees, by and through a labor organization or labor union, to bargain collectively with their employer.[6]

Although most states have followed Florida's lead, in granting protection to both members and non-members, Arizona and Nevada have decided to emphasise the right of non-membership alone: 'No person shall be denied the opportunity to obtain or retain employment because of non-membership in a labor organization . . . '.[7] Of course, state prohibitions with regard to discrimination on the basis of union membership are probably pre-empted by the federal statute.

The majority of states further extend the principle of the Florida statute to include a monetary provision similar to that adopted by Virginia: 'No employer shall require any person as a condition of employment or continuation of employment to pay any dues, fees or other charges of any kind to any labor union or labor organization'.[8] Such provisions must be construed as prohibiting both the union shop and the agency shop. In those states which do not explicitly ban the agency shop it has nevertheless been prohibited by judicial interpretation or in accordance with a state attorney general opinion.[9] Only the state of Indiana, whose statute has been repealed, has interpreted its legislation to exclude the agency shop from coverage. In addition to banning the agency shop, most states provide that contracts which include agreements in violation of the right to work are declared void and some provisions designate such violation a criminal offence.[10]

The coverage of right to work statutes

Under section 14(b) the states have both the right to prohibit agreements requiring membership in a labour organisation and the power to enforce prohibition. However, the states' right of enforcement is not without federal limitation. The Supreme Court has construed that 'state power, recognised by section 14(b), begins only with the actual negotiation and execution of the type of agreement described by section 14(b)'.[11] States are entitled, therefore, to enforce their laws by providing remedies and sanctions such as injunctions, damages and criminal penalties.

There are in addition several clear exceptions to the coverage of right to work laws; they cannot, for example, invalidate union shop agreements negotiated in accordance with section 2, eleventh, of the RLA 1951 or prohibit check-off or hiring hall arrangements sanctioned by Taft-Hartley, nor may they permit what federal law restricts, for example the closed shop. In line with the Taft-Hartley Act, section 14(b) laws may only apply to the private sector, although many states, including those without right to work legislation, have provisions prohibiting union security arrangements which apply to public employees. It is worth considering the coverage of section 14(b) in greater detail.

Section 2, eleventh, of the Railway Labor Act 1951

Until 1951 the RLA did not permit union shop contracts in the railway or airline industries, but in that year Congress passed section 2, eleventh, to amend the Act and bring it into conformity with the Taft-Hartley provisions. Right to work laws were, however, held to be non-effective with regard to the new section. A proposed amendment which would have made right to work legislation applicable to railway and airline employees was defeated in Congress, while the validity of section 2, eleventh, was confirmed by the Supreme Court in 1956.[12] Congress made an exception of the RLA employers and employees because it considered that the union shop could provide the industrial stability necessary to protect inter-state commerce.

The agency shop

Section 14(b) permits the states to prohibit union security agreements requiring membership in a labour organisation. In right to work states union lawyers have attempted to employ the agency shop, which requires not union membership but payment of a collective bargaining fee, as an alternative to the banned union shop. However, in *NLRB v General Motors Corp.*[13] it was made plain that the agency shop is within the scope of section 8(a)(3), and thus open to state regulation in accordance with section 14(b). The agency shop requirement of payment of initiation fees and dues was held by the court to be the practical equivalent of union membership.[14] In *Local 1625 Retail Clerks v Schermerhorn*[15] the legality of the agency shop with regard to the Florida right to work statute was in question. The Supreme Court followed the ruling in *General Motors* and held that despite the fact that the agency shop clause did not use the term 'membership' it was nevertheless the equivalent of membership, as defined by section 8(a)(3), and thus came within the scope of section 14(b).[16]

The states have been virtually unanimous in holding the agency shop invalid under their respective right to work statutes. The only decision to the contrary was reached in an Indiana ruling in *Meade Electric Co. v Hagberg.*[17] The Indiana statute under consideration, since repealed, referred only to 'membership' and the court concluded that since the agency shop did not require formal membership as a condition of employment it was beyond the reach of the statute.

Had the judiciary construed the agency shop to be a permissible form of union security it could be said that the right to work laws would have been left with no function. There is a difference between the 'modified union shop' and the agency shop, albeit a small one. Membership in a Taft-Hartley modified union shop requires the full payment of dues and fees, whereas the agency shop (or 'service fee shop') requires that the employee pay only a contribution towards the cost of bargaining. In practice, however, the agency shop and the modified union shop tend to be one and the same thing and represent the maximum kind of union security allowed by federal law.

Section 9(a) of the NLRA laid down the principle of exclusive representation (by a union, following a majority vote) of *all* the employees in an appropriate bargaining unit, and in section 8(a)(3)

Congress attempted to resolve the 'free-rider' problem by redefining 'membership' as the payment of dues and fees. Clearly the provision of the section 14(b) right for individual states to prevent the compulsory payment of dues and fees brings into focus the conflict between the collectivists, who argue that the right to work laws unduly favour the individual, and the individualists who argue that it is wrong to require all employees to pay for a service which some of them do not want. It is this argument which has often caused a bitter clash of opinion between opponents and proponents of the right to work laws.

Hiring halls under section 14(b)

None of the state right to work statutes refer directly to hiring hall arrangements but several state legislatures obviously bore them in mind when drafting their restrictive provisions. The Arkansas provision, for example, declares that contracts which 'exclude from employment . . . persons who are not members of or who fail or refuse to join or affiliate with a labor union . . . '[18] are prohibited. A non-discriminatory hiring hall — one which does not favour union members at the expense of non-members — is not, however, open to state control. According to the 8th Circuit Court of Appeals:

> Section 14(b) does not empower states to ban all involuntary relationships between workers and unions. It merely allows the prohibition of "agreements requiring membership in a labor organization as a condition of employment . . . " 29 USC s.14(b). A hiring hall which though exclusive does not require union membership, does not violate the closed shop prohibition of s.8(a)(3) [Local 357, *Int'l B'hood Teamsters* v *NLRB*, 365 US 667, 47 LRRM 2906 (1961)] and thus, a fortiori, it is not within the ambit of s.14(b).[19]

In *Kaiser* v *Price-Tewell Inc.*[20] the Arkansas Supreme Court, in accordance with its statutory provision prohibiting compulsory union affiliation, struck down an exclusive but non-discriminatory hiring hall. The 8th Circuit Court of Appeals held the *Price-Tewell* decision to be pre-empted by federal law. The 9th Circuit likewise held that a Nevada decision banning a non-discriminatory hiring hall, though a correct interpretation of state law, was overruled by federal law.[21]

The check-off

Section 302 of the Taft-Hartley Act authorises a check-off irrevocable for a period of one year. This provision, according to Haggard, has

> the same effect as an agreement that requires an employee who becomes a member of the union to maintain that membership for a fixed term. Since all of the state right-to-work statutes prohibit membership in a union as a condition of employment, and since in all the states membership has been construed to include the mere payment of money, it necessarily follows that fixed-term check off authorisations are implicitly prohibited by all state right-to-work laws.[22]

Certainly, some states have laws regulating the circumstances and tenure of check-off authorisations; in Georgia they are revocable 'at will', in Iowa on 30 days' notice but in Louisiana and Nebraska they are only regulated with regard to public employees.

The states are not, in fact, the controlling body with regard to fixed term check-off authorisations. Section 302 of the Taft-Hartley Act was not an amendment to the Wagner Act and does not fall within the scope of section 8(a)(3) which was; section 302 is not, therefore, subject to state legislation enacted under section 14(b). In *Sea Pak* v *Professional Employees*[23] the Supreme Court confirmed that federal law had fully occupied the field and added the opinion that the inability of an employee to withdraw when he wished from a check-off agreement did not constitute compulsory unionism.

Workforce location and 'job situs'

The lack of uniformity in state union security legislation has, inevitably, raised the question of which state has jurisdiction over the contract of an employee who works in both right to work and non right to work territories in the course of his employment. In *re Northland Greyhound Lines Inc.*,[24] an NLRB case, the bargaining unit of the employees (inter-state bus drivers, office, station and maintenance staff) covered an eight-state area, four of which prohibited or regulated union security arrangements. The Board considered such factors as where the employees were hired, in which states they were resident and in which state their headquarters was situated. The place where the employees received wages and reported for work was held by the Board to be the deciding factor in determining which state had jurisdiction. In *re Western Electric Co.*[25] the workers involved were a group of mobile telephone installation employees who performed their work in 45 states. The headquarters test was applied with the result that the NLRB found that 'the headquarters of the employees . . . would appear to be at their job site . . . therefore, each employee is subject to the laws of the state in which his job site is located . . . '.[26] It should be noted that both of these decisions were reached by the NLRB which does not have the authority to decide the scope of right to work laws; the real authority rests with the state and federal courts.

It was more difficult for the court to achieve a solution in *Oil, Chemical and Atomic Workers' Union* v *Mobil Oil Corp.*[27] The employees were seamen who performed the majority of their work at sea. Their employers, a Texas-based company, and their union entered into a union security agreement which the company later asserted was void and unenforceable under the Texas right to work statute. The union in response argued that the seamen's 'job situs' was on the high seas and, therefore, was outside the state's territorial boundaries. The court concluded that if the job situs is outside the boundaries of all states, no state 'has sufficient interest in the employment relationship to be able to apply its own right-to-work laws'.[28] This conclusion effectively creates another exemption to section 14(b) by excluding all seamen from state right to work laws. Application of the 'job-situs' test prevents a state with a right to work statute from imposing its restrictive provisions upon the employees of a non right to work state.

The location of right to work state

It has been observed that right to work campaigns have been most successful in those states which are primarily agricultural.[29] The map of the USA — figure 10.1 — shows the distribution of right to work laws among the states; most of the southern and western agricultural states have introduced legislation while the northern industrial and the Pacific sun-belt states have unanimously resisted it, the one exception to this general rule being Indiana which eventually repealed its right to work legislation. The reasons for this fairly clear-cut territorial division are debatable but one important factor is the relative levels of union organisation.

Table 10.1 makes it plain that right to work laws are generally in force in states with low percentages of union and employee association membership.[30] Nevada is the only right to work state with a union density rating of above 20 per cent. North and South Carolina achieved respectively just 6.5 and 6.7 per cent density, well below the New York figure of 39.2 per cent. The exceptionally high trade union density of 22.9 per cent in right to work Nevada is largely accounted for by the

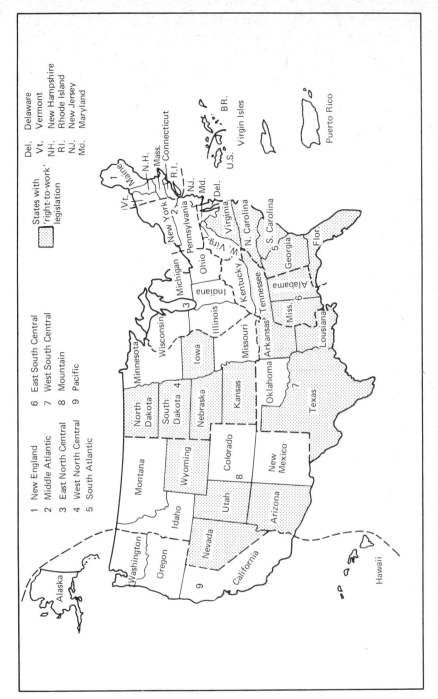

States with
'right-to-work'
legislation

Del.   Delaware
Vt.   Vermont
N.H.   New Hampshire
R.I.   Rhode Island
N.J.   New Jersey
Md.   Maryland

1 New England   6 East South Central
2 Middle Atlantic   7 West South Central
3 East North Central   8 Mountain
4 West North Central   9 Pacific
5 South Atlantic

Figure 10.1   The United States of America

151

Table 10.1
Trade union membership and density of employees on non-agricultural payrolls 1978
R = ranking in terms of trade union membership and density

Non right to work states	Membership (thousands)	R	Density %	R	Right to work states	Membership (thousands)	R	Density %	R
All states	20,402	–	23.6	–	All states	20,402	–	23.6	–
All non RTW states	16,932	–	–	–	All RTW states	3,470	–	–	–
Alaska	43	46	26.2	13	Alabama	257	22	19.2	25 =
California	2,184	2	23.7	17	Arizona	122	30	13.8	37
Colorado	172	27	15.2	32	Arkansas	109	33	15.0	33
Connecticut	296	18	21.9	22	Florida	367	16	11.7	46
Delaware	52	43	21.1	23	Georgia	271	20	13.6	38
Hawaii	120	31	32.1	6	Iowa	212	26	19.2	25 =
Idaho	47	45	14.3	36	Kansas	117	32	12.8	42
Illinois	1,497	4	31.5	7	Louisiana	227	24	16.0	30
Indiana	643	8	29.3	10	Mississippi	103	35	12.7	43 =
Kentucky	274	19	22.4	21	Nebraska	92	36	15.3	31
Maine	74	39	18.3	27	Nevada	80	37	22.9	20
Maryland, DC	458	14	21.0	24	North Carolina	147	28	6.5	50
Massachusetts	611	9	24.4	14 =	North Dakota	34	47	14.7	35
Michigan	1,223	6	34.6	3	South Carolina	76	38	6.7	49
Minnesota	411	15	24.4	14 =	South Dakota	24	50	10.3	48
Missouri	578	10	30.0	8	Tennessee	303	17	17.7	28
Montana	67	41	24.1	16	Texas	575	11	11.0	47
New Hampshire	48	44	13.3	40	Utah	68	40	13.0	41
New Jersey	683	7	23.0	19	Virginia	258	21	12.7	43 =
New Mexico	54	42	12.1	45	Wyoming	28	49	14.9	34
New York	2,753	1	39.2	1					
Ohio	1,294	5	29.5	9					
Oklahoma	138	29	13.5	39					
Oregon	232	23	23.1	18					
Pennsylvania	1,595	3	34.2	4					
Rhode Island	108	34	27.1	12					
Vermont	33	48	17.5	29					
Washington	496	13	33.1	5					
West Virginia	226	25	36.8	2					
Wisconsin	522	12	27.8	11					

Source: Bureau of Labor Statistics.

fact that unique conditions involving the mining industry and politics prevail there.[31] The states with low percentage membership but no right to work law — Colorado, Delaware, Idaho, New Hampshire, New Mexico and Oklahoma — are all regions in which such a law existed or where there is pressure to pass legislation.[32] Texas has 575,000 union members but despite substantial industrialisation it remains politically dominated by agricultural interests and has a low union density rating of 11 per cent. The states with high trade union density also tend to be the most heavily populated and highly urbanised states — the three factors being closely interlinked.

Why are right to work laws enacted?

The objectives of right to work legislation have become obscured in a maze of emotive and often meaningless phrases. However, the crux of the matter is often held to be dependent upon the freedom to associate or not to associate. That is, the

> . . . conflict between labour's right to organize, solidify its strength and preserve the group interest, and the individual worker's right to obtain and keep his job (depending only on the job's continuing availability and the worker's willingness and ability to do the work) unfettered by organizational entanglements he may not want. Essentially the cleavage comes when the group and the individual attempt to exercise fully their respective rights.[33]

For many right to work proponents compulsory union membership, even as limited by section 8(a)(3) to a monetary basis, is contrary to the individual's right to freedom of association.

Other more pragmatic, less philosophical reasoning has encouraged the spread of right to work laws among the agriculturally dominated states. Many of these states desire to attract new industry and increase their level of industrialisation; it is believed that the introduction of a right to work law encourages companies to locate within the area. This belief is allied to what is perhaps the real driving force behind the right to work movement, that is the desire to control the strength, and thus the growth, of organised labour. It is assumed, rightly or wrongly, that unions are harmful to economic progress. It is genuinely felt that 'a "right-to-work" law is the best assurance that a state government is not "labor dominated", that union organization is very slight, and in any event that community "cooperativeness" will forestall militant union organization'.[34] Proponents hope that the introduction of these laws will frustrate union efforts to organise and both proponents and opponents believe that these laws have had some effect upon unionisation in right to work states. In fact there is little evidence to indicate that this is true, but the belief in itself is a useful indicator of the forces behind the right to work movement. A peripheral argument advanced in support of the legislation is that it reduces industrial strife and increases economic efficiency, presumably by controlling union power.

The effectiveness of right to work laws

The question of individual rights with regard to section 14(b) may be to a large extent academic, because in practice union membership is often required and achieved both in right to work and non right to work states. 'Once a union is in and a collective agreement is consummated, virtually all employees covered by that contract will become dues check-off, card-carrying members . . . '.[35] According to Meyers, in his study of the operation of the Texas Act, only a small proportion of workers, at least in manufacturing, have escaped membership as a result of the right to work law. He maintains that such measures are not effective because

> The simple fact is that a union strong enough to negotiate a union security agreement is in little danger of losing out . . . . A union so weak that its existence is threatened by loss of the loyalty of its members is unlikely to gain or hold a union security agreement, except by the grace of the employer.[36]

In a right to work state the union will, of course, negotiate for the greatest level of union security allowed by the law. Even the existence of a mere check-off agreement is sometimes sufficient security to enable a strong union to enforce a maintenance of membership among employees. Basically, where a union is strong enough, its members will exercise their right to refrain from working with non-members irrespective of the statutory regulations. This is as true of federal law as it is of state law, and the sometimes wide division between legislative theory and industrial practice will be discussed in depth in the next chapter.

Right to work laws are purported to attract new industry to a region but it is impossible to prove that they, as opposed to other factors, affect industrialisation to any marked degree. It is true that manufacturing industry has tended to move towards many of the right to work states, but this is not necessarily a consequence of the legislation. Certainly many firms do consider the industrial relations climate of a state before locating there, and employers often prefer to work with non-unionised labour, but it is unlikely that these factors alone are a sufficient incentive to encourage industrialisation. In fact it is difficult in theory to assess the relative merits of the union and open shops, and 'the question of the relative efficiency of alternative union security arrangements remains an unsettled issue'.[37] Similarly, it is not possible to discover any relationship between right to work laws and the relative level of industrial conflict existing from state to state.[38]

Right to work states tend to be the least populated and lack the level of cultural, technical and educational facilities available in the highly industrialised states. There has been a recent shift in population towards these states, however, as table 10.2 indicates, which suggests that, given the poor standard of social facilities and lack of urbanisation, other factors must be in force.

Table 10.2
Population changes, 1 April 1970 to 1 July 1976

Section	Increase	Per cent increase
United States − total	11,354,000	5.6
North east (New England and mid-Atlantic)	443,000	0.9
North central (E. north central and W. north central)	1,146,000	2.0
South (S. Atlantic, east s. central and west s. central)	6,042,000	9.6
West (Mountain and Pacific)	3,724,000	10.7

Source: Current Population Reports, December 1976, US Department of Commerce, Bureau of the Census.

'Transportation, energy supply and quantity of labour supply, marketing channels and material availability'[39] are all taken into account when reaching a decision and the right to work states are usually found to possess one or more of them.

Non-monetary attractions, such as a good climate, also feature high upon the list for relocating employees, and it is notable that the workforce has been eager to move to the non right to work Pacific sun-belt states. There are in addition many non-urban areas in non right to work states which are equally resistant to unionisation, a fact more noticeable in recent years with the increased desire on the part of employers to operate non-union plants and companies. The only advantage of a right to work law in this case lies in its appeal to anti-union employers, but again whether this alone is sufficient to attract new business is doubtful.

It is equally difficult to assess the effect of right to work legislation upon trade union strength, in particular upon union growth. In many states the laws are simply not being enforced. Novit examined the Indiana statute and concluded that it was eventually repealed because the unions successfully circumvented its restrictions.[40] According to Lumsden and Peterson, if the laws are in any way effective they work by making unionism more costly; members who could have been coerced into membership have now to be persuaded.[41]

The statistical impact of right to work laws on unionisation is particularly confusing. According to Bloom and Northrup the loss of union membership varies from 10 to 40 per cent; Miller places the loss at between 6 and 8 per cent and 10 and 15 per cent; while Hirsch places it at only 0.3 or 0.6 of one percentage point.[42] There is, in fact, no proof of a significant correlation between the right to work and low levels of unionisation except insofar as the level of unionisation in a state is a determinant in the enactment of a right to work statute. According to Eliot 'the right to work variable is insignificant once all other explanatory variables have been properly specified'.[43]

Even more interesting is the evidence (table 10.3) that union membership in those states with right to work laws has been steadily growing, so that between 1964 and 1978 there was a percentage increase of 45.6. Overall union and employee association membership also increased by 20.7 per cent in the period 1970-78, which is far greater than the 4 per cent growth experienced by the other states. Because of the low levels of membership in right to work states, unions have, in fact, greater scope for organisation there than in the already relatively highly unionised north.

In practice section 14(b) would appear to be of limited importance to industrial relations in the USA, although both unions and right to work proponents insist that the issue is significant. In one respect, at least, they are correct. The presence or absence of right to work laws is an excellent indication of the attitudes towards trade unionism which exist within a given state. Right to work states could be said to have a high level of anti-union sentiment among their populations, while the reverse is true of those states which have not adopted the legislation. What would appear to be 'at stake is the political power and public support of management and unionism'.[44]

After 33 years the controversy continues unabated but it is possible that the right to work movement has reached a state of equilibrium. The majority of states likely to pass such legislation, that is those with low union density and strong anti-union feelings, have already done so

Table 10.3
Summary table of trade union and employee association membership in the USA 1964-78
(all figures are in thousands or percentages)

	1	2	3	4	5	6	7	8
Year	Union membership in 20 RTW states	Union membership in 30 non RTW states	Total union membership	Total union density (per cent)	Union and employee association membership in 20 RTW states	Union and employee association membership in 30 non RTW states	Total union and employee association membership	Total union and employee association density (per cent)
1964	2,389	14,799	17,188	29.5	–	–	–	–
1966	2,516	15,785	18,301	28.6	–	–	–	–
1968	2,873	16,424	19,297	28.4	–	–	–	–
1970	3,067	16,690	19,757	27.9	3,497	18,355	21,852	30.8
1972	3,126	16,663	19,789	26.9	3,603	18,636	22,239	30.2
1974	3,294	17,272	20,566	26.3	3,863	19,545	23,408	29.9
1976	3,093	16,781	19,874	25.0	3,957	19,157	23,114	29.1
1978	3,470	16,989	20,402	23.6	4,221	19,085	23,306	26.9
Percentage change 1964-78	+45.6	+14.8	+19.0	Percentage change 1970-78	+20.7	+4.0	+6.8	–
Actual change 1964-78	+1,081	+2,190	+3,271	Actual change 1970-78	+724	+730	+1,454	–

Source: Bureau of Labor Statistics.

(see table 10.1) and it now seems unlikely that many more, if any, states will follow suit in the near future.

References

1   H. Cong. Rept. 510 80th Cong. 1947, p.60.
2   US and Pub. Welf. Proceedings of 2nd Annual Ind. Rel. Conf. Indust. Report AFL-CIO 1959, p.95.
3   Essinger, J., 'The Right-to-Work Imbroglio', *North Dakota Law Rev.*, vol.51, spring 1975, p.573.
4   Pollitt, D.H., 'Right to Work Law Issues: An Evidentiary Approach', *N. Car. Law Rev.*, vol.37, 1959, p.235.
5   *AFL* v *American Sash & Door Co.*, 335 US, 1949, 538; *Lincoln Fed. Labor Union* v *Northwestern Iron & Metal Co.* 335 US, 1949, 525.
6   Fla. Const. Art 1 s.12, 1944, revised Art 1 s.6, 1968.
7   Ariz. Const. Art XXIV.
8   Va. Code Ann. 540-77; a similar provision is included by Alabama, Arkansas, Georgia, Iowa, Louisiana, Mississippi, Nebraska, North Carolina, South Carolina, Tennessee and Wyoming.
9   Court decisions: Arizona, Florida, Kansas, Nevada and North Dakota. Attorney-general opinions: South Dakota and Texas.
10 Georgia, Mississippi, Nevada and Texas declare void any provision in a contract contrary to the right to work. Alabama, Arizona, Arkansas, Iowa, Nebraska, North Carolina, South Dakota, Tennessee, Utah and Virginia declare such a contract provision illegal. Arkansas, Iowa, Nebraska, South Dakota, Tennessee, Utah, Virginia and Wyoming further attach a criminal penalty to violation of the right to work law.
11 *Retail Clerks Local 1625* v *Schermerhorn* 373 US 746, 1963.
12 *Railway Employees' Department* v *Hanson*, 351 US 225, 1956.
13 373 US 734, 1963, at pp. 741-2.
14 Ibid., p.743.
15 373 US 746, 1963.
16 Ibid., pp. 755-6.
17 159 NE 2d 408, IND 1959.
18 Ark. Stat. ss. 81-201 to 81-207, 1960.
19 *Laborers' Local 107* v *Kunco Inc*, 472 F 2d, 456, CA8, 1973.
20 235 Ark. 295, 359 SW 2d 449, 1962.
21 *Painters' Local 567* v *Tom Joyce Floors Inc.*, 81 Nev 1,398 P 2d 245, 1965. *NLRB* v *Tom Joyce Floors Inc.*, 353 F2d 768, 9th Cir, 1965.
22 Haggard, T.R., 'Compulsory Unionism, the NLRB, and the Courts: A Legal Analysis of Union Security Agreements', Lab. Rels. and Pub. Policy Series Report No.15, Univ. of Pennsylvania Ind. Research Unit 1977, p.178.
23 SD Georg 1969, 300 F.Supp, 1197; Affil 423 F2d 1229 (CA5) 1970.

24   80 NLRB 288, 1948, p.290.

25   84 NLRB 1019, 1949.

26   Ibid., pp. 1022-3.

27   96 SC 2140, 1956, p.2151.

28   Ibid., p.2147.

29   Sultan, P., 'Right-to-Work Laws', Californian Inst. for Industrial Rels, Monograph No.2, 1958, pp. 58, 59. The economic constitution of each right to work state is briefly described in Colberg, M.R., *The Consumer Impact of S14B*, The Heritage Foundation, Washington DC, 1978.

30   Miller, R.L., 'Right to Work and Compulsory Union Membership in the US', *B.J.I.R.*, vol.XIV, no.2, 1976, p.188.

31   Ibid., p.188.

32   Ibid.

33   Essinger, J., op.cit., p.575.

34   Soffer, B. and Korenich, M., 'Right to Work Laws and Location', *Journal of Reg. Sci.*, vol.3, no.2, 1961, p.44.

35   Willis, R.N., 'Georgia's Right to Work Laws: Their Meaning and Effect', *Georgia State Bar Journal*, vol.13, no.4, April 1977.

36   Meyers, F., *Right to Work in Practice*, The Fund for the Republic, New York, 1959, p.31.

37   Page, W.P. and Delorme, C., 'Economic Efficiency and Right to Work Laws: An Issue in a Muddle', *So. Econ. Journal*, vol.37 (1970-71), p.359.

38   Gilbert, D., 'A Statistical Analysis of the Right-to-Work Conflict', *Industrial and Lab. Rels. Rev.*, vol.19, July 1966, p.533.

39   Miller, R.L., op.cit., p.192.

40   Novit, M.S., 'Right to Work: Before and after the Indiana Experience', *Business Horizons*, October 1969, pp. 15-18.

41   Lumsden, K. and Peterson C., 'The Effect of Right-to-Work Laws on Unionization in the United States', *Journal of Pol. Economy*, vol.83, no.6, 1975, p.1237.

42   Bloom, G.F. and Northrup, H.R., op.cit., p.179; Miller, R.L., op.cit., p.188; Hirsch, B.T., 'Unionization and the South: Do Right-to-Work Laws Matter?', *North Carolina Review of Business and Economics*, April 1978, p.7.

43   Elliot, R.D., 'The Impact of Right to Work Laws on Union Activity', A National Right-to-Work Legal Defense Foundation Study, unpublished, 1979, p.43. See also Moore, W.J., 'Membership and Wage Impact of Right-to-Work Laws' and comments by Palomba, N.A. and Kuhn, J.W., *Journal of Labor Research*, vol.I, no.2, fall 1980, pp. 349-71.

44   Meyers, F., op.cit., p.45.

11 Union security in practice

The Taft-Hartley and Landrum-Griffin amendments to the Wagner Act have ostensibly eliminated the closed shop and severely restricted all other forms of union security in the USA. However, many of the prohibited union security arrangements such as the closed shop, the true union shop and the discriminatory hiring hall continue to exist in practice. This chapter is, therefore, concerned with two questions: firstly, what effect, if any has the legislation had upon union security arrangements? Secondly, what tactics have the unions used to circumvent the legislation and how successful have these tactics been?

Union security provisions in major collective bargaining agreements

There is a serious lack of empirical data with regard to the extent and operation of union security agreements in the USA. Nevertheless, information concerning the prevalence of different types of union security and check-off provisions in major collective bargaining agreements (those covering 1,000 or more workers) is collected and collated by the Bureau of Labor Statistics. Before considering the Bureau's figures it is necessary to place them firmly in perspective. The contracts under study are drawn exclusively from the private sector (the public sector is not subject to the provisions of the Taft-Hartley Act). The resulting statistics cover virtually all major collective bargaining contracts in the private sector and represent roughly half of all employees subject to such agreements in the USA, with the notable exception of those workers under contract in the airline and railroad industries. It is important to note that the Bureau's figures are only relevant to large agreements. They do not reflect the policies prevailing in small bargaining units and, as can be appreciated in table 11.2, represent only a small proportion of the total industrial labour force. Consequently, these figures are not comparable to those in the UK section.

The number of workers covered by major collective bargaining agreements has remained relatively stable, at around the 7 million mark, for over twenty years (see table 11.1). The majority of these workers have also been subject to some form of union membership requirement, the most popular being the union shop clause. Prior to the enactment of the Taft-Hartley Act the most popular type of union security arrangement was the closed shop which included approximately one-third of all workers covered by such provisions in 1946 (see chart 11.1). Immediately after the passage of the Act the now illegal closed shop clauses were rapidly replaced by union shop agreements which accounted for almost half of the union security provisions in major agreements between 1949 and 1950. It should be noted that although industries subject to the amended NLRA are prohibited from including closed shop provisions in collective contracts, such provisions are still to be found in industries not covered by the Act, such as local trade and service industries. These agreements seldom cover over 1,000 workers and are, therefore, included in the union shop statistics.

The Bureau figures may also include a number of workers who are not in fact affected by a union security clause. As a result of the ban on union and agency shop provisions in states with right to work legislation, agreements negotiated on a multi-state level include a general saving-clause. This is usually a statement to the effect that any contract provisions found to conflict with the laws of a state, in which the contract might be applied, shall be invalid within that state. It should be said, however, that agreements in right to work states account for only a small proportion of the total studied by the Bureau — not more than 10 per cent.

As noted, following Taft-Hartley the most striking trend in major collective bargaining agreements, as revealed in chart 11.1, was the percentage increase in workers covered by union shop provisions; in 1972 the proportion was over three-quarters. This proportion has since dropped to roughly two-thirds, although the union shop clause still remains the most frequently employed type of union security provision in major collective contracts. The rise of the union shop appears to have been largely at the expense of the maintenance of membership clause,

Table 11.1

Union security and check-off provisions in agreements covering 1,000 or more workers

Year	Number of agreements studied		Number containing a union security clause		Number containing a union shop clause		Number containing a check-off provision	
	Agreements	Workers (thousands)	Agreements	Workers (thousands)	Agreements	Workers (thousands)	Agreements	Workers (thousands)
1954	1,716	7,404.6	—	—	1,222	4,752.8	1,275	5,756.1
1958-59	1,631	7,472.0	1,287	6,079.4	1,162	5,532.6	1,163	5,728.7
1972	1,300	6,312.8	1,085	5,552.0	868	4,190.2	1,050	5,263.6
1973	1,339	6,723.0	1,116	6,030.8	809	3,750.0	1,075	5,533.0
1974	1,550	7,218.0	1,270	6,329.3	943	4,346.4	1,261	6,018.7
1975	1,514	7,069.7	1,251	6,193.6	945	4,441.3	1,228	5,789.6
1976	1,570	6,741.7	1,290	5,841.4	971	4,060.7	1,277	5,519.3

Source: Bureau of Labor Statistics, various years.

163

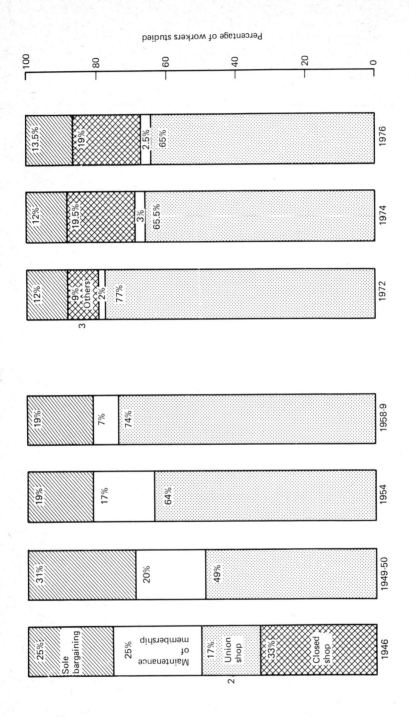

Percentage of workers studied

13.5%	12%	12%	19%	19%	31%	25% Sole bargaining
19%	19.5%	9%	7%	17%	20%	25% Maintenance of membership
2.5%	3%	2% Others / 2%	74%	64%	49%	17% Union shop
65%	65.5%	77%				33% Closed shop
1976	1974	1972	1958-9	1954	1949-50	1946

Chart 11.1   Union security provisions in major collective bargaining agreements[1]

Table 11.2

Percentage of the non-agricultural, civilian labour force covered by union security and check-off provisions in collective bargaining agreements covering 1,000 or more workers

Year	Non-agricultural labour force *	Union security %			Check-off %		
		All industries	Manufacturing	Non-manufacturing	All industries	Manufacturing	Non-manufacturing
1972	78,230,000	7.1	3.9	3.2	6.7	4.3	2.4
1973	80,957,000	7.4	3.7	3.7	6.9	4.1	2.8
1974	82,443,000	7.7	3.9	3.7	7.3	4.3	3.0
1975	81,403,000	7.6	4.0	3.6	7.1	4.3	2.8
1976	84,188,000	7.0	3.5	3.5	6.5	3.8	2.8

Source: Labour force figures: Bureau of the Census, various years. Percentages calculated from Bureau of Labor Statistics figures in table 11.1.

* The non-agricultural labour force excludes agricultural workers, the armed forces and the unemployed. The fall in the non-agricultural labour force in 1975 was due to a substantial increase in unemployment.

Table 11.3
Union shop provisions by industry 1972-76 (in agreements covering 1,000 workers or more)[4]

Industry	1972 Agreements	1972 Workers	1973 Agreements	1973 Workers	1974 Agreements	1974 Workers	1975 Agreements	1975 Workers	1976 Agreements	1976 Workers
All industries	868	4,190,200	809	3,750,050	943	4,346,400	945	4,441,350	971	4,060,750
Manufacturing	472	2,338,250	417	1,715,700	465	2,209,050	475	2,188,350	475	1,885,350
Ordnance accessories	11	44,450	8	18,650	8	21,350	4	9,100	6	13,900
Food, kindred products	69	213,400	65	213,300	70	211,450	77	220,950	72	214,050
Tobacco manufacturing	—	—	—	—	1	3,850	2	5,400	2	5,400
Textile mill products	8	25,100	7	22,400	7	14,200	5	20,500	6	19,850
Apparel	38	353,100	29	365,800	41	457,500	42	416,550	32	275,650
Lumber, wood products	8	12,900	6	8,900	5	7,100	3	5,900	6	9,600
Furniture, fixtures	9	17,000	6	13,650	12	21,900	12	20,200	9	15,600
Paper, allied products	22	42,150	23	38,550	31	59,300	33	61,450	30	51,950
Printing and publishing	15	37,150	11	23,450	16	37,700	20	43,750	17	37,950
Chemicals	18	32,850	15	24,950	17	34,500	16	32,950	13	30,700
Petroleum refining	—	—	—	—	—	—	1	2,000	—	—
Rubber and plastics	17	100,600	9	33,350	11	47,700	13	46,500	9	13,150
Leather products	17	46,400	13	33,200	11	34,850	12	36,600	12	31,700
Stone, clay and glass	24	51,150	18	38,100	22	53,750	20	44,900	22	47,000
Primary metals	26	64,250	36	82,800	37	94,200	35	83,850	38	86,550
Fabricated metals	27	75,350	24	41,650	21	33,450	18	33,800	22	38,700
Machinery	45	206,650	51	156,250	60	219,350	63	222,200	70	219,350
Electrical machinery	46	147,250	33	119,600	36	117,200	40	130,700	39	120,050
Transportation equipment	59	824,750	51	443,900	42	703,200	48	721,550	57	619,000
Instruments	7	18,250	6	13,700	9	17,000	5	12,900	6	17,600
Misc. manufacturing	6	25,500	6	24,000	8	19,500	6	16,600	7	17,600
Non-manufacturing	396	1,851,950	392	2,034,350	478	2,137,350	470	2,253,000	496	2,175,400
Mining, crude petroleum and natural gas	6	88,000	6	90,700	7	91,800	5	134,450	6	136,450
Transportation[5]	60	473,700	38	385,400	44	318,650	38	370,450	37	279,400
Communications	9	109,700	5	79,250	3	27,550	5	58,950	3	4,300
Utilities, elec. and gas	21	38,700	15	28,950	26	72,600	24	66,000	25	68,300
Wholesale trade	16	55,150	12	21,250	14	24,700	11	20,900	14	26,100
Retail trade	74	272,850	76	326,400	85	327,500	82	281,100	100	385,950
Hotels and restaurants	34	141,400	31	124,300	36	149,200	37	159,500	38	163,300
Services	29	124,800	46	280,900	57	357,400	57	321,700	51	253,450
Construction	146	546,450	162	696,000	205	766,850	211	839,950	222	858,150
Misc. non-manufacturing	1	1,200	1	1,200	1	1,100	—	—	—	—

Table 11.4
Check-off provisions by industry 1976,
in agreements covering 1,000 or more workers

Industry	All agreements		Check-off total	
	Agreements	Workers	Agreements	Workers
All industries	1,570	6,741,750	1,277	5,519,300
Manufacturing	826	3,398,500	770	3,220,400
Ordnance, accessories	14	36,300	13	34,350
Food, kindred products	104	301,250	92	271,150
Tobacco manufacturing	9	27,700	9	27,700
Textile mill products	15	42,450	14	34,950
Apparel	41	298,700	33	235,950
Lumber, wood products	9	14,750	7	11,050
Furniture, fixtures	17	27,650	16	25,850
Paper, allied products	53	98,600	51	94,400
Printing and publishing	22	44,800	15	35,650
Chemicals	42	103,750	40	99,350
Petroleum refining	13	26,850	13	26,850
Rubber and plastics	13	34,800	13	34,800
Leather products	14	34,900	13	33,700
Stone, clay and glass	35	94,600	33	88,300
Primary metals	90	506,500	88	504,000
Fabricated metals	36	83,600	33	77,550
Machinery	95	274,100	92	269,900
Electrical machinery	86	313,850	86	313,850
Transportation equipment	98	986,400	91	956,600
Instruments	10	24,550	8	22,050
Miscellaneous manufacturing	10	22,400	10	22,400
Non-manufacturing	744	3,343,250	507	2,298,900
Mining, crude petroleum and natural gas	14	152,450	14	152,450
Transportation	62	573,000	55	532,100
Communications	63	437,450	63	437,450
Utilities, electric and gas	57	166,950	49	137,300
Wholesale trade	16	28,600	10	15,600
Retail trade	120	432,350	95	308,400
Hotels and restaurants	42	177,600	26	106,900
Services	64	304,900	47	192,050
Construction	303	1,066,200	144	413,950
Miscellaneous non-manufacturing	3	3,750	2	2,700

Source: Bureau of Labor Statistics 1979.

which has declined significantly since the Second World War from 25 per cent in 1946 to just 2.5 per cent in 1976. Similarly, the ground lost by the union shop in recent years has been taken over by an assortment of other arrangements, in particular the agency shop.

In the manufacturing sector the union shop is most commonly found in the apparel, transportation equipment, electrical machinery, food and primary metal industries (table 11.3). Union shop agreements have become more prevalent in non-manufacturing where they are to be found especially in construction, transportation, hotels and restaurants, services and the retail trade.

Union security is closely allied with check-off provisions and 82 per cent of workers covered by major collective agreements in 1976 were also subject to some form of check-off (table 11.4). These figures apply to just 6.5 per cent of the non-agricultural labour force (table 11.2). Nevertheless, the check-off is fairly common in manufacturing with the 1976 figures revealing that 95 per cent of manufacturing employees under major agreements were covered by the check-off. The percentage in non-manufacturing is lower, just 69 per cent, a fact related to the type of work engaged in by employees in the non-manufacturing sector. Check-off arrangements are less common in industries such as construction, printing and maritime where multi-employer bargaining is the rule; that is agreements are not negotiated with a simple firm or company but with a group or association of employers. It is also true that where work tends to be sporadic, as in the construction and maritime industries, it is difficult to arrange the mechanics of the check-off.

On the face of it the Bureau statistics would appear to indicate that the legislation concerning union security is being complied with. No major agreements, except those not subject to Taft-Hartley, include a closed shop provision. Nevertheless, several industries, such as construction and printing, still operate *de facto* closed shops.[6] The question must therefore be raised: if the unions can no longer legally negotiate closed shop and true union shop clauses what methods do they use to achieve these conditions in practice?

The requirement of union membership

As will be recalled, the amended NLRA prohibits 'full membership' in a labour organisation as a condition of employment. Thus legal union shop agreements can only require employees to pay dues and fees to the union. The language of many union shop agreements tends to suggest, however, that actual membership in the union is required. Nor does the 'model clause' drafted by the NLRB help to clarify the situation:

> It shall be a condition of employment that all employees of the
> employer covered by this agreement who are members of the
> union in good standing on the effective date of this agreement
> shall remain members in good standing and those who are not
> members . . . shall on the thirtieth day [or such longer period as
> the parties may specify] following the effective date of this agree-
> ment, become and remain members in good standing in the union.
> It shall also be a condition of employment that all employees
> covered by this agreement and hired on or after its effective date
> shall, on the thirtieth day following the beginning of such employ-
> ment . . . become and remain members in good standing of the
> union.[7]

Phrases such as 'member in good standing' tend to encourage the belief
that something more than payment of fees and dues is required. Unless
an employee was well versed in the provisions of the law it is unlikely
he would realise that he is not required to join the union formally. And
indeed 'it would appear that many unions, with the acquiescence of
contracting employers, insist upon more — and get it'.[8]

Hiring halls

Hiring halls have traditionally been associated with the closed shop, but
although the closed shop was banned by the Taft-Hartley Act the
legality of the hiring hall was a matter of judicial interpretation. The
Supreme Court determination in *Local 357, Teamsters v NLRB*,[9] that
only non-discriminatory hiring halls were permitted under federal law,
was statutorily codified in section 8(f) of Landrum-Griffin. Industries
which have traditionally operated the hiring hall referral system have
also had high levels of unionisation. Not unnaturally, where the union
is the chief source of employment allocation, union members would
seem to stand a greater chance of gaining employment, or at least the
better jobs, than non-union workers.

Typical hiring hall unions tend to be craft based and representative
of one specific trade such as carpenters, plumbers, electricians, typo-
graphers, truck-drivers, merchant seamen and longshoremen. Of course,
referral unions are not totally craft based; semi-skilled men, such as
labourers on building sites, are also represented. The type of work
performed by such unions tends to be casual, sporadic and not tied to
any specific location for any length of time. Members of these unions
have, moreover, traditionally objected to working with non-members.

Perhaps not surprisingly, these unions have proved relatively successful in circumventing the prohibition upon closed shop agreements.

The largest proportion of union members to be found in hiring halls are construction workers, almost 60 per cent of whom are dependent upon the union for employment opportunities (table 11.5). In transportation, mainly trucking and longshore workers, 15 per cent of members are referred through hiring halls while in trade and services, chiefly hotels and restaurants and the retail trade, the figure is 16 per cent. Relatively few hiring halls are found in manufacturing and those workers who are covered by them are chiefly concentrated in printing.[10] The majority of industries with hiring halls also seem to have negotiated a high level of union security provisions. Table 11.3 shows, for example, that the number of agreements negotiated, and the number of workers affected in the construction industry, have been steadily increasing. The printing trades, construction and trucking are, of course, industries where the closed shop is considered a necessary method of organisation.

Table 11.5
Referral union membership compared with
total membership by industry 1969
(numbers in thousands)[11]

Industry group	Union membership		Referrals as a percentage of total
	Total[12]	Referral	
Total	20,210	2,551	13
Contract construction	2,541	1,495	59
Manufacturing and mining	9,560	248	3
Transportation	2,503	385	15
Trade and service	2,485	386	16
Government	2,155	–	0
Miscellaneous	966	37	4

Union security is achieved in many ways other than the enforcement of formal closed shop or union shop clauses. One method particularly used by referral unions is the manipulation of seniority clauses. These generally provide that employees should be laid off and re-employed in the order in which they were employed. In 1959, for example, the

Bureau of Labor Statistics found that many preferential hiring agreements:

> . . . did not contain any explicit statement as to non-discrimination between members and nonmembers. Many of the clauses were ambiguous and difficult to interpret. For instance some required preference in employment to workers with previous training and experience in the industry and often referred to employment prior to 1947, when closed shop arrangements may have prevailed. Such clauses, even when incorporated in agreements otherwise limited to sole bargaining, could result in virtually closed shop conditions since applicants with previous experience in industries with a history of extensive unionization would presumably be union members.[13]

Section 8(f) of the NLRA was, of course, specifically added by Landrum-Griffin to provide that workers previously employed in construction could legitimately be given preference over others.

In many cases the employer co-operates with the union to exclude non-members or unions may operate an inter-union blacklist. Unions may also seek to affect the seniority rights of non-members. Seniority does not depend upon union membership but a union can call attention to the poor standard of work of a non-member and thus reduce the employee's seniority rights through employer penalties. It should be pointed out that a non-member can, of course, be made to look inefficient when the union allocates the most difficult and dirty jobs to him.

Other informal pressures are applied and they can be, and often are, extremely effective, particularly when there is a strong union community. Thus, union members may refuse to work with the non-member, or refuse to socialise with him. Where union members live in the same area this may be extended beyond working hours and applied to the non-member's family also. Some union members may even resort to violence, thus making such areas as building sites and docks dangerous for non-members.

Union bylaws

Some unions have introduced union bylaws into their constitutions prohibiting union members from working with non-members. Despite what may be an unlawful purpose the courts have generally held that the unions are entitled under section 8(b)(1)(A) to prescribe their own rules and the bylaws are not, therefore, prohibited by Taft-Hartley.[14]

Bylaws perform the same function as a union security clause by preventing the replacement of union members with non-unionists and by encouraging union members to maintain membership. Moreover, 'Employers expecting a substantial percentage of employees to comply with such bylaws often seek to avoid labor problems by hiring only union men'.[15]

Closed shop bylaws are common in industries such as construction and entertainment, where jobs are often temporary and the maintenance of closed shop conditions is important to ensure stability of employment. Members generally comply with the bylaws by protesting at the presence of non-union employees, by walking off the job where non-unionists are present or by refusing to work with employers using non-union labour. In the *Musicians Local 802* case[16] union members would not work with expelled members of the musicians' union. The hiring agent, who was also a union member, was informed by the union president: 'You are familiar with the bylaw. The bylaw speaks for itself. It is perfectly all right for those . . . nonmembers to play but if they play and you play with them, . . . you will be brought up on charges'.[17] Thus union members cannot work with non-members without jeopardising their own position. Of course employers must not be seen to agree to co-operate with a union bylaw since this would constitute an unfair labour practice, but in *International Typographical Union* v *NLRB*[18] such a situation was avoided because the bylaws were not part of the collective contract.

These bylaws 'by informing qualified nonmembers that they are unwelcome . . . may deter nonmembers from applying to work without first seeking to join the union'.[19] Furthermore a bylaw, by indicating that non-members are likely to cause problems may effectively limit their chances for employment. Closely allied to closed shop bylaws are clauses included in the collective agreement which permit the union to object to any employee who adversely affects employer and employee relations. The union will object to a non-member and the employer in compliance with the collective agreement will dismiss him. It would, of course, be extremely difficult to prove that dismissal was a result of non-membership in the union and, thus, discriminatory.

Right to work states

In right to work states the unions have to contend with not just the federal prohibitions but also additional state regulations with regard to union security. Very little empirical evidence exists on the operation of right to work legislation, but what does exist suggests that unions which can resist the provisions of the federal law are also likely to ignore right to work legislation. A survey conducted in 1958, although the response was poor, suggests that right to work laws have little effect in practice. One state Federation of Labor for example stated: 'Some closed shops continue to exist but not in writing. Employers just continue to hire all union employees'.[20] While an Industrial Relations Council pointed out:

> Some closed shops, closed unions . . . still exist in violation of both Taft-Hartley and the right to work laws but these are limited to heavy industry such as highway, big commercial building, the easy money federal construction jobs and that sort of thing.[21]

Frederic Meyers, in a detailed study of the operation of the Texas Act, found similarly that in the areas where the closed shop was traditional the law, both federal and state, was disregarded. Closed shops existed throughout organised construction in Texas. Meyers discovered from questionnaires received from about half of organised labour in the building trades that 'in two out of three bargaining units all eligible employees were members'[22] of the union. Bargaining units which possessed less than 60 per cent union members were almost invariably small units working for small contractors.

Meyers found similar situations existing in other traditional closed shop trades such as motion picture theatres and the printing trades. In the latter 130 out of the 148 bargaining units reported on had 100 per cent union membership. Thus, the traditional hiring and employment conditions persisted in organised printing in Texas. 'In this respect Texas is no different from those states in which there is no state right-to-work statute.'[23]

If the law was disregarded in the established closed shop areas Meyers also found units in manufacturing with 100 per cent membership. However, while the employers in industries like construction often formed a conspiracy with the unions to exclude non-members, those in manufacturing tended to maintain the right of non-membership. Nevertheless, in the units covered by Meyers' survey, union membership was 100 per cent in 30 per cent of the bargaining units with almost half reporting 95 per cent union membership.[24]

Illegal provisions are enforced in right to work states in much the same way as in other states. Union members apply pressure upon non-unionists in the same way as their non right to work counterparts. Meyers noted that in 'a strongly unionized community, such as Port Arthur, extremes of nonconformity might provoke widespread community retaliation. Instances were reported in which nonunionists who crossed a picket line were totally ostracized in the community'.[25] Several employers who were operating under a union shop when this legislation was passed had not subsequently been challenged and since their agreements worked reasonably they made no change.[26] It is, of course, far harder to remove an existing union or closed shop than to prevent the negotiation of a new one.

Those unions unable to negotiate a full union shop agreement have, nevertheless, made use of the agreements within their reach. Since none of the right to work states are free to prohibit the check-off, unions can negotiate such arrangements. The majority of such agreements, studied by the Bureau of Labor Statistics in 1959, provided for automatic renewal of the check-off authorisation unless the employee gives written notice of intention to cancel during the escape period at the end of the term of authorisation.[27] Many agreements also provided that the automatic renewal was effective from year to year unless the employee gave written notice. Such agreements operate effectively as maintenance of membership clauses. Whether many of these agreements exist in right to work states is difficult to assess, but since they are not illegal it is reasonable to suppose that they are used by the unions.

Certain unions, most notably the construction, transportation, maritime, longshore and printing unions, would seem to a large extent to have successfully avoided the provisions of both federal and state legislation (table 11.6 shows that construction and transportation have a high proportion of union members). However, the statutes have had a

Table 11.6
Labour force and unionisation, by industrial category 1960-72

		1960	1964	1966	1968	1970	1972
Manufacturing	†	16,796	17,304	19,081	19,781	19,300	18,933
	%	51.1	48.2	46.0	46.6	47.5	47.1
Mining	†	712	635	628	606	600	607
	%	83.3	49.1	51.6	56.4	61.5	54.5
Construction	†	2,885	3,106	3,281	3,306	3,500	3,521
	%	78.7	74.8	75.1	76.9	78.1	78.2
Transportation	†	4,004	3,976	4,137	4,311	4,500	4,495
	%	81.2	79.8	81.3	76.6	73.0	71.4
Trade	†	11,391	12,188	13,220	14,099	15,000	15,683
	%	7.4	10.0	10.2	9.9	10.0	8.2
Finance	†	2,669	2,944	3,086	3,381	3,700	3,927
	%	2.7	2.1	2.0	1.5	1.5	0.9
Services and miscellaneous	†	7,423	8,533	9,582	10,622	11,600	12,309
	%	18.1	12.1	11.2	11.4	11.8	13.4
Government	†	8,353	9,502	10,850	11,845	12,600	13,290
	%	12.8	15.3	15.8	18.2	18.4	18.5

In thousands   †Labour force   % Percentage of the labour force unionised.

Source: Thieblot, A.J., 'Patterns and Trends in Labor Organization', Baltimore, Maryland, June 1978, unpublished.

diversifying effect and not all unions have been equally successful in circumventing them. Their effect upon union growth has been far more significant than their effect upon established unions' bargaining power.

The effect of the legislation upon trade union organisation

Undeniably labour organisations in the USA, with a few exceptions, have been faced with declining membership density (see table 8.1); thus total density is now roughly 20 per cent. Although the total union membership of the USA continues to grow, unions are definitely less successful in gaining new members. The effect of the Taft-Hartley legislation upon union membership is difficult to assess, but certain provisions of the Act would appear to have affected the unions' ability to organise effectively. To the representation elections provided by the Wagner Act, Taft-Hartley added two other elections — the decertification election, in which employees decide if they wish to continue to be represented by their union, and the deauthorisation election, in which employees vote as to whether they wish to continue authorising a union shop contract. It will be recalled that the Act also included an authorisation poll, which determined whether a group of employees wished to allow their union to negotiate a union shop clause, but this was removed in 1951.

Before a union can negotiate any collective conditions it must represent a majority of employees. This usually involves a representation (or certification) election but that may not be necessary if the employer voluntarily recognises and bargains with a union representing the majority of his employees. The NLRB can use employee 'union authorisation cards' as an alternative to the representation election. This method is generally used by the Board where an employer's unfair conduct has made a secret ballot unreliable. Employees are, therefore, required to indicate their consent, or otherwise, to the union acting as bargaining agent by presenting authorisation cards to the Board. The Board's right to use these cards was upheld by the Supreme Court in *NLRB* v *Gissel Packing Co.*[28]

Table 11.7 shows that there has been an increase in the number of certification elections but that unions have been less successful. Reasons for their lack of success are varied but chief among them is the inclination on the part of management to drag out the elections. Normally management and labour would agree to conduct a 'consent election', that is when both parties consent to the election; balloting can then occur quite quickly and any difficulties can be settled in the region. Other forms of union representation elections take much longer and are more likely to undermine the organisational drive of the

Table 11.7
NLRB decertification and certification elections, 1954-55 and 1976-77

Type of NLRB elections	Number of elections		Number of units lost/gained (retained)		Number of eligible voters		Number of voters lost/gained (retained)	
	1954-55	1976-77	1954-55	1976-77	1954-55	1976-77	1954-55	1976-77
Decertification	154	735	102	545	11,623	35,138	4,917	18,850
Certification								
Total	4,439	8,331	2,955	4,076	513,697	487,922	361,029	182,285
New organising	3,563	8,039	2,178	3,906	292,388	466,672	142,864	165,146

Source: *Monthly Labor Review*, November 1979, p.31.

union. Management has thus been refusing the consent and delays have resulted.

The longer the delay the less chance the union has of winning the election. It has been calculated that for each month of delay the union's chance of victory drops by 2.5 per cent[29] (table 11.8). In general 95 per cent of elections are concluded within the initial six months' time period but delays are added to by post-election conditions. Thus, even when a union is certified it may not be in a position to start collective bargaining; in fact, 23.35 per cent of the units won in NLRB elections in 1970 were never brought under contract 'because in most situations where there was no contract five years after the election the absence of an agreement referred to an employer who had exploited the weaknesses of the NLRA to frustrate the results of the election'.[30]

Table 11.8

Calender months elapsed between filing and election	Percentage of units won by unions during indicated month
Month of filing	59.0
1	56.3
2	51.7
3	50.0
4	49.0
5	46.5

Source: *Monthly Labor Review*, November 1979, p.38.

Certain unions tend to be most successful in winning representation elections, notably craft unions and in particular the construction unions. Seven unions were engaged in over half of the elections surveyed in 1966.[31]

Table 11.9

Union	Elections won	Elections lost	Percentage of all elections in sample
Total	191	145	51.9
Teamsters	104	67	26.4
Machinists	23	26	7.6
Steelworkers	14	13	4.2
Auto workers	13	12	3.9
Operating engineers	14	8	3.4
Carpenters	13	8	3.2
Meat cutters	10	11	3.2

Source: *Monthly Labor Review*, October 1972, p.49.

'Unions tended to be more successful in those industries and types of units which they had traditionally organised'.[32] Thus the steelworkers won in primary metal units and the teamsters were most successful among truckdriver units. Those unions which are successful in maintaining closed or union shop agreements also seem capable of winning a large proportion of their representation elections.

Surprisingly, table 11.10 reveals that there are few variations amongst geographical regions and between urban and metropolitan areas. In fact there was a slightly higher percentage of union triumphs in the south which has traditionally been harder to organise.

Table 11.10
Election outcome by location of firm
(based on a sample of 1,000 union petitions filed with the NLRB in 1966)

Region or area	Number of elections	Union won election		Union lost election	
		Number	Percentage of total	Number	Percentage of total
Total	647	377	58.3	270	41.7
North east	137	78	56.9	59	43.1
North central	225	130	57.8	95	42.2
West	102	60	58.8	42	41.2
South	170	103	60.6	67	39.4
Outlying areas*	13	6	46.2	7	53.8
Total	646†	376	58.2	270	41.8
Metropolitan	417	236	56.6	181	43.4
Non-metropolitan	229	140	61.1	89	38.9

*Includes Puerto Rico and the Virgin Islands.

†Excludes one case not specified by area.

Source: *Monthly Labor Review*, October 1972.

Similarly, union decertification elections have been increasing (table 11.7) from 154 in 1954-55 to 735 in 1976-77. Unions have been less successful in retaining units and again differences can be perceived among various unions in the area of decertification. Those unions which are relatively successful in certification elections also tend to have a high percentage of units decertifying. In 1976-77 the teamsters' union accounted for almost one-third of all decertification elections and the machinists, the steelworkers, the electrical workers, the auto workers and the carpenters also had a fair share of the table.[33] In fact, 'units represented by the Auto Workers were least likely to be decertified while Retail Clerks, Teamsters and Hotel and Restaurant Employee units were most likely to be decertified'.[34] However, where two unions were involved the petitioning union was more likely to win the election in construction and transportation.

The other type of election authorised by Taft-Hartley is the de-authorisation election — or deauthorisation poll as it is often called. The poll is, of course, associated with the issue of union security. Thirty per cent of interested employees can call for a deauthorisation election, and if the majority of employees eligible to vote (as opposed to the majority who actually vote) cast ballots in favour of deauthorisation then the effect is immediately to remove the union shop clause from the collective bargaining contract.

There has been an upward trend in the number of petitions, and the number of deauthorisation elections actually held, over the last 25 years (table 11.11). However, a large proportion of petitions are withdrawn prior to the election; in practice roughly one election is held for every two petitions filed. As can be seen in table 11.11, petitions are running at approximately 300 per year while actual polls have increased from just 17 in 1953 to 140 in 1978. In every year except 1953 the majority of polls resulted in deauthorisation, with roughly 6 out of every 10 elections producing this result. The number of eligible voters who actually vote for deauthorisation in any year is usually less than 50 per cent; in 1978 only 28 per cent of eligible voters cast votes in favour of deauthorisation.[35]

Table 11.11

Union shop deauthorisation polls, selected years 1953-78

Year	Petitions received	Polls held	Deauthorisations	Eligible voters	Actual voters	Votes for deauthorisation
1953	44	17	8	3,394	2,110	1,343
1955	55	20	12	1,814	1,542	842
1960	40	16	10	2,522	1,232	891
1965	106	48	35	3,975	3,426	2,196
1970	158	87	54	8,652	6,371	4,353
1975	209	110	61	7,616	6,035	2,519
1978	298	140	89	9,060	7,116	2,451

Source: National Labor Relations Board Annual Reports, 1953-78.

The probability of deauthorisation, as opposed to decertification where the reverse is true, appears to be much greater for small bargaining units than for large ones.[36] For instance in 1978 the average number of workers in bargaining units where deauthorisation occurred was

34.7.[37] Although the majority of polls are decided in favour of de-authorisation, larger bargaining units are more likely to vote in favour of allowing their union to maintain a union shop clause (in larger units the number of abstentions will naturally be significant to the outcome). It would be reasonable to suppose, therefore, that the type of arrangements collated by the Bureau of Labor Statistics would be least likely to be deauthorised. Managers have not attempted to influence the outcome of deauthorisation polls as they have with certification elections. The general lack of success of deauthorisation elections in larger units may account for their reluctance to interfere.

As noted previously, management in the USA is not normally favourable to unionism, although employers in industries like construction are most likely to co-operate with unions. Recently there has been an increase in management hostility to unionisation in manufacturing and even in some union-dominated industries such as construction. This may in part be:

> . . . the more visible resistance of the most anti-union employers who are now the focus of organizing campaigns in already heavily organized sectors. This wave of resistance is consistent with the longstanding preference and ideology of American business to operate non-union.[38]

It is, of course, difficult to determine the effectiveness of management opposition. Certainly the determination of management, perhaps more in the south than the north, to remain non-union is becoming increasingly apparent. One of the most visible manifestations is the 'new profession' of 'union-busting' management consultants which has grown up to advise companies how to fend off unions.[39] 'Union-busting' has become more common in recent years and management consultancy firms, specialising in advising employers how to prevent new union organisation and how to remove already established unions, are now a part of the American industrial relations scene. One of the largest consultancies is Modern Management Methods which had 450-500 major companies on its books in 1979.[40] These methods may not seriously affect strongly established unions in construction and transport, but they no doubt frustrate the efforts of less secure unions to organise or negotiate union security provisions.

The unions in traditional closed shop industries appear to be capable of maintaining their high level of union membership density but, as in Britain, the number of workers involved in such employment is shrinking. In recent years there has been a general shift away from blue-collar to white-collar employment. Between 1960 and 1970 craft workers as an occupational group dropped from 13.8 per cent to 12.9

per cent of the labour force, while blue-collar workers in general dropped from 36.5 per cent to 33.4 per cent.[41] The obvious conclusion to be drawn from this is that unions will have to organise the white-collar sector if they are to consolidate or improve their present position, and so far they have been reasonably successful in doing just that. In 1976 it was estimated that almost half of the 9.5 million full-time employees in state and local government were union or employee association members, and table 11.12 reveals that teachers and firemen have high density ratings (teachers are usually the largest group of employees employed by state and local governments). As will be recalled, the National Education Association is the second largest labour group in the US after the teamsters. Whether the unions can continue to organise white-collar workers, and in particular the public sector, has yet to be seen.

Table 11.12
Percentage of full-time employees organised,
by function and level of government, 1976

Function	State and local governments	State governments	Local governments
Total	49.8	38.2	54.1
For selected functions:			
Education	58.3	28.6	64.9
Teachers	63.6	34.3	72.1
Other	37.9	25.6	44.8
Highways	44.3	53.5	36.0
Public welfare	41.3	39.3	43.0
Hospitals	39.5	47.7	30.3
Police protection	54.3	51.8	54.7
Local fire protection	71.6	–	71.6
Sanitation other than sewerage	49.2	–	49.2
All other functions	36.9	36.2	37.3

Source: *Monthly Labor Review*, August 1978, p.43.

The extent to which legislation has affected the ability of unions to negotiate and enforce union security provisions is extremely difficult to assess. Despite legislation, the closed shop still persists in industries in which it has always been the traditional method of organisation. In the area of new organisation the determination of many American employers to operate non-union and the decrease in blue-collar and craft employment are among the factors which makes it impossible to estimate exactly what part the legal restrictions have played in determining the level of union membership.

References

1   The chart for 1946-1958/9 is taken from Theodore, R., 'Union Security and Checkoff Provisions in Major Union Contracts 1958-59', Bulletin No. 1272, March 1960, United States Department of Labor, Bureau of Labor Statistics (BLS), p.2.
     The chart for 1972-76 has been calculated using BLS statistics taken from various editions of 'Characteristics of Major Collective Bargaining Agreements'.
2   The union shop also includes the modified union shop.
3   'Others' encompasses both the agency shop and all combinations of provisions such as the agency shop and maintenance of membership.
4   Table 11.3 was compiled using BLS statistics taken from various editions of 'Characteristics of Major Collective Bargaining Agreements'.
5   Transportation does not include the railroad or airline industries.
6   See, for example, Bloom, G.F. and Northrup, H.R., op.cit., p.615: '. . . closed shop industries have either ignored or circumvented the prohibition', and Meyers, F., *The Right to Work in Practice*, op.cit.
7   Keystone Coat, Apron and Towel Supply Co. 121 NLRB 880 (1958), p.885, footnote omitted.
8   Haggard, T.R., 'A Clarification of the Types of Union Security Agreements Affirmatively Permitted by Federal Statutes', *Rutgers Camden Law Journal*, vol.5, 1974, p.451.
9   365 US 667 (1961).
10   Hammerman, H., 'Minority Workers in Construction Referral Unions', *Monthly Labor Review*, May 1971, p.17.
11   Ibid., p.19, from 'National and International Labor Unions in the United States, 1969', BLS Bulletin 1665, 1970, p.73, table 8.
12   Total membership includes membership in Canada.
13   Theodore, R., op.cit., note 1 at p.9.
14   *Glasser* v *NLRB* 395 F. 2d 401 (2d CIR 1968); *American Newspaper Publishers Association* v *NLRB* 193 F. 2d 782 (7th Cir 1951).
15   Closed Shop Union Bylaws under the NLRA, *University of Chicago Law Review*, vol.37, summer 1970, p.778.
16   176 NLRB 76, 71 LRRM 1228 (1968).
17   Ibid., p.1228.
18   365 US 705, 1961.
19   *Chicago Law Review*, op.cit., p.794.

20   Cohen, S., 'Operating Under Right-to-Work Laws', *Labor Law Journal*, August 1958, p.575.
21   Ibid., p.576.
22   Meyers, F., op.cit., p.14.
23   Ibid., p.16.
24   Ibid., p.24.
25   Ibid., p.29.
26   Cohen, S., op.cit., p.576.
27   Theodore, R., op.cit., p.15.
28   395 US 575 (1969).
29   Prosten, R., 'The Rise in NLRB Election Delays: Measuring Business's New Resistance', *Monthly Labor Review*, February 1979, p.38.
30   Ibid., p.40.
31   Rose, J.B., 'What Factors Influence Union Representation Elections?', *Monthly Labor Review*, October 1972, p.49.
32   Ibid., p.50.
33   Anderson, J.C., Busman, G. and O'Reilly, C.A., 'What Factors Influence the Outcome of Union Decertification Elections?' *Monthly Labor Review*, November 1979, p.33.
34   Ibid., p.33.
35   Dworkin, J.B. and Extejt, M.M., 'The Union Shop Deauthorization Poll : a New Look after 20 Years', *Monthly Labor Review*, November 1979.
36   Morgan, C.A., 'The Union Shop Deauthorization Poll', *Industrial and Labor Relations Review*, October 1958, pp. 79-85.
37   Dworkin, J.B. and Extejt, M.M., op.cit., p.38.
38   Roomkin, M. and Juris, H.A., 'The Changing Character of Unionism in Traditionally Organized Sectors', *Monthly Labor Review*, February 1979, p.36.
39   'American Union-busting: Crisis? What Crisis?', *The Economist*, 17 November 1979, p.39.
40   Geddes, P., 'The New American Waterfront', *The Listener*, 6 December 1979.
41   *Monthly Labor Review*, March 1978, p.24.

PART IV

UNION SECURITY IN THE FEDERAL REPUBLIC OF GERMANY

12 Union security and collective bargaining in the post-war context

In the area of union security, and more specifically the closed shop, the Federal Republic provides an intriguing comparison with Britain and the USA although the fundamental problem is exactly the same. On the one hand the constitutional guarantees of individual liberty, established under the Basic Law of 1949, have made the question of compulsory membership in particular, and union security in general, just as sensitive an issue for unions, employers and government in Germany as in the UK and the USA, although the debate has not been as public or intense. On the other hand union security has historically been an objective of some German trade unions. For example, under Weimar closed shop agreements were considered desirable by a number of craft and professional unions.[1] It should also be remembered that the Nazis imposed compulsory membership on all workers through the German Labour Front (*Deutsche Arbeitsfront*), and this principle of an organisation embracing the whole working class on the basis of compulsory membership was briefly advocated by some leading German trade unionists immediately after the Second World War,[2] before a structure of industrial unionism was introduced under allied supervision.

Industrial unionism does not in itself generate a need for control over entry, particularly to crafts, since these barriers are transcended by such a trade union structure. However craft and professional traditions inevitably live on, even where a new structure has been artificially imposed from above. Thus, the absence of the closed shop and union security from public debate need not necessarily preclude the existence of certain workplace practices which effect compulsory membership, or other forms of union security which have arisen as a result of the particular structure of collective bargaining in West Germany.

The main question of comparative interest, then, in this section is why, given the open and at times passionate interest of the unions in establishing and maintaining union security in Britain and the USA, trade unions in the Federal Republic have never viewed this as an organising device fundamental to their existence and hence central to their bargaining policy. There are two subsidiary questions. First, do such practices exist on an informal basis? Second, if they do, why are they tolerated?

Before attempting to answer these questions in detail it is necessary to say something about the institutional, economic and political context within which trade unions have developed in the FRG since 1945.

After the war organised labour in what is now West Germany was in a state of disarray. It was divided administratively between the three Allied zones and there was no coherent organisational structure. Ideologically, however, there were, particularly in the British zone, definite conceptions of the future role of trade unions in German society. These were based on demands for nationalisation of key industries, the introduction of worker participation on the supervisory boards of companies (*Mitbestimmung*) and a new Works Constitution Act to regulate industrial relations at plant level.[3]

At the outset the situation in war-torn Germany created possibilities for the German labour movement to consolidate its position at a key level in the economy — namely the level of the enterprise; but attempts at rekindling an organic development from below, i.e. at the workplace, were soon quashed by a number of developments. Firstly in 1949 the DGB — the German trades union congress — was founded on the principle of a new union structure — industrial unionism. The formation of 16 industrial unions under the aegis of the Allies as an alternative to the demands from some trade union leaders for an all-embracing single union with compulsory membership (*Einheitsgewerkschaft*) was to transcend the craft, occupational and denominational interests which had characterised the structure of unionism under Weimar. Some organisations, however, retained their identity, notably the Teachers' Union (GEW) which has remained the only professional association within the DGB, and journalists (DJV) who have their own organisation within the Printing Union (IG Drupa). Furthermore the Fine Arts Union has two affiliated organisations, the RFFU (*Rundfunk Fernseh Union*) in broadcasting and the GDBA (*Gewerkschaft Deutscher Bühnenarbeiter*) for the theatrical professions. Secondly, although the passing of the Basic Law in 1949 gave individuals the right to join the organisation of their choice, that choice was effectively restricted by the artificial establishment of industrial unionism from above.

This factor led early on to a split within the white-collar sections of the DGB, as more professionally oriented trade unionists gravitated towards the German Union of Salaried Employees (DAG, *Deutsche Angestelltengewerkschaft*). This union now has eight affiliated organisations and competes with the staff sections of the DGB unions for membership in private industry.

Furthermore, senior white-collar workers in the private sector are organised by nine managers' associations affiliated to the Union of Senior Managerial Staff Association (ULA).

In the public sector the same phenomenon has occurred with senior civil servants, or *Beamte* as they are known. Here the German Civil Servants Federation (DBB) competes with the DGB public sector unions, notably the Teacher's Union, the Public Services, Transport and Communications Union, the Railwaymen's Union, the Post Office Workers' Union and the Policemen's Union. The DBB now has 44 affiliated organisations which recruit in the public sector.

Finally there are also denominational alignments grouped under the Confederation of Christian Unions (CGB) in both the public and private sectors.

Although the CGB and the ULA have members, and in some cases representatives, on works councils, only unions affiliated to the DGB, the DAG and the DBB have been recognised for the purposes of collective bargaining in the Federal Republic.

The year 1949 also saw the passing of the first Collective Agreements Act by the Allied authorities which effectively predetermined the nature of union security in the Federal Republic, since it gave a bargaining monopoly to trade unions *outside* the plant only. It followed that all important collective bargaining and job regulation also took place outside the plant, and that there was initially no *direct* need for strong organisation in the plant itself.

In the following years two enactments during this formative period were to have significant implications — both positive and negative — for union security. On the one hand the Codetermination Act of 1951 (*Montanmitbestimmungsgesetz*) gave the unions substantial access at company level in the coal and steel industries. On the other hand the Works Constitution Act (*Betriebsverfassungsgesetz*) of 1952 organisationally and institutionally dismembered the trade unions from the workplace and weakened their access at company level in non coal and steel industries. The implications of this legislation for union security now need to be considered in some detail.

Codetermination and union security

Under the Codetermination Act of 1951, which applies to the coal and iron and steel industries only, trade unions have virtually direct access to the company. The Act provides for a supervisory board to be made up of an equal number of elected shareholder and employee representatives, with an independent member being elected by the other members. The supervisory board appoints the management board which is responsible for the day-to-day running of the company. One of the members of this board — the so-called labour director — cannot be appointed against the wishes of the employee representatives on the supervisory board. In practice this means that the trade union has a veto over the appointment of the labour director since three of the employee representatives are put forward by the trade unionists after consultation with the works councils in the company and two by the works councils themselves.

The significance of codetermination in these industries for union security is twofold. Firstly, the union can ensure via the labour director, who in most cases is a trade unionist himself, that its organisational interests are acknowledged within the company (this will be dealt with in more detail in chapter 15). Secondly, because of the constellation of the supervisory board a close link is established between the trade union and the works council in each plant.[4]

Since 1951 legislation in the area of codetermination has been retrograde, with different and weaker provisions in other industries, which inevitably have an effect on the degree of union presence in a company.

In 1952 the Works Constitution Act provided for only one-third employee representation on the supervisory board of firms outside the coal and steel industries. In addition no provision was made for a labour director, the office being filled by a personnel director appointed by the company.

In 1976 the legislation was amended for firms with over 2,000 employees to provide parity, that is equal employee/shareholder representation on the supervisory board, with the complicating factors of a senior managerial representative on the employee side of the board and a chairman with a casting vote elected by the shareholder representatives.

Furthermore the labour director need not necessarily be elected with the consent of the employee representatives.[5] Of the 460 labour directors appointed since the Act only seven have been appointed in accordance with the wishes of the employee board representatives,[6] which leads to the speculation (given that there is little empirical evidence) that the legislation will not bring about the same degree of union security as that enjoyed in the *Montan* sectors.

The works constitution and union security

A tradition in German labour relations which started with the Works Councils Act of 1920 (*Betriebsrätegesetz*), and continued through legislation passed by the Allied Control Commission[7] to the Works Constitution Act of 1952, has sought to establish the workplace as a locus of employee representation *independent* of trade union influence.

In the Federal Republic all firms with more than five employees are entitled to a works council which is elected by all the workforce by secret ballot for three years. The works council has a number of bargaining rights which encompass disclosure of information, consultation and full bargaining. Accompanying these rights are a set of obligations under which works councils must refrain from initiating industrial action and divulging confidential information (Ss. 74 and 79 WCA). Against this employers are obliged to recognise the works councils as their negotiating partners and to provide them with the necessary facilities, including full-time release, offices and clerical assistance (Ss. 38, 39, 40 WCA). Thus at the outset the works council embraces all workers irrespective of trade union membership — a factor obviating (in contrast to the UK) any managerial need for compulsory membership as a means of stabilising workplace relations.

In contrast to these arrangements at the workplace, collective bargaining is conducted at supra plant level between the trade union and the relevant employers' association. At this level different rules operate, with both trade unions and employers free to resort to industrial action (inasmuch as they are not restricted by case law). Furthermore collective agreements are legally binding and have a normative effect on trade union members only under S.3 (1) of the Collective Contracts Act (CCA).

It is this dual system which confronts the trade union with two different organisational forms which, on the face of it, appear to stand in competition with one another. In contrast to the UK and the USA there is no direct link in the FRG between union security in the plant and immediate gain for the trade union member from such an arrangement. Because the locus of union activity in terms of collective bargaining is outside the plant, trade unions naturally find it very difficult to convince non-members of the direct benefits of union membership except for strike pay and legal aid for representation at a labour court, of which there is a common awareness. This has been found to be the case in a recent empirical survey carried out in the food, drink, tobacco and hotel and catering industries,[8] although the problem is common to other industries.

Have unions been able to attract members via the status of collective agreements? It has already been stated that legally terms and conditions negotiated in collective agreements apply only to union members. In practice, however, employers offer non-members the same terms and conditions and in most large firms and in the public sector the terms and conditions will be incorporated in the contract of employment which applies to all employees in a particular establishment.

Collective agreements may, in addition to pay and general terms and conditions, be concluded to regulate issues pertaining to the Works Constitution Act. However under S.3 ss. 2 CCA these agreements must apply to *all* employees in the establishment. The Collective Contracts Act also provides under Section 5 for the possibility of an extension of the terms and conditions of collective agreements. This means that all the employees in a particular industry and region covered by the collective agreement may fall under the jurisdiction of that agreement regardless of whether they are trade union members or not, or whether their employers are federated or not. Generally an extension is declared by the appropriate Federal or State Minister for Employment and is commonly found in the case of blanket agreements (*Manteltarifverträge*) establishing minimum basic terms and conditions. Understandably extension is to be found in those industries where trade union organisation is weak, namely construction, textiles, clothing, baking, confectionery, wholesale, hotel and catering and the retail trade.[9]

The 'dual system' of collective bargaining briefly outlined above reflects at crucial points the constitutional guarantees for individual rights established under the Basic Law of 1949. Article 9 Section 3 of the Constitution explicitly grants a person a positive right to associate. By 1952 consensus had been reached by academic lawyers that this meant by implication that employees had a complementary right to dissociate.

Hence it can be argued that both institutionally and constitutionally there were at the outset considerable constraints on unions wishing to expand and protect their power base at the workplace by both voluntary and compulsory means. British trade unions have traditionally scorned legislation which threatened to curtail their potential for organisation and action and have sometimes turned their scorn into effective political activity. Why were the German unions different in their response? There were a number of reasons, of which two in particular can be singled out. Firstly, the boom conditions following the Korean war in the early 1950s and the subsidised economic recovery shifted the emphasis of trade union policy towards more overtly economic demands. The 1950s were marked by periodic wage rounds and unco-ordinated strikes across industry as left-wing trade unionists came to expect that a militant policy, oriented towards pay, would bring improved standards of living and political concessions from the government.

Secondly, trade unions began to realise that despite its constraints the works council system had important functions in maintaining the stability of industrial unionism, in performing vital organisational services for the union and in allowing for flexibility in supplementary pay bargaining.[10] Thus from the outset there has been a *de facto* identity between statutory representation and union organisation at the workplace. (The average percentage of trade union works councillors has been consistently high throughout the post-war period — at 80 per cent).

By the early 1960s, then, a distinct centralisation of bargaining and an acceptance of the status quo by the unions against a backdrop of sustained economic growth and low inflation heralded a new 'co-operative' style of industrial relations at both supra-plant and plant level.

These developments, reinforced by a situation in which the inorganic development of collective bargaining meant that union security did not appear as a goal central to the bargaining process itself (unlike the UK and the USA), generally created conditions which were unfavourable for union growth.[11] Overall density of DGB unions stagnated and even fell during the 1950s and 1960s to 30 per cent or less (see table 12.1) — a low level in comparison with some other countries.[12] Some unions, notably the Construction Workers' Union, did make concerted efforts during this period to improve membership by means of certain union security measures,[13] but the co-operative stance adopted by most unions must have been a factor contributing to the overall stagnation in density and the lack of interest in improving organisation from below.[14]

The absence of conflict during the period from the late 1950s to the mid 1960s meant that in terms of public policy there was no overt 'trade union problem'. However, this situation was to change in the late 1960s with a wave of unofficial stoppages over pay in the mining, steel and engineering industries and a reaction to wage cuts and redundancies in the wake of the 1967 recession. This was followed by further unofficial action over cost of living supplements in 1971 and 1973.[15] This period of heightened bargaining awareness (between 1970 and 1975 the share of wages and salaries in the national income rose by 5 per cent)[16] was also marked by increases in membership and density in a number of DGB unions (cf. table 12.2). It is neither possible nor appropriate to present here an analysis of all the factors which were responsible for these increases. This has been done admirably elsewhere in comprehensive studies by Streeck et al.[17] and Herbammer et al.[18] It is however possible to make some observations with regard to developments in organisational security during the above period.

In the mid 1960s unions in textiles and wood processing were making concerted efforts, in some cases leading to strike action, to extend their

Table 12.1
Trade union membership and density
in the Federal Republic 1950-78

Year	Membership (000's)			DGB Density (per cent of employees)[2]				
	DAG[1]	DBB[1]	DGB	1	2	3	4	5
1950	225	120	5,073	31.1	28.8	43.0	34.8	3.9
1951	343	234	5,543	33.1	31.0	44.3	37.0	5.2
1955	421	517	5,517	29.5	27.4	41.0	32.2	4.7
1960	450	650	5,599	27.5	25.2	38.7	29.0	4.5
1965	476	703	5,658	26.0	24.0	34.9	28.2	3.7
1970	461	721	5,702	25.6	23.9	32.5	28.9	3.9
1975	470	727	6,326	28.4	27.3	32.3	33.6	6.5
1978	482	801	6,661	29.7	29.0	32.3		

Columns 1-5 show the density of DGB unions disaggregated as follows:

Column 1 — The economy as a whole
Column 2 — Private sector
Column 3 — Public sector
Column 4 — Manufacturing sector
Column 5 — Commercial (includes Banking and Insurance)

NOTE: Addition of the DAG and DBB membership to the DGB figures would, of course, increase overall union density quite substantially, but the effect would vary greatly from one sector to another.

Sources: (1) Statistische Jahrbücher; (2) T. Hagelstange 'Die Entwicklung der Mitglieder-zahlen der DGB — Gewerkschaften' in *Gewerkschaftliche Monatshefte* 11/79, pp. 734-43. The discrepancy between the above density figures for the DGB and those in table 12.2 can be explained by the fact that the above calculations do not include pensioners, students and trainees which together can account for yearly differences of between 7 and 15.6 per cent.

Table 12.2
Union density in the DGB and twelve selected industries 1960-75

Year	DGB	(a) IG Bau, Steine Erden	(b) IG Bergbau u. Energie	(c) IG Chemie Papier, Keramik		(d) Gewerkschaft Handel, Banken u. Versicherungen		(e) IG Metall				(f) Gewerkschaft Textil u. Bekleidung	
		1	2	3	4	5	6	7	8	9	10	11	12
1960	31.7	27.0	65.0	–	–	4.4	3.9	–	–	–	–	44.7	23.7
1961	31.0	25.9	66.7	41.9	54.2	4.2	3.9	76.0	34.5	53.1	26.0	45.4	23.0
1962	30.8	25.6	67.7	–	–	4.0	3.9	–	–	–	–	45.2	22.3
1963	30.4	25.3	66.5	–	–	3.9	4.2	70.7	36.6	47.9	25.8	–	–
1964	30.4	26.6	66.9	–	–	3.7	4.1	–	–	–	–	44.6	22.3
1965	30.4	27.1	63.9	39.0	50.6	3.9	4.5	–	33.1	50.4	23.4	–	–
1966	30.2	29.1	65.7	–	–	3.9	4.8	–	–	–	–	–	–
1967	30.6	29.4	71.2	–	–	3.9	4.9	–	–	–	–	45.3	23.7
1968	30.3	26.7	75.9	37.5	44.6	4.0	5.4	67.7	28.5	51.0	21.6	–	–
1969	30.0	28.7	80.0	–	–	3.9	5.9	–	–	–	–	–	–
1970	30.3	27.9	83.4	–	–	4.0	6.4	–	–	–	–	44.3	21.1
1971	30.8	28.6	82.8	42.0	48.9	4.2	7.3	–	–	–	–	43.7	0
1972	31.2	28.9	84.7	–	–	4.6	8.3	76.4	34.1	60.4	21.7	–	–
1973	31.8	30.7	88.6	–	–	5.1	9.0	–	–	–	–	50.1	25.7
1974	33.4	34.7	88.5	–	–	6.0	10.1	–	–	–	–	53.7	28.5
1975	36.4	36.3	91.9	46.4	51.9	6.8	10.6	78.6	37.7	68.7	30.7	56.5	30.4

Key to industries:

1 Construction	5 Commerce	9 Automobiles	
2 Coalmining	6 Banking and insurance	10 Electricals	
3 Chemicals	7 Iron and steel	11 Textiles	
4 Rubber and asbestos	8 Engineering	12 Clothing	

Key to unions:

(a) Construction Workers' Union
(b) Mining Union
(c) Chemical and Paper Workers' Union
(d) Banking, Commerce and Insurance Union
(e) Metalworkers' Union
(f) Textile and Garment Workers' Union

Source: Wolfgang Streeck, 'Politischer Wandel und Organisatorische Reformen – zur Überwindung der Gewerkschaftlichen Organisationskrise der sechziger Jahre' in GMH, 10/78, pp. 632-3.

membership by means of clauses in collective agreements differentiating in favour of union members. The subsequent academic and legal debate culminated in the decision of the Federal Labour Court of 1967 which banned such agreements and brought the issue of union security into the open for the first time.

Because of this decision these unions and others faced with similar organisational problems prompted a debate within the DGB towards achieving a corresponding amendment in the Collective Contracts Act. Other unions saw fit to pursue more indirect ways of achieving union security. The Metalworkers' Union (*IG Metall*) and the Post Office Workers' Union (*Deutsche Postgewerkschaft*), for example, attempted to improve their position at the workplace by drafting agreements which recognise and grant facilities to their lay officials at the workplace — so-called *Vertrauensleute* (shop stewards) — as a support system for their works councillors and as a surrogate means of improving union security. Other unions followed suit so that by the end of 1974 there were 50 such agreements registered with the Federal Ministry of Employment.[19]

The question of the practical effectiveness of this second column has been critically assessed elsewhere,[20] but it can be argued that where there is a strong *Vertrauensleute* organisation supporting the works council at the point of production it is likely that there will be a high union density in the plant in question. However, attempts to extend facilities for *Vertrauensleute* have faltered in recent years as other more substantive issues have taken priority in the worsening economic climate. Furthermore some unions, notably the *IG Metall*, have met with total opposition from the employers with regard to an extension of union shop-floor facilities and some unions may fear that a second column of workplace representation would pose a threat to the internal stability of their organisation. By the mid 1970s interest within the DGB for some change in legislation to permit union security arrangements was at its height. However, that interest was expressed only by those unions which needed an injection of membership and which found it particularly difficult to recruit for structural reasons. Whilst the 1975 DGB congress passed a motion calling for a change in the Collective Contracts Law to allow differentiation, this was not vigorously taken up either by individual unions or by the Social Democrat/Liberal coalition government.

Without doubt the passage of an amended Works Constitution Act in 1972 was a factor which held back any aggressive pursuit of the above policy. Not only did the Act increase the coverage and numbers of works councillors and improve union access to the plant to attend works council meetings and works and department meetings, it also greatly enhanced the organisational position of the trade union which in part solved the *Vertrauensleute* problem.

The 'capture' of the works councils by DGB unions does not in itself have any great implications for union security. Under the Works Constitution Act there is no such concept as the non-member. Works agreements concluded between management and the works council apply to all employees (S.77 ss. 1 WCA 1972). A differentiation in the terms and conditions of such agreements based on membership of a trade union would constitute an infringement of S.75 ss. 1 WCA which prescribes the fair and equitable treatment of all individuals in the establishment.

However *de facto* works councils have become workplace trade union organs carrying out organisational tasks often with the tacit approval of management. In some cases this may be extended to include some form of pressure on non-members in the day-to-day processing of grievances or personnel issues, a point which will be taken up in more detail in chapter 15.

From the mid 1970s onwards the industrial relations climate has changed markedly. Firstly, union bargaining policy has focused on qualitative rather than quantitative demands.[21] Whereas the beginning of the decade was marked by a quite aggressive official policy on pay, in response to the unofficial stoppages over pay in 1969 and 1971, the emphasis later shifted to the area of job security. This was a logical consequence of changed circumstances, as industry responded to the mounting problems of oil price increases, over-accumulation and structural change by increased rationalisation, concentration and the movement of capital abroad. The effects of these measures on employment and the status of skilled workers have rendered it increasingly necessary for unions to negotiate, often aggressively, agreements securing certain guarantees. Agreements have been concluded in printing over manning (1978), in engineering over downgrading (1973 and 1978), in steelmaking over a reduction in working hours (1979) and in other industries such as chemicals and leather to protect union members from the effects of rationalisation. Secondly, this new bargaining strategy has led to a hardening of attitudes between the 'social partners' as employers have sought to resist any advance which might extend the 'frontier of control'. It is against this backdrop that the action brought by the BDA (German Employers Federation) before the Federal Constitutional Court against the Codetermination Act of 1976, the subsequent withdrawal of the DGB from the Concerted Action pay talks in 1977, and the increase in industrial conflict by both employers and trade unions must be viewed.

These developments have been accompanied by a public debate about trade union power. However, unlike Britain, where the debate has focused primarily on union power at the workplace, discussion in

Germany has revolved around the manifestations of union power at a macro level. In particular there has been concern about the inter-relationship between the SPD/FDP coalition and the ideologically neutral DGB[22] and the implications for control in industry of an extension of codetermination following the model operating in the coal and steel industries.[23] This 'March into the Union State'[24] has been seen as the inevitable outcome of an extended period in government of the SPD/FDP coalition which had come to power in 1969. It was argued that from that time onwards tacitly favourable conditions existed for union growth and consolidation to take place at a number of levels.

This debate, which was initiated principally from conservative quarters, was given an added dimension in 1976 with the publication by the CDU of a compilation of cases of misuse of union power at the workplace. The so-called *Biedenkopf-Dokumentation*, released during the run-up to the 1976 federal elections, was a party political manoevre which met with a barrage of opposition and litigation from the cited trade unions. In the latter half of the 1970s attention has shifted away from the more politically sensitive area of union discrimination at the workplace to the discussion about legislation to control the internal structure of the unions (*Verbändegesetz*)[25] and the removal of the alleged 'political monopoly' of the DGB unions.[26]

For the reasons which have been discussed it may be seen that union security has never emerged either as a union policy issue or as a public policy issue to the same extent as in Britain or the USA. Yet, as already stated, the absence of union security as an issue is not a denial of its existence in practice. In the Federal Republic a relatively stable, prosperous, capitalist economic system functions under a tightly knit legal framework of collective bargaining which emanates from a catalogue of constitutional safeguards. In these circumstances it is understandable that neither trade unions nor employers nor the government would wish to reveal aspects of more traditional trade union behaviour which are incompatible with constitutionally guaranteed individual liberties and a public and international image of social partnership. In the Federal Republic trade unionism has not normally appeared as a problem deemed central to the country's economic or political fabric as in the respective cases of Britain and the USA. Consequently research into the topic of union security has been virtually non-existent. It is only recently that the question has received any serious empirical treatment as part of a wider study of the effects of organisational change on union growth in the Federal Republic.[27]

However, the particular nature of the factors shaping the West German system contain contradictions which have a central bearing on the supposed absence of the closed shop and union security in West Germany. Firstly, the right to associate as guaranteed under the Basic

Law is not complemented by an explicit right to dissociate. Instead the courts have interpreted the right *not* to join as being implicit in the right to join. The question which this poses is why, given such a tightly knit normative system, a right to dissociate has not been explicitly spelt out.

Secondly, the different traditions and structural factors operating in different industries mean that certain unions may want to approach the question of organisational security in their own particular way. Their approach may be determined by the legal or extra-legal options open to them. The following chapters will, therefore, be concerned with the ways in which the Constitution, and more specifically labour law, has determined the pattern of union security in the Federal Republic and the methods which the unions have used to circumvent that law.

References

1   Gamillscheg, F., *Die Differenzierung nach der Gewerkschafts-zugehörigkeit*, 1966, p.9.
2   Kolb, J., *Metallgewerkschaften in der Nachkriegszeit*, Frankfurt am Main 1970, p.15.
3   Schmidt, E., *Die verhinderte Neuordnung*, Frankfurt am Main 1970.
4   Streeck, W., Bayer, E., Treu, E., *Organisationsstrukturelle Wandlungsprozesse in westdeutschen Gewerkschaften 1960-75*, University of Münster, unpublished report 1978. For an English summary see: Streeck, W., 'Organisational consequences of Corporatist Co-operation in West German Labour Unions. A Case Study', *International Institute of Management: Discussion Paper 1978*, op.cit., pp. 31-3.
5   Section 33 subsection 2, *Mitbestimmungsgesetz* 1976.
6   *Handelsblatt* 5 December 1978.
7   Gesetz 22 des Kontrollrates 10.4.1946: Works Councils provided for elected committees of worker representatives safeguarding worker interests in the sphere of social and personnel issues and disclosure of the relevant information by management. Under this Act works councils were to pursue their duties in co-operation with the relevant trade union or unions.
8   Wiedenhofer, H., 'Fragen der Integration gewerkschaftlicher Tarif- und Betriebspolitik', *Gewerkschaftliche Monatshefte* 11/1979, pp. 702-4. Findings of an empirical survey carried out in the hotel, catering and foodstuffs industries.
9   Between 1968 and 1975 the number of extended collective agreements increased from 158 to 446. In 1977 there were 504 extended agreements covering 4 million employees (2.5 million manual and 1.5

million staff). This constitutes roughly one-sixth of the working population of the Federal Republic.

10 Streeck, W., 'Qualitative Demands and the Neo-Corporatist Manageability of Industrial Relations', *BJIR*, vol. XIX, no.2, July 1981.

11 Altvater, E., Hoffman, J., Semmler, W., *Vom Wirtschaftswunder zur Wirtschaftskrise*, Berlin 1979, pp. 342-70.

12 Streeck, W., 'Gewerkschaften als Mitgliederverbände. Probleme gewerkschaftlicher Mitgliederrekrutierung', in Bergmann, J. (ed.), *Beiträge zur Soziologie der Gewerkschaften*, Frankfurt 1979, pp. 72-3; also table V, p.106.

13 Seitenzahl, R., Zachert, U., Pütz, H.D., *Vorteilsregelungen für Gewerkschaftsmitglieder*, WSI Studien Nr. 33, Cologne 1976, pp. 3-6.

14 Miller, D., 'Trade Union Workplace Representation in the Federal Republic of Germany: An analysis of the Postwar Vertrauensleute policy of the German Metalworkers' Union (1952-77)', *BJIR*, November 1978.

15 Müller-Jentsch, W., *Streiks und Streikbewegungen in der Bundesrepublik 1950-78*, Bergmann, J., op.cit., p.44.

16 *Jahresgutachten des Sachverständigenrates*, 1979, p.76.

17 Streeck, W., Treu, E. and Bayer, H., op.cit. Discusses union growth as a function of organisational change.

18 Herbammer, S., Bischoff, J., Lohauss, P., Maldauer, K.H., Steinfield, F., 'Organisationsgrad und Bewusstsein', *Gewerkschaftliche Monatshefte* 11/79, pp. 709-20. Links changes in density with changes in workers' consciousness.

19 Wlotzke, O., 'Zur Zulässigkeit von Tarifverträgen über den Schutz und die Erleichterung der Tätigkeit gewerkschaftlicher Vertrauensleute', *Recht der Arbeit* 1976, p.80.

20 Miller, D., op.cit.

21 Müller-Jentsch, op.cit., pp. 34-50, Streeck, op.cit.

22 Beyme, K. von, 'The Changing Relations between Trade Unions and the Social Democratic Party in West Germany', *Government and Opposition*, 13,4.

23 *Mitbestimmungsgesetz* 1976.

24 Meyer, E., 'Zur Polemik über den Gewerkschaftsstaat' in Jacobi, O., Müller-Jentsch, W., Schmidt, E., *Gewerkschaften und Klassenkampf, Kritisches Jahrbuch*, 1975, p.128. 'Zeit-Forum, Marsch in den Gewerkschaftsstaat?', *Die Zeit*, 49 and 50, 29 November 1974 and 6 December 1974.

25 Blum, N., 'Reform der Gesellschaft durch Reform der Gewerkschaft', *Gewerkschaftliche Monatshefte* 1979/8.

26 Stoiber, E., *Rohmaterialen zur DGB Diskussion*, CSU 1979.

27 Streeck et al., op.cit.

13 Union security and the constitution

In Germany the freedom to join a trade union, and conversely not to join a trade union, was first guaranteed under the Trade Regulations (*Gewerbeordnung*) of 1869. Under Section 153 of these Regulations it was rendered a criminal offence to force individuals to join or remain a member of a trade union. Since 1918, however, when these Regulations were repealed, the right not to join a trade union has ceased to be explicit in German law. Following on from the Weimar Constitution of 1919, Article 9(3) of the West German Constitution (or Basic Law of 1949 as it is known) explicitly guarantees only a positive right to associate.

> The right to form associations to safeguard and improve working and economic conditions is guaranteed to everyone and to all trades and professions. Agreements which restrict or seek to hinder this right shall be null and void, measures directed to this end shall be illegal.[1]

At the drafting stage of the Federal Constitution and in particular Article 9 there was considerable discussion over the spelling out of the right not to join (*die negative Koalitionsfreiheit*). In reaction to the compulsory membership of the Labour Front under the Nazi regime two Länder, notably Hessen and Bremen, had set precedents by including an explicit right to dissociate in their respective constitutions.[2] However, this example was not followed by the Senior Drafting Committee of the Constitution which voted by 12 votes to 6 to delete a provision declaring that no one was to be forced to become a member of an organisation.

What was the reasoning behind this decision? It was held that a certain constraint was implicit already in Article 9(3) since a positive right to join embodies the element of choice. Trade unions were to be voluntary associations and a worker was to have the right to choose which union she or he wished to join. It followed from this that it would already be unlawful to force an individual to join a different organisation from that to which she or he already belonged.[3] Whilst Article 9(3) envisaged a pluralism of unions, in practice the structure of industrial unionism, as Wedderburn says, has meant that for blue-collar workers,[4] choice has been limited to one union only (the DAG competes with DGB unions for staff employees).

The more general question, namely whether an individual has the right to belong to no organisation at all was, it seems, left open by the members of the drafting committee. Their decision not to render this principle explicit was based on a number of primarily pragmatic reasons. Firstly, it was felt that certain union measures such as 'moral suasion' and 'appeals for solidarity', whilst representing a degree of compulsion, had been acknowledged and sanctioned by the courts in the past[5] and had probably contributed 'towards achieving stability in certain sectors of the economy'.[6] Stability in the economy had 'a higher priority than obstinacy and obstructionism', this latter statement being addressed principally to the Lower Courts which the Committee feared might interpret and apply an explicit right to dissociate in too rigorous a manner.[7] Furthermore the question was raised about the compulsory membership of those organisations representing the legal and medical professions, engineers, veterinary surgeons, chemists, architects and accountants. Misgivings were expressed that the explicit right to dissociate might have detrimental effects on these organisations of public law.[8]

Although it can be argued that pragmatism underlies the absence of an explicit right to dissociate, the abstract formulation of the basic rights grants to the judges the power to read anything or nothing into or out of them. Concerning this issue of the constitutional guarantee of the right to dissociate, there appear to be three main interpretations by the courts and legal scholars: (a) the first, to which the Federal Labour Court adheres, is that the right to dissociate is derived from Article 9(3) of the Basic Law — an individual having the right to decide whether to join any organisation at all as well as the right to choose the organisation which he or she wishes to join;[9] (b) the second position which tends to predominate in the legal literature on the subject is that the right to dissociate derives from Article 2(1) of the Basic Law which guarantees to the individual the right to the free development of his or her personality.[10] Historically, it is argued, the right to dissociate has never been in doubt, although the 'desire to enjoy personal freedom emerged much stronger from the experience of the Hitler era than it had been at the time of the creation of the Weimar Constitution';[11] (c) finally, a third group of legal scholars maintain that the right to dissociate has no constitutional basis whatsoever.[12] This of course, does not imply that these scholars reject a general right to dissociate. Indeed the writers who take this standpoint are very few.[13] Thus the argument about the right to dissociate in the Federal Republic is not about whether or not it exists but about the basis from which it is derived.

As has been made clear in the previous chapter, the question of union security did not become an issue of any legal import until the mid 1960s when several of the smaller unions with low memberships attempted to expand their base by concluding agreements which differentiated in favour of union members and which effectively prevented employers from making supplementary payments by means of a 'differential clause'. Matters came to a head in 1965 when the Westphalian Clothing Employers' Association brought an action against the Textile Workers' Union for striking to enforce such an agreement. After protracted labour court hearings at local and Land level the issue came before the Federal Labour Court for clarification because of its fundamental nature. In its ruling[14] the Federal Labour Court declared differentiation by collective agreement and the negotiations of differential clauses unlawful for reasons grounded in both collective bargaining and constitutional law.

In terms of collective bargaining law it was considered unacceptable to charge a 'fee' (in this particular case the loss of holiday pay) for union services. Furthermore, relating holiday pay to union membership was held to 'grossly violate the feeling of justice' of the non-union member, in that holiday pay was something to be calculated on the basis of category of work, age of the employee, family status and need for rest rather than on the basis of membership of a trade union. An employer who sought to differentiate in such a manner might run the risk of endangering 'industrial harmony' at the workplace. In addition the court held that it was unacceptable to expect an employer or employers' association to co-operate with a union in discriminating between union members and non-members. This constituted a breakdown in the legitimacy of the collective bargaining system.[15]

In terms of an infringement of the Constitution, differentiation and differential clauses were ruled to be a 'socially inadequate' way of putting pressure on individuals[16] for the reasons set out above, and as such they violated Article 9(3) of the Basic Law which guarantees a *voluntary* right to join a trade union. Elsewhere in its decision the Upper Senate interpreted Article 9(3) as implying a right not to join a trade union,[17] drawing on previous related decisions of the Federal Constitutional Court. This view is still questioned by the majority of legal writers.

The decision of the Federal Labour Court was heavily criticised by the DGB[18] which promptly appealed to the Federal Constitutional Court. However, the latter rejected the appeal on formal grounds because it had not been asked for a ruling over a concrete legal situation but had been called upon to clarify legally a number of fundamental issues. Hence the DGB was not directly affected by the decision of the Upper Senate.

For practical purposes the 1967 ruling of the Federal Labour Court has remained the prevailing doctrine of the right not to associate, since the highest court in the land, the Federal Constitutional Court, has not yet made a ruling on the issue of the closed shop or discrimination in favour of union members. Because the ruling defines a right to dissociate as being implicit in Article 9(3) of the Basic Law, it has Federal application since the basic rights guaranteed in Articles 1-19 of the West German Constitution bind the executive and the judiciary and serve as limitations not only on the Federal Government but also upon the exercise of Länder authority. The constraint is reinforced in the latter case by a Supremacy Clause in the Constitution (Article 31) under which Federal law overrides Land law. In the case of the Hessen and Bremen Constitutions the formalised right to dissociate does not represent an infringement of the Basic Law since it is deemed compatible with the catalogue of basic rights in the Constitution.

Although it is clear that these fundamental rights serve to protect the individual in relation to the State, there is doubt as to whether they operate between individual citizens. Whereas in the USA, as has been seen, the Bill of Rights protects the individual against governmental action but not directly against actions of other individuals, in the Federal Republic the fundamental constitutional guarantee of freedom of organisation has been expressly extended to apply between citizens. This extended effect, known as *Drittwirkung*, has been maintained by the Federal Labour Court since 1955 in its recognition that the parties to collective bargaining wield a rule-making power which is a legislative power delegated to them by law. In using this doctrine the courts have been able to exert a decisive and formative influence on the political effect of the catalogue of basic rights in practice. The interpretation of Article 9(3) is a case in point, although the severity of the interpretation is, as Kahn-Freund says, tempered by the fact that the illegality of the closed shop is recognised on other grounds, principally the infringement of the free development of the individual.[19]

Beyond court rulings on the issue there has been no legislation explicitly dealing with the question of the closed shop or union security during the post-war period in the Federal Republic, although the Länder may legislate under Article 74(12) of the Basic Law on matters of employment and labour relations as long as, and to the extent that, the Federation does not exercise its right to legislate in this area. In practice legislative jurisdiction for industrial relations has been almost entirely absorbed by the Federation.[20] This stands in contrast to section 14(b) of the US National Labor Relations Act, as amended, which exceptionally allows individual states to ban most forms of union security if they wish to do so.

Although the Federal Constitutional Court has not made any precise ruling in the area of the closed shop and discrimination in favour of union members, there has been a decision on the constitutional nature of compulsory membership in related 'non-union' employee organisations. In the Federal Republic it is generally accepted that professional associations (*berufständische Kammern*) and worker chambers (*Arbeitnehmerkammern*) operate closed shops as institutions of public law. Under Federal Law the *berufständische Kammern* exist for the legal and accountancy professions as well as the professional and craft trades (so-called Handwerk). Under Land law similar associations exist for the medical professions and for architects. Generally all employees in these professions are obliged to join their respective associations which administer and supervise vocational training, draft and enforce professional codes of practice and maintain welfare funds for retired members.

In the case of the worker chambers (*Arbeitnehmerkammern*) these exist only in two Länder — Bremen and Saarland — although there are examples in Austria. In Bremen, where *Arbeitnehmerkammern* were re-established by law in 1956, there are separate chambers for manual and salaried employees. In the Saarland there has been one joint chamber for manual and salaried workers since 1951. Attempts to extend worker chambers to other Länder in Germany have continually met with resistance from the trade unions[21] on the grounds that they are incompatible with the DGB's concept of establishing economic and social committees with worker representation, as a means of achieving codetermination at regional and national levels in the economy.

Early in the 1960s actions were brought by individuals against the respective worker chambers in Bremen and the Saarland on the grounds that it was unconstitutional to force employees to pay a monthly subscription. The actions, dealt with in the finance and administrative courts respectively, were unsuccessful but the plaintiffs appealed and their cases were brought before the Federal Constitutional Court which failed to recognise their claims. In essence the Court ruled that compulsory membership in worker chambers did not constitute an infringement of Article 9(3) of the Basic Law since these organisations did not fall under *private* but *public* law.[22] Worker chambers, in contrast to trade unions, do not negotiate on behalf of their members with employers' associations over terms and conditions of employment, and hence cannot be classed as collective bargaining agents.

The general legal position with regard to the closed shop and union security in the Federal Republic may be summed up as follows. There is no statutory legislation which regulates union security in the Federal Republic. The legal position is derived from the Basic Law and its interpretation by the courts. Whereas the closed shop is held by all parties and the majority of legal commentators to be unlawful, there is uncertainty about the right to 'dissociate' being implicit in the right to join a trade union. On the question of discrimination in collective agreements in favour of trade unionists as a means of improving membership, the courts have ruled this to be unlawful, much to the chagrin of the unions.

References

1   The West German Constitution (Basic Law) is printed in full, in English, in Brownlie, I. (ed.), *Basic Documents on Human Rights*, Oxford University Press 1971, pp. 18-24.
2   Art. 36(2) Hessen Constitution 1946 and Art. 48 Bremen Constitution 1947.
3   Schaub, G., *Arbeitsrechtshandbuch*, Munich 1977, p.878.
4   Wedderburn, Lord, in Schmidt, F., *Discrimination in Employment*, Stockholm 1978, p.449.
5   Hueck, A., Nipperdey, C., *Lehrbuch des Arbeitsrechts*, vol.II (7th edn. 1967), p.157.
6   Ibid.
7   Gernandt, O., 'Die negative Koalitionsfreiheit', *der Arbeitgeber*, 1954, p.154.
8   Report of Senior Committee quoted in A. Lenhoff, 'Compulsory Unionism in Europe', *The American Journal of Comparative Law*, 1956, p.32.
9   Federal Labour Court Decision 29 November 1967, 42: BAG 20 175: AP Nr 13 zu Art 9 GG.
10   Hueck, A., Nipperdey, C., *Grundriss*, 5th edn. section 43 1; Söllner, A., *Arbeitsrecht*, 6th edn., p.60.
11   Nikisch, A., *Arbeitsrecht*, 1951, p.268.
12   Gamillscheg, F., op.cit., p.53 ff; Biedenkopf, K., *Grenzen der Tarifautonomie*, 1964, p.93 ff.

13   Däubler, W., *Das Grundrecht auf Mitbestimmung*, Frankfurt/
Cologne 1973, p.280 ff.
14   BAG 20 175 AP Nr 13 24 Art 9. GG. (29 November 1967).
15   Ibid., p.218-24.
16   Ibid., p.228.
17   Ibid., p.215.
18   Minutes of the 8th Congress of the DGB, 1969, Motions tabled
p.151 ff.
19   Kahn-Freund, O., 'The Impact of Constitutions on Labour Law',
Cambridge Law Journal, November 1976, p.269.
20   There are a few exceptions to this. The Hessen Constitution, for
instance prohibits the lock-out, and the terms and conditions of
employment for public service workers are determined by Länder law
but within an overall framework established by the Federal law.
21   Peters, J., *Arbeitnehmerkammern in der Bundesrepublik Deutschland?*, Olzog, Munich 1973, p.90 ff.
22   Decision of the Federal Constitutional Court 18 December 1974,
no.24, 297 ff.

14 Union security: policies and possibilities

From what has already been said about the closed shop in the FRG it might be thought that there could be little doubt about its illegality there, or about the obstacles in the way of unions attempting to negotiate formally about union security at the workplace. Nevertheless the matter has sometimes been the subject of considerable discussion and controversy within the trade union movement and this indicates that there is no uniform approach to union security within the DGB. The stance of particular unions in the debate will shortly be considered, but first it is necessary to specify those options open to trade unions in exerting influence over the extension of their membership.

One of the features of trade union bargaining strategy in the last two decades has been the negotiation of specific plant oriented collective agreements at a sectoral level which can be a vital means of formally, and thus legally, extending union influence at the workplace. Certainly the discussion on union security has tended to be an assessment of the various kinds of clauses in sectoral collective agreements by which unions might increase membership. What kind of agreements have been suggested or made?

Straightforward membership clauses (*Organisations — or Absperrk-lauseln*) are legally impracticable, as has been seen, because of the serious constitutional objections which exist. Thus the formal type of closed shop agreement, or union membership agreement as it is known in Britain is, from the outset, unlawful and hence unknown in the Federal Republic. Discussion has therefore centred around modified forms of such provisions in agreements like the *Ausschlussklausel*, which is a clause placing the employer under a legal obligation not to extend the terms and conditions of an agreement negotiated by the union to non-members.[1] This may be accompanied by an *Aussenseiterklausel* which is a provision permitting the otherwise unlawful regulation of the employment relationship of workers not subject to the terms of the collective agreement. Such a clause would allow the respective trade union and employers' association to agree on inferior terms and conditions for non-members and thus avoid individual employers undercutting the agreement.

Similar to the *Ausschlussklausel* in effect is the *Differenzierungsklausel*, a provision in a collective agreement which differentiates between union members and non-members, for example by providing for a holiday or Christmas bonus to be awarded to union members only. However, since all workers must be treated equitably under S.75(1) of the Works Constitution Act an employer on his own could not award such benefits. So 'differentiation clauses' are usually linked to the creation of a regional fund[2] jointly administered by both the employers and trade unions. But in order for such provisions to have any effect there must be some mechanism by which individual employers can be prevented from offering non-members the same benefits as those accruing to union members from such a fund. The 'differential clause' (the *Spannensicherungsklausel* or *Benachteiligungsverbot*) is just such a mechanism. In essence it obliges the employer to pay union members any additional payments made to non-members to bring them onto a par with union members. Quite clearly such clauses neutralise the individual employer's attempt not to differentiate between members and non-members, since their effect is to maintain the differential between the two categories of employees.[3] Such supplementary agreements were rendered unlawful by a decision of the Upper Senate of the Federal Labour Court in 1967,[4] although some academic lawyers question this judgement.[5]

Finally solidarity contributions — *Solidaritätsbeiträge* — were seriously considered by the Construction Union in the 1950s as a means of improving union security. Based on the Swiss model[6] non-members would have been obliged to pay an amount equivalent to the union subscription to acquire a job card necessary to obtain employment under the same terms and conditions as union members. The subscriptions paid by the non-members would have been used to finance union costs and support training schemes.

The establishment of solidarity contributions would, however, have created legal and organisational problems because collective agreements between trade unions and employers calling on third parties to make such contributions have little foundation in German law. In addition they would have presented union members with a means of 'buying themselves out of the union'[7] thus infringing the basic right of individuals to associate as guaranteed in Article 9 section 3 of the Basic Law. For these reasons, then, and because of employer resistance, solidarity contributions were never introduced.

Finally the problem of the wage gap, that is the disbursement by some firms of supplementary payments in addition to the wages negotiated by the union, and the effect which this may have on membership, has prompted certain unions, in particular the *IG Chemie*, to propose the introduction of clauses in collective agreements which prevent employers from setting off the supplementary payment against the annual wage increase. These clauses provide for the supplementary payment made to the employee before the wage increase to be added on to the newly agreed rate of pay.

In addition to these limited 'take home pay guarantee' clauses, or *begrenzte Effektivklauseln*, there is another variety of guarantee clause, or *Effektivgarantieklausel*, which would oblige employers to relate negotiated wage increases to total take-home pay, which includes the supplementary payments. As a result the supplementary payments would become legally binding rather than subject to the discretion of the employer. Whereas this latter type of guarantee clause has traditionally been held to be unlawful, limited take-home pay guarantee clauses were originally deemed to be lawful by both the Reich Labour Court (*Reichsarbeitsgericht*)[8] and the Federal Labour Court (*Bundesarbeitsgericht*).[9] However, in 1968 the Federal Labour Court declared limited take-home pay clauses unlawful.[10] A number of reasons were advanced for this decision, but only one is of interest here. It is that trade unions would be able to differentiate between their members and non-members, in that higher wages would only be guaranteed for those employees bound by the collective agreement, but not for employees who were not members of the relevant unions.[11]

Union security: union policy and attitudes

Although the DGB is officially opposed to the closed shop in the form in which it is practised in the UK,[12] there is nevertheless interest among affiliated unions in the feasibility of the 'differentiation clause' linked with the establishment of jointly administered funds, and the 'take-home pay guarantee' clause.

In 1973, a study was commissioned by Heinz Kluncker, general secretary of the Public Services, Transport and Communications Union, to examine thoroughly the legal, political and organisational implications of an amendment of the Collective Contract Law to include differentiation clauses. The final report, completed by a research team of the Institute of Economic and Social Research at the DGB (WSI),[13] included short reports from twelve of the major affiliates of the DGB, outlining their respective attitudes towards the question of union security. Their varying standpoints are included in table 14.1. From the table it can be seen that the majority of DGB unions which submitted evidence support some form of discrimination in collective agreements in favour of their members. However, notable exceptions are the two big unions, the *IG Metall* (metalworkers) and the *ÖTV* (public services, transport and communications).

Of those unions in favour only four are committed to a policy of legislative change in favour of differentiation clauses and jointly administered funds. One of these — the Foodstuffs, Tobacco, Hotel and Catering Union — had eight motions carried at its 1974 Conference to amend the Collective Contracts Act and has carried out a survey which reveals that a small majority of non-unionists would join the union if there was differentiation in collective agreements.[14] The other three are the Textile and Clothing Union, the Wood and Plastics Union and the Construction Workers' Union; the last named also supports a policy of solidarity contributions. However, four other unions — the Railwaymen, the Banking and Insurance Section of the Wholesale and Retail, Banking and Insurance Union, the Metalworkers and the Public Services, Transport and Communications Union — are categorically opposed to union security via differentiation clauses and jointly administered funds.

How can these differences in policy towards union security be explained? It will be seen that the four unions which support differentiation clauses all have low densities. This is largely the result of the structure of the workforce (a high proportion of female labour in foodstuffs and textiles), the small size of establishments, as in the case of construction, hotel and catering and the wood and plastics industries, and high turnover rates, as in construction and hotel and catering. But how can the rejection of this policy by the banking and insurance section of the HBV and the Public Services, Transport and Communications Union, which have to recruit in areas of the economy facing similar problems, be explained?

The answer lies in the particular situation of white-collar staff in these service sectors and in the special position of senior civil servants (*Beamten*). In the Federal Republic of Germany, in contrast to manual workers, white-collar employees can join a number of competing organisations. Firstly there are the relevant white-collar sections of the DGB affiliated unions — in this case the HBV and the ÖTV. In the ÖTV there is also a section for senior civil servants. Alternatively staff employees may join the DAG — the German white-collar employees'

Table 14.1
Policy of twelve DGB unions on union security

Trade union	Density (1977)	General principle of discrimination via collective agreement	Differentiation clauses via jointly administered funds	Solidarity contributions	Extension of rights for *Vertrauensleute*	Take-home pay guarantee clauses
Construction	20.8%	√	√	√	x	+
Mining and energy	88.9%	+	+	+	+	+
Chemicals, paper and ceramics	41.3%	√	+	+	√	√
Printing and paper	36.7%	√	o	+	+	+
Railwaymen	70.0%	√	x	+	+	+
Commerce, banking and insurance	17.0%	√	Banking & insurance x / Co-ops √	+	√	+
Wood and plastics	19.0%	√	√	+	+	+
Metalworkers	45.4%	+	x	+	√	√
Food, drink, tobacco, hotels and catering	17.5%	√	√	+	+	+
Public services, transport and communications	30.0%	+	x	x	+	√
Post office workers	70.0%	+	o	x	√	+
Textiles and clothing	34.6%	√	√	+	+	+

√   advocates
x   rejects
o   acceptance in principle but uncertainty as to whether it would or could be implemented
+   no comment

Table compiled by the author from Seitenzahl et al., op.cit.

union which recruits across industry. In the higher echelons of the public sector civil servants may join the German Civil Servants Union — *Deutscher Beamtenbund* — or one of its affiliates. The relevant unions fear that differentiation could lead to a situation where the unions would try to 'outsell' each other in the form of competitive subscriptions, and membership of a union would come to be regarded entirely in terms of its cost effectiveness. In addition the ÖTV in particular sees serious difficulties in introducing differentiation into the senior civil service where the terms and conditions of employees regarded as servants of the state and the public are regulated by special legislation. Other groups of employees, notably the railwaymen and the post office workers, have senior civil servant status and the unions recruit accordingly, but density in these organisations has traditionally been high (see chapter 15) so that the question of differentiation has never had to be seriously considered.

One cannot make the converse assumption with those unions which do not favour discrimination, that they do so against a background of organisational strength. Whilst this certainly is the case in the Coal Mining Union, the iron and steel section of the Metalworkers' Union and the Railway Union, the arguments which they advance are in the main political ones. The most important is the effect which the formation of employer/trade union administered funds could have on the independence of the parties concerned. The *IG Metall* is particularly opposed to this on the grounds that differentiation and solidarity payments would undermine the role of the union 'as an organisation of struggle and interest' and that involvement with employers in joint arrangements could compromise the independence of the union, although rank and file members appear to be of a different opinion.[15] A similar but less hard-line stance is taken by the Public Services, Transport and Communications Union. This body sees the trade union traditionally as an organisation which *de facto* represents the interests of all workers and is therefore wary of differentiation. Furthermore this union sees the danger of compromise in the formation of joint arrangements.[16] Despite the controversy within the DGB as to the methods by which union security could be achieved, all unions favour some form of modification of the Collective Contracts Law to the extent that differentiation *may* be legally permissible. This was ratified at the 1975 and 1978 DGB congresses[17] and has been incorporated into a draft amendment which reads as follows:

Section 1: Content and Form of the Collective Agreement
Subsection (1) The collective agreement can regulate rights and obligations of the parties to the contract and norms relating to the content, commencement and termination of the employment re-

lationship as well as matters relating to the establishment and the Works Constitution Act.

(2) It shall be lawful to negotiate agreements and legal norms which ensure that benefits or payments awarded by joint arrangement of the contractual parties or other such expressedly defined benefits are to be awarded to employees who are bound by those agreements only.

(3) The parties can agree that supplementary payments are to be guaranteed along with the newly negotiated rates of pay.

(4) It shall be lawful to negotiate agreements which reserve the right for additional contractual negotiations to be conducted over certain specified terms and conditions outlined in a collective agreement.

(5) Collective Agreements must be in writing.[18]

Finally the question of differentiation on the basis of union membership has been drafted as an objective in the new DGB action programme of 1979. Less specific than the above draft amendment it reads:

Employers' associations and trade unions must be given the opportunity to negotiate agreements which provide benefits from jointly administered arrangements or other specific benefits to only those employees directly bound by the agreement.[19]

Union security: employer policy

It is clear that the German employers' association, the *Bundesvereinigung der Deutschen Arbeitgeberverbände*, is formally opposed to any change in the law governing the existing collective bargaining system which would improve the organisational position of a union; but it is difficult to assess whether some member firms and associations differ in their approach to the overall question of union security. Public statements outlining policy on this issue were, until recently, virtually non-existent. It was not until the leak in 1978 of the so-called 'Taboo Catalogue', which outlined the frontier in collective bargaining beyond which the BDA recommends employers not to advance, that a picture of the official employers' position in this area could be formulated. The verbatim text of the catalogue is reproduced below.

. . . The trade unions are increasingly forwarding claims for an improvement in union security at plant level. These involve
(a)   Check off arrangements
(b)   Paid release for members of negotiating committees

214

(c) The concession of a special status for their lay representatives (*Vertrauensleute*) at plant level.

Considerable objections relating to constitutional law as well as collective bargaining law can be advanced against these demands. For these reasons such claims are to be rejected.

III *Consultation with the Executive*

The following basic issues are of particular importance with regard to collective bargaining policy. Consequently they fall under a special executive guideline which may not be deviated from unless prior consultation with the executive has taken place.

In order to guarantee the freedom of association as laid down in the Constitution and to maintain industrial peace it is necessary to ensure that all employees are treated equitably regardless of whether they are members of a trade union or not.

As part of their general demands for union security trade unions are increasingly calling for preferential treatment for their members in the form of benefits awarded by special funds financed by the employers. The same legal misgivings relating both to the Constitution as well as to the law of collective bargaining as mentioned in the previous section apply here also.

By concluding such agreements the parties would be exceeding the limits of their power as defined both by the Constitution and by the law of collective contract, and would thereby infringe the freedom of workers to associate. *Such agreements should therefore be rejected* since they contradict the principle of equal treatment for all employees regardless of membership of any organisation.

Included in these demands is the restriction of the scope of a collective agreement to trade unionists only by placing an obligation on employers not to allow non-members the same terms and conditions as negotiated in the collective agreement (*Tarifausschlussklauseln or Aussenseiterklauseln*). Such clauses must not be incorporated into collective agreements since they are clearly unlawful.[20]

From the text it can be seen that member employers are strongly urged to resist all attempts by trade unions to seek collective agreements which extend union security. (At the level of the enterprise and/or plant individual employers may of course practise a different policy.)

Government policy

Although the motion tabled by the Textile Workers' Union for an amendment of the Collective Contracts Law to include the possibility of differentiation clauses was accepted at the 10th DGB Congress in 1975 there has been little progress since then at government level. The predicament for the policy-makers was outlined in a speech given by Helmut Schmidt at the 10th Congress of the Construction Workers Union[21] and reiterated by Rudolf Sperner, General Secretary of the Union. In his speech Schmidt outlined the difficulties which the SPD faced in achieving support from its coalition partner, the FDP, in the area of union security legislation. Since then there have been no public statements on the issue by members of the government, although it is interesting to note that recent legislation providing for extra court legal aid for German citizens on low incomes specifically excludes the field of labour law.[22] This was the result of extensive lobbying by the trade unions, who were clearly concerned that the free provision of legal aid in industrial relations matters would undermine their position vis-à-vis prospective members.

The law relating to union security in the FRG and the respective public policies of the parties involved have been explored. It is now necessary to consider how well the legal norm and the public policies of the parties are matched by what actually happens in practice.

References

1   Hueck, A., *Tarifausschlussklauseln und verwandte Klauseln im Tarifvertragsrecht*, München 1966.
2   Bötticher, E., *Die gemeinsamen Einrichtungen der Tarifvertragsparteien*, Heidelberg 1966.
3   Hueck, A., *Tarifliche Differenzierungsklauseln*, Düsseldorf 1967; Gamillscheg, F., op.cit.
4   Reference BAG E 20, 175.
5   For a survey cf. Seitenzahl et al., op.cit., pp. 60-99.
6   Ibid., p.62.
7   Ibid., pp. 102-3.
8   BAG, *Arbeitsrechtsammlung* 5,50; 6,90; 7,23; 8,484.
9   BAG, Arbeitsrechtliche Praxis (AP), Nr. 1 on section 4 Collective Contracts Act (TG), decision of 1 March 1956, BAG AP Nr. 5 decision dated 26 April 1961.
10   BAG AP Nr. 7 re. s.4. Collective Contracts Act. Decision dated 14 February 1968 and confirmed by a further decision 26 April 1961 in BAG AP Nr. 5.

11 Cf. Däubler, W., *Arbeitsrecht*, Hamburg 1976, pp. 89-94.

12 The DGB considers the Worker Chambers Act to be unconstitutional on the grounds that it provides for compulsory membership for all workers.

13 Seitenzahl et al. op.cit., cf. note 5.

14 Wiedenhofer, H., *Probleme gewerkschaftlicher Interessenvertretung*, Bonn 1979, p.120.

15 Ibid., p.17, cf. Bergmann, J., Müller-Jentsch, W., *Gewerkschaften in der Bundesrepublik*, vol.2, Frankfurt 1977, table 18, p.229.

16 Ibid., p.24.

17 Motions 160 at the 10th DGB Congress Hamburg 1975, and 235 at the 11th DGB Congress, Hamburg 1978.

18 In Zachert, U., *Tarifvertrag*, Cologne 1979, p.189.

19 DGB Aktionsprogramm 13 June 1979 in *GMH* 12/79.

20 Bundesvereinigung der Deutschen Arbeitgeberverbände. *Katalog der zu koordinierenden lohn — und tarifpolitischen Fragen — von 12.10.1965, in der Fassung von 15.12.1968, von 6.5.1975, und von 16.3.1978.*

21 Minutes of the 10th Conference of the IGBSE held at Hamburg 1975, p.14, quoted in Streeck, W., 'Gewerkschaften als Mitgliederverbände. Probleme gewerkschaftlicher Mitgliederrekrutierung', in Bergmann, J., *Beiträge zur Soziologie der Gewerkschaften*, Frankfurt 1979, p.85.

22 Rechtsberatung und Vertretung für Bürger mit geringem Einkommen (Beratungshilfegesetz 18 June 1980). Bundestagsdrucksache 8/3695. The upper house of the German Parliament (Bundesrat) and the CDU (Bundestagsdrucksache 8/1713) wanted the inclusion of labour law in the Act but the SPD/FDP bill (BT/Drucksache 404/79) was finally accepted.

15 The closed shop and union security in practice

It has been shown in the preceding chapters that there are very considerable institutional and legal constraints on union security in the Federal Republic. Similarly the public policy of the respective parties gives an indication formally of the lack of willingness on both sides of industry to pursue this question as a collective bargaining issue. But what does the situation look like in practice?

A useful indicator is, of course, trade union density, but even the disaggregated densities in table 12.2 give no indication of the level of organisation in particular sections of industry, establishments, professions and/or groups of employees. Comprehensive disaggregated figures are unavailable so it is necessary to piece together a picture from the available research data. Table 12.2 does indicate, however, that by 1975 high union densities existed in mining (91.9 per cent), iron and steel (78.6 per cent) and automobiles (68.7 per cent). Broken down according to employment status, it was found that manual workers in both mining and iron and steel were virtually 100 per cent organised.[1]

The picture in automobiles is somewhat more differentiated, but there has been an increase in density among manual workers from 57.1 per cent in 1961 to 76.2 per cent in 1975.[2] Trade union density is also high, at 90 per cent,[3] in the corsetry section (*Miederindustrie*) of the textile industry and on the railways. In that industry the density ratio among manual workers increased from 86 per cent in 1970 to 93 per cent by 1975. More important, during the same time the density among rail *Beamte* (staff with civil servant status) increased from between

92 per cent and 94 per cent to between 96 per cent and 98 per cent.[4] It is also known that density is high among postmen (90.4 per cent) and trainee post office workers (99.3 per cent),[5] in certain sectors of printing,[6] the docks,[7] and among certain groups of workers such as polishers in the construction industry.[8] As far as employees in the theatre and the arts are concerned, density in the GDBA — the theatrical workers' union affiliated to the Fine Arts Union — is said to have reached a maximum amongst dancers, opera singers and technicians.[9] It is also at a maximum among employees of co-operative/trade union enterprises.[10]

Thus it will be seen that there are a number of areas of employment where a high density of trade union organisation exists. It must be noted that the data, with the exception of the railways and the post office, refer primarily to manual labour. The particular situation of white-collar employees will be discussed in a later section.

What factors can be advanced as an explanation of these high membership ratios? Clearly it is not now intended to offer a comprehensive explanation of union growth and membership patterns in the Federal Republic. As already stated, this ambitious task has been undertaken elsewhere.[11] The aim here is strictly to correlate those aforementioned industries and employee groups with union security measures prevalent in the same sectors. In so doing it will be necessary to look at both the formal and the informal strategies employed by trade unions to maintain organisational security.

Formal union security arrangements

It has been shown that formal collective agreements rendering union membership a condition for employment are unlawful in the Federal Republic on constitutional grounds. It is interesting, however, to note that attempts were made to introduce membership clauses in book printing as early as 1906,[12] laying down that members' companies should only employ members of the said union and conversely that union members should only take up employment in those firms which were party to the collective agreement. Furthermore, during the Weimar Republic, when the legal framework of industrial relations was not dissimilar to that of the Federal Republic today, local railway companies, co-operative societies and the German theatrical profession[13] negotiated membership agreements with their employers.

In the post-war period there has been only one known membership agreement. This was concluded in 1960 for co-operative societies (*Konsumgenossenschaften*) in the Federal Republic.[14] The membership clause in the said blanket agreement was generally applicable; that is, it stipulated that employees were to be members of a recognised trade union. In the case of the co-operative societies, the relevant organisations are the HBV, the DAG and the NGG. According to Streeck, in 1960 these three unions accounted for all the employees in the industry. This membership clause was abandoned in 1966, but the parties still recommend membership of the relevant trade unions in a clause of the blanket agreement for the trade,[15] negotiated on 30 November 1973: 'The parties to the above agreement and the co-operative societies will endeavour to see that employees of such societies become members of one of the recognised trade unions. Similarly the trade unions party to the agreement shall promote the co-operative spirit in their sphere of influence'.

In later framework agreements the unions and employers concerned have sought to consolidate union membership in this sector by including differentiation clauses in collective agreements. There are examples of such agreements in the textile, construction and confectionery trades.

Differentiation according to union membership is not new. During the Weimar period unions were not averse to improving their membership by means of contractual clauses which forbade employers to hire non-members on the same terms as union members. Such agreements were known to operate in coalmining in the Ruhr and Central Germany in the 1920s.[16] There appears to have been little consensus as to the legality of these provisions in the collective agreements, but generally clauses of this kind became neither widespread nor effective.

In the post-war period the first attempt at discrimination was made by the Building Trades Union in 1960. After unsuccessful attempts to introduce a form of agency shop through solidarity contributions based on the Swiss model (see previous chapter) and then holiday pay for members only, the union was able to negotiate a higher supplementary pension for its members. The basis for this arrangement was a welfare fund established in 1957 for the building trades which awards financial assistance in the case of disability and a widow's pension in the event of death of a member. The fund is jointly administered by the union and employers' association, but financed entirely by the latter.

After industrial action, an agreement on a supplementary pension was concluded in 1962, providing the additional benefit to union members only. Because the fund was contractually the sole payer of the supplementary pension the employers could not undermine the agreement by paying similar supplements to non-members. However, in 1969 the additional pension was abandoned after the adverse decision of the Federal Labour Court on 29 November 1967[17] over the question of differentiation clauses in collective agreements.

The next union to succeed in gaining differentiation between members and non-members was the Textile and Clothing Union. In June 1963 a collective agreement concluded with the corsetry employers' association provided for a jointly administered fund financed by the employers and similar to that in the building industry to be established. In addition to a number of welfare benefits the fund was to provide a supplementary holiday bonus exclusively to union members.

A similar contract was concluded between the GTB and the textile and leather employers' association in the Saarland in September 1963, but in attempting to extend the scope of the agreement to other bargaining regions the union was resisted by the employers' associations. As a result the union switched its strategy to concluding company agreements and succeeded in establishing 25 contracts providing holiday pay according to length of service and trade union membership. Where funds were established in these firms, in some cases the union was sole administrator, in others it was a joint administrator with the employer and the works council. For the first time these agreements included so-called *Spannensicherungklauseln*, a type of safety or differential clause which prevented the employer from paying non-members a similar benefit in that it obliged him to pay union members any additional benefits which he paid to non-members.

In two clothing firms in Westphalia the union resorted to industrial action to press home the agreement. As a result in March 1965 the Westphalian clothing employers' association brought an action against the GTB at the Düsseldorf labour court on the grounds that it was unlawful to strike in pursuit of union security agreements. The action was then reformulated to a suit for damages resulting from the strike and in a later phase again to declaring void eight of the company agreements hitherto concluded. The court issued an injunction against the strike and in June 1965 decided on all points against the union, a decision which was later confirmed by the State Labour Court (*Landesarbeitsgericht Düsseldorf*).

A similar action followed in the case of *Messrs. B. and W. in the Saarland* v *the Wood and Plastic Workers' Union*, I.G. Holz und Kunststoff. In June 1966 the union took industrial action against the above firm and others in an attempt to achieve a holiday bonus for its members only. The firm in question applied to the labour court in Neunkirchen/Saar for an injunction to stop the strike, and this was granted.

The Düsseldorf and Neunkirchen decisions unleashed a legal controversy over the question of discrimination against non-members in collective agreements which was finally resolved by the decision of the Federal Labour Court in 1967, discussed in chapter 12.

However, the adverse decision of the Federal Labour Court has had little apparent influence on the level of density in the corsetry industry and the Saarland clothing industry, which both employ a high proportion of female labour. Density, which was said to be 20 per cent in 1963, had increased to over 90 per cent in the 1970s.[18] The joint funds operating in these industries have been reorganised, but they still continue to offer training schemes and supplementary holiday bonus to union members only.[19]

Similar provisions are known to exist in baking and confectionery. Here the NGG, the union which organises in the hotel and catering and foodstuffs industries, has concluded agreements with the relevant employers' associations (*Bundesverband der Deutschen Brot- und Backwarenindustrie VVag* and the *Zentralverband des Deutschen Bäckerhandwerks*) for the bread and confectionery trades. These agreements establish jointly administered funds which provide supplementary pensions in the case of retirement and occupational invalidity. In addition the latter agreed in 1970 to establish a joint fund for the educational advancement of employees in the trade as well as the provision of recreational facilities.[20] Whilst these agreements contain no discriminatory clauses, the union is nevertheless in practice able to discriminate in favour of union members in the operation of these schemes.[21]

Although the decision of the Federal Labour Court in 1967 generally caused trade unions formally to refrain from insisting on discriminatory provisions in collective agreements, the preceding examples would seem to suggest that certain trade unions are still able, in practice, to exert indirect pressure on employees to join the union. In the case of worker-owned enterprises, for example the co-operative societies, formal discrimination on the basis of union membership is still carried out by means of a provision in the blanket agreement for the payment of a Christmas bonus.[22] These arrangements are also tolerated in similar sectors, e.g. trade union enterprises like *Bank für Gemeinwirtschaft, Neue Heimat* and *Volksfürsorge*. It is important to note here that the respective agreements do not contain a clause which prevents the employer from paying non-members the same as trade union members. However, since the employers themselves are trade unions it is unlikely that non-members will receive the same treatment. Despite the absence of this clause, these agreements have still sometimes been the cause of disputes, and non-members have successfully brought an action against the employer over a failure to pay the Christmas bonus.[23]

Generally it can be said that although, as already stated, the DGB is committed to changing the Collective Contracts Law to permit differentiation in accordance with trade union membership, the present legal situation means that union security must be sought, if at all, predominantly by informal means. It is in this way, it can be argued, that some trade unions seem to have made their biggest gains.

Informal union security arrangements

At the formal level we have dealt with the limits and possibilities of securing membership by means of a legally binding collective agreement which can form the terms and conditions of employment for a large number of employees, since these agreements are generally negotiated on a regional or industry-wide basis. What, however, does the situation look like in the individual firm or more specifically in each plant? As was shown in chapter 12, the Works Constitution Act, which regulates labour relations at establishment level, provides for a works council to be elected by all employees. Thus there can be no non-members in terms of formal representation under the Works Constitution Act, because the trade union does not formally represent the workforce, or even its own members, at the level of the establishment. Similarly under Section 75 ss. 1 and Section 77 ss. 4 of the WCA discriminatory treatment of employees is unlawful. From the legal point of view one would, therefore, expect that there would be little pressure on employees, including newly recruited employees, to join the relevant trade union for their establishment.

However, trade union density among works councillors is extremely high and it would, therefore, not be unreasonable to expect that organised works councillors will attempt to influence the level of union membership in their sphere of activity. Essentially there are three areas where works councils can indirectly 'force' recruitment. These are at the hiring stage of new labour; during the representation of the day-to-day interests of the workforce; and when operating the dismissals procedure. These areas will now be considered in turn, but it must be stressed that where evidence of such practices exists it relates to specific establishments only. The extent of such practices in German industry as a whole can thus only remain a matter for sheer speculation.

It is through the involvement of the works council in the engagement of new labour that some unions are able to apply in practice a closed shop among manual workers in a number of establishments in various branches of industry. Under Section 99 ss. 1 WCA the employer is obliged to notify the works council 'in advance of any hiring, grading, regrading and transfer, (to) submit to it the appropriate recruitment documents and in particular supply information on the persons concerned'. Under Section 99 ss. 2 the works council may refuse its consent to a hiring if it should breach any statute or health and safety regulation, or prejudice any other employees or disrupt 'good' industrial relations or if the employer has failed to advertise the vacancy within the establishment.

In larger establishments where hiring has become a formalised procedure the recruitment of new labour may require the applicant to appear before the works council with a form handed to him by the personnel department. In his appearance before the works council (usually a works councillor) a question regarding trade union membership may be asked. This could take the form 'We are 100 per cent organised in this firm. Do you want to become a member?' This question is, of course, perfectly legitimate although it clearly places the individual under a certain degree of psychological pressure. What happens when applicants answer 'No' to the question posed above? There is actually little documentary evidence over this kind of eventuality, partly due to the extremely sensitive nature of the issue. During the run-up to the Federal election in the autumn of 1976 the CDU published a documentation of a number of cases of works councils misusing their legal position to influence trade membership in the plant. The unions cited in the documentation responded with a wave of injunctions against the CDU.[24] Another cause of the lack of evidence is the fact that a refusal to consent to the hiring of a person who declines to join the union may be conveniently masked by one of the legal pretexts under Section 99 ss. 2 of the Works Constitution Act. However, in research carried out in a steel plant in the Ruhr it was reported that if a worker refused to join the union the works council would refuse its consent to the hiring.[25] There are other examples recorded in iron and steel,[26] and in an interview at the headquarters of the mining union it was reported that there were examples of similar practices in this industry.[27]

There are a number of factors which can explain the existence of such a practice among manual workers in mining and iron and steel. As can be seen from table 12.2, these industries have traditionally had a high union density, which in itself acts as a strong pressure on new labour to join the union. Furthermore the localised community-based organisation of the IGBE (mining union) has traditionally meant that union membership represented an entitlement to a number of benefits extending beyond the area of work. Hence withdrawal of membership could mean ostracism at a social level for the individual concerned.

Equally important is the structure of management in the two industries. Iron and steel and coal mining are both codetermination industries under the 1951 *Montanmitbestimmungsgesetz*. As outlined in chapter 12, a particular feature of this Act is the consolidation of the union at company level via the person of the labour director and the employee representatives on the supervisory board. In coal mining this legislation is supplemented by a Codetermination Agreement signed 18 July 1968 between the IGBE and the Ruhrkohle AG (the nationalised coal concern), section 4 of which provides for codetermination at a lower level through the appointment of a personnel director for each plant, dependent on the consent of the labour director.[28]

These provisions are crucial for an understanding of the attitude of management towards union security in the codetermination industries. Since union interests are received favourably on the personnel side, it is understandable that works councils, which exert pressure to join the union on individual applicants for employment, will be tacitly supported by their counterparts in the personnel department. It is difficult at present to assess the extent of union influence in those firms covered by the 1976 legislation, but it seems unlikely that the 'Montan' style of industrial relations will evolve in these firms.

An additional factor influencing the position of the trade union, particularly in the codetermination industries, has been the extent of government support and recognition of trade union needs. Treu (1978) has shown that it was not until the Grand Coalition government of 1965, which first gave the SPD access to power, and the subsequent formation of the coalition between the Liberals and the Social Democrats in 1969, that trade unions could consolidate and extend their position at company and plant level. This seems to have been particularly the case in mining, where from 1967 the check-off was established for the Ruhrkohle AG. Similarly at Volkswagen the state interest in the firm has meant that the IG Metall has had greater influence on the supervisory board than in other automobile firms and in practice the personnel director (now labour director) has been appointed with the approval of the union. Consequently almost the whole workforce is organised in this union. Similarly in the case of the nationalised sectors, where comparable management structures and government involvement exist, such as the railways and the post office, the division between employers and employees becomes blurred.[29] In the case of the Bundesbahn a situation not unlike that in codetermination industries exists, in that the personnel director was a former executive member of the GdED (the main railway trade union). Similarly most managerial employees are unionised, so that an identity of interest may often exist when it comes to the recruitment of new members at the hiring stage.

The study of trade unionism in the Bundesbahn, from which the above findings were taken, also shows that only in very rare cases would a staff council be asked by the management to give its reason for rejecting an applicant for employment. Although under the Staff Representation Act (the corresponding legislation to the Works Constitution Act for the public sector) staff councils are not permitted to recruit union members on the office premises, it was found in the study that applicants for posts were informed that their engagement would not be advocated unless they agreed to join the union. In a number of cases, it was reported, the staff council was spared this task because recruitment had already been carried out by the responsible officer in the personnel department. On the basis of this the authors of the report came to the conclusion that union membership in the Bundesbahn is no less compulsory than it is in British Rail.[30]

In the case of the Bundesbahn, however, the presence of rival unions (the GDBA and the GDL,[31] small organisations which recruit and campaign for staff council elections in addition to the GdED, but are not recognised for the purpose of collective bargaining) has led to cases of GdED staff councillors being taken to court by their rivals for violation of the Staff Representation Act on the grounds that they have used the facilities of the staff council for trade union purposes. Under Section 67 ss. 2 para.1 of the Staff Representation Act (*Personalvertretungsgesetz*) 1965, staff councillors may be deposed if they violate the Act by using the premises of the Staff Council for trade union activities. This provision is not contained in the WCA. Some councillors have been removed from office after labour court hearings, a factor which has caused the GdED to switch its efforts regarding union security to increasing the number of workplace representatives (*Vertrauensleute*).[32]

In the Federal Post Office similar structures in management, namely DPG membership among departmental heads and personnel officers, ensure that there will be little objection to staff councils turning down job applicants who are unwilling to join the union.[33]

Thus it is clear that some form of compulsory recruitment can in fact be practised among railwaymen and post office workers. But the organisation of most white-collar employees in private industry is complicated by structures arising out of the system of collective bargaining. Generally speaking clerical, technical, commercial and supervisory staffs are divided in the FRG into those whose terms and conditions are determined essentially by collective agreement (whether they are union members or not), so-called *Tarifangestellte*, who are the less senior staffs, and those whose contracts do not incorporate these terms but are negotiated individually between the employee and the employer, so-called *aussertarifliche Angestellte* (meaning outside and above the scope of the union agreements). This distinction is clear-cut on the one hand in that collective agreements establish the limits, i.e. the top grades for salaried staff, and define the starting point in salary terms for the *aussertarifliche Angestellte*. In the plant, however, the situation is complicated by the fact that in terms of the representation of white-collar employees the Works Constitution Act is applicable to all employees up to the rank of senior managerial staff, so-called *leitende Angestellte*. This term, as defined under Section 5 of the Act, is open to a considerable variety of interpretation and employers endeavour to define this group of staff as widely as possible in order to exclude them formally from representation by the works council and thus from the indirect influence of the trade union. It has been reported that some unions, notably the *IG Bergbau* (mining union), have retaliated by having their works councillors demand works agreements to regulate the hitherto grey area of staff between the top grade of *Tarifangestellte* and the *leitende Angestellte*. In this way it is hoped to exert some influence on the recruitment of these employees.[34]

A further industrial sector which is known to have high density ratios and an informal closed shop is the docks.[35] Again it is important to note that special circumstances in the docks have led to an unusual type of management and style of labour relations. The peculiar problems of dock work, especially fluctuations in the level of work and casual labour leading to difficulties over entitlement to benefits and holidays, have made it necessary to bring together the various dock sections into one recognised establishment or port (*Gesamthafen-betrieb*)[36] and to establish some form of security of employment for dock-workers. During the Nazi period the docks were established and administered by the central labour ministry (*Reichstreuhänder der Arbeit*). In the immediate post-war period the Allied Control Commission began to allow the employers and trade unions freedom to regulate employment in the *Gesamthafenbetrieb*. In 1950 a Federal Act[37] formally sanctioned this trend and in 1951 the Central Federation of German Port Authorities and the ÖTV concluded a framework agreement, Section 3 of which established joint trade union and employer committees to administer each port. Job security is guaranteed in the docks and mobility between different docks in one port is permitted through the holding of a job card which is issued by the joint committee on commencement of employment. It is through these committees that the ÖTV can exert a considerable degree of influence on membership,[38] although it must be noted that they do not act as surrogate works councils.

We have seen that in all the above four sectors — iron and steel, coal-mining, the railways and the docks — where a form of 'closed shop' exists the structure of management is an important factor. Yet it is known that informal closed shops exist in other sectors, including printing and some engineering establishments, where traditional management structures prevail. Clearly the strength of the existing union organisation in the plant is a significant variable, but the behaviour of management over the question of union recruitment is of central importance. What sanctions does an employer have at his disposal to oppose the informal closed shop?

Under Section 99 ss. 4 WCA management may apply to the labour court for a decision in lieu of consent if the works council refuses approval for a hiring. However, there is no obligation in the WCA on the employer to assert his rights. In practice a number of factors may militate against him doing so. Firstly, the time factor involved in bringing an action before the labour court is considerable. Secondly, works councils in larger establishments where union density is high can wield considerable power, by using the law and in other ways. Thus employers may have an interest in maintaining 'industrial peace' at the expense of what amounts to a closed shop.[39] A third related reason is that employers may have a positive interest in organisational strength and discipline, because they can then rely on a certain degree of union control over the workforce. This was found to be the case particularly after the wave of unofficial stoppages in 1969.[40]

Trade union membership may be vital not only for employment but also for representation of day-to-day interests by the works council. For example, it is known in the Bundesbahn that trade union membership is crucial for promotion,[41] a factor which no doubt partially explains the high union density among white-collar employees in that industry. Generally, however, there is little evidence to suggest that works councils discriminate between non-members and union members when it comes to representation of day-to-day interests. This is partly because organised works councillors may not wish to lose potential members, and partly because individuals who feel badly treated have little recourse to legal sanctions against the works council.

The possession of a union card may be significant in determining the stance which a works council adopts towards the proposed dismissal of an individual. Formally, of course, the works council may not take the question of union membership into account and there are no legal cases bearing on this issue. With regard to dismissal, the German situation differs markedly from the British, in that the German employer may not dismiss an employee for not belonging to a union and trade union expulsions cannot, therefore, lead automatically to dismissal. However, under Section 104 WCA works councils may initiate dismissal proceedings of an employee or employees who are seen to be disturbing the peace of the enterprise 'through unlawful conduct or gross violation of the principles laid down in Section 75 (1)'. Indirectly the union represented in the plant may defend itself against militants by virtue of its dominance of the works council, with individual rights succumbing to an overriding interest in 'order'.[42] However, this rarely occurs, and a dismissal initiative for reasons of a closed shop would definitely not be accepted by the courts. Generally it can be said that whereas in the UK the polemical nature of the controversy about the closed shop is usually connected with the fact that non-membership may automatically lead to dismissal, in the FRG, by contrast, the non-member is more likely to face problems over recruitment and day-to-day representation. But this is not to deny that non-membership of the FRG may lead to dismissal through informal pressures.[43]

Finally, a brief comment about the check-off and union subscriptions. The extent of check-off in the FRG, that is the collection of union dues by the employer, is unknown. In the early 1960s the textile union concluded agreements on check-off with the respective employers' associations in Bavaria (19 December 1962), Westphalia (15 January 1963), Hessen (30 January 1963), Baden Würtemburg (1 February 1963), Aschaffenburg and Lower Franconia (18 January 1963). These are the only known collective agreements on check-off.[44] Under these agreements essentially union dues were to be deducted from members free of charge by the employer if a majority of union members had declared their approval. In textiles in 1975 65 per cent of the membership had their dues deducted in this way.[45] In the case of IG Metall some 30 per cent of the members are on check-off[46] and while the comparable figure for trade union members in the chemical industry is 11.8 per cent,[47] in coalmining nearly all members have their dues paid by the Ruhrkohle AG on the basis of an agreement made in 1968.[48] In these latter cases check-off has come about as the result of pressure from works councils and may have been secured informally or in the form of a works agreement.

It is important to note that these agreements relate to *union members only* and do not embrace all the employees in a particular establishment, as in the case of the US agency shop. Nevertheless, it has been found that check-off agreements do have a positive effect on membership in that they reduce the turnover rate in dues-paying members.[49]

At a further level works councils may occasionally use check-off arrangements with employers to attempt to enforce membership in their sphere of influence. Thus there have been a number of cases where union dues have been involuntarily paid by employees[50] and a case where the works council in a chemical firm issued a statement to the workforce that all unorganised workers were to become members. Those individuals who had not lodged a formal objection at the works council office were to be taken as having agreed to the resolution and their subscriptions were to be deducted accordingly.[51]

References

1   Treu, H.E., 'Probleme der gewerkschaftlichen Mitglieder-rekrutierung in ausgewählten Industriezweigen', *Soziale Welt*, Heft 4, 1978, p.428.
2   Ibid., p.430.
3   Ibid., p.434.
4   Streeck, W., Seglow, P., Bayley, P., 'Railway Unions in Britain and West Germany. Structural sources of cross national differences and

similarities', *International Institute of Management Discussion Paper 78/80*, Berlin 1978, p.25.

5   Internal statistics of the German Post Office Workers' Union (DPG), 28 February 1976.

6   Erd, R., Müller-Jentsch, W., *Innovation in the Printing Industry in the Federal Republic*, Research paper (B0179/4), Anglo German Foundation for the Study of Industrial Society 1978, p.20.

7   Abendroth, M., Beckenbach, N., Braun, S., Dombois, R., *Hafenarbeit: Eine industriesoziologische Untersuchung der Arbeits — und Betriebs verhältnisse in den bremischen Häfen*, Campus, Frankfurt 1979, p.526.

8   Bayer, H., 'Die Integration heterogener Mitgliedergruppen in Industriegewerkschaften 1960-1975', *Soziale Welt*, Heft 3 Jahrgang 30 1979, p.354.

9   *Die Quelle*, November 1978, p.645.

10   Such enterprises include co-operative societies, the trade union bank (Bank für Gemeinwirtschaft — BFG), the unions' housing corporation (Neue Heimat) and the unions' insurance company (Volksfürsorge).

11   See Streeck, 1978, for a discussion of the factors involved in trade union growth in the Federal Republic post-1945.

12   Erd and Müller-Jentsch, op.cit., pp. 2-3.

13   Gamillscheg, op.cit., p.9.

14   Streeck, W., Bayer, H., Treu, H.E., op.cit., 1978, vol.1, pp. 434-5.

15   Section 23 subsection 4 of the Blanket Agreement for the Co-operative Societies of West Germany (30 November 1973).

16   Gamillscheg, op.cit., pp. 10-11.

17   Reference BAG. E 20, 175.

18   Seitenzahl et al., p.32.

19   Treu, op.cit., pp. 434-5. See also the relevant collective agreement establishing funds in the corsetry industry (*Tarifvereinbarung über die Errichtung eines Vereins und einer Stiftung für die Arbeitnehmer der Miederindustrie 25.3.1974*) negotiated by the Textile Union (GTB) and the employers' association (Arbeitsgemeinschaft der Miederindustrie).

20   The collective agreement negotiated between the Hotel, Foodstuffs and Catering Union and the Federation of Bakery Employers establishing a supplementary benefit fund (20 February 1970) and an agreement providing a joint training fund for employees in the industry (Seitenzahl et al., pp. 215-21).

21   Ibid., pp. 22-3.

22   Section 21 subsection 1, of Blanket Agreement for the Co-operative Societies of the Federal Republic (30 November 1973).

23   Zachert, U., *Tarifvertrag*, Bund, Cologne 1979, pp. 182-3, cf. Stuttgart Labour Court Decision 4 Ca 15/75 (6 February 1975).

24   CDU Bundesgeschäftsstelle, *Dokumentation über den Missbrauch gewerkschaftlicher und politischer Macht durch SPD — und Gewerkschaftsfunktionäre, Parts I & II*, Bonn 1976.

25   Marsh, A., Hackmann, M., Miller, D., *Workplace Relations in the Engineering Industry in the UK and the Federal Republic of Germany, A Comparison*, Anglo German Foundation for the Study of Industrial Society 1981.

26   IMSF Autorenkollektiv, *Mitbestimmung als Kampfaufgabe*, Pahl Rugenstein, Cologne 1972, pp. 121-2; Herding, R., *Job Control and Union Structure*, Rotterdam, University Press, 1973, p.322.

27   Interview with an official at the IGBE, 14 August 1979.

28   Beer, W., 'Die Mitbestimmungssituation im Steinkohlenbergbau', *Das Mitbestimmungsgespräch*, 1973, pp. 162-4.

29   Streeck, W., Seglow, P., Bayley, P., op.cit., p.26.

30   Ibid., p.27.

31   The *Gewerkschaft Deutscher Bundesbahnbeamter und Anwärter* (principally white-collar) and the *Gewerkschaft Deutscher Lokomotivführer* (similar to ASLEF).

32   Streeck, Bayer, Treu, op.cit., p.393.

33   Seitenzahl, et al., op.cit., p.27.

34   Cf. IG Bergbau Vorstand, *Betriebsvereinbarung für AT Angestellte bei der Ruhrkohl AG October 1978*.

35   Spiegel, Nr 6, 1973, pp. 99-100.

36   Assmann, J., Rechtsfragen zum Gesamthafenbetrieb, Dissertation, Cologne University 1965, pp. 1-11.

37   *Bundesgesetz über die Schaffung eines besonderen Arbeitgebers für Hafenarbeiter. Gesamthafenbetrieb von 3.8.1950.*

38   Spiegel, Nr 6, 1978; Abendroth et al., op.cit., pp. 522 and 526.

39   Streeck, Bayer, Treu, op.cit., vol.1, p.362.

40   Ibid., p.364.

41   Streeck, Seglow, Bayley, op.cit., p.27.

42   Lord Wedderburn of Charlton, 'Discrimination in West Germany', in Folke Schmidt (ed.), *Discrimination in Employment*, Stockholm 1978, pp. 450-1. Trade union expulsions are on the whole more frequent in the Federal Republic than in the UK. Cf. J. Reents Verlag, *Rotbuch zu den Gewerkschaftsausschlüssen*, Hamburg 1978.

43   CDU *Erweiterte Dokumentation* 1976, p.27 (cf. note 22 above).

44   Report by Prof. H.C. Nipperdey on the question of check-off agreements and the payment by employers of lay union officers for their attendance on negotiating committees commissioned by the BDA, Cologne 3 May 1963.

45   Streeck, Bayer, Treu, op.cit., vol.1, p.279.

46   Handelsblatt Nr 66, 1979.

47   Streeck, Bayer, Treu, op.cit., p.138.

48 Treu, H.E., 'Gewerkschaftliche Organisation in einer schrumpfenden Branche', *Soziale Welt*, Heft 1/2 1977, p.174.
49 Streeck, Bayer, Treu, op.cit., vol.II, p.337.
50 CDU Dokumentation II, pp. 29-31.
51 Ibid., pp. 24-5.

PART V

CONCLUSION

16 Summary and conclusion

Comparative studies in the field of industrial relations are notorious for their inability to reach practical conclusions. They inevitably stress differences in tradition, culture, language, social and political structures and attitudes as well as economic organisation, all of which render fruitful comparison difficult.[1] However, this study has been concerned with an aspect of industrial life which would appear to transcend national boundaries — namely the desire of trade unions on the one hand to expand and protect their organisation and the obligation of the state on the other hand to promote and protect the rights of the individual. In this brief conclusion, therefore, attention will be focused as much on those features of the problem which are common to all three countries as on the differences which make it difficult for one country to learn from another.

It was argued in the introduction that in most western industrialised economies there are groups of workers which may be regarded as 'closed shop prone'. The empirical analysis has indeed revealed that despite widely differing institutional and legal frameworks of collective bargaining, and different formal approaches to the closed shop, there are examples of similar groups of employees having established and maintained a high degree of union security, often by means of a pre-entry closed shop of some form, in all three countries covered by this study. These are to be found in industries like printing, the docks, shipping, entertainment, steel, coalmining and construction, although that is not to suggest that all these industries are closed to non-unionists in all three countries. Where other factors such as establishment size and workforce structure are broadly similar, differences in the nature and extent of the closed shop will be explained largely by differences in the collective bargaining system. How far can public policy affect the operation of the closed shop among groups of workers of this kind?

The evidence from all three countries suggests that where the law has sought to restrict or abolish the pre-entry closed shop it has been largely ineffective. Those groups which are capable of enforcing forms of the pre-entry closed shop are equally capable of circumventing restrictive legislation in a way which usually involves a tacit understanding between the union and the employer. In these industries the attitude of the employer plays a significant part in the effectiveness or ineffectiveness of public policy. In the UK many employers may openly encourage the closed shop. In the USA and Germany, while employers generally are hostile to the closed shop, they are willing to condone or even encourage it where special conditions prevail. For example, the existence of special arrangements for codetermination in coal and steel in West Germany means that unions are able to influence personnel policies in these industries.

In contrast to the closed shop prone groups discussed above, which may have the capacity to enforce union security arrangements irrespective of public policy, there are many other groups of employees for whom an extension of union security would depend on some degree of state support. In the UK the growth of the formal (normally post-entry) closed shop accelerated significantly in certain areas following the 1974 TULRA. Some industries, such as the railways and electricity supply, have become completely closed to non-unionists and for a large number of manual and white-collar local authority employees union membership has become a condition of employment. Similarly, in the USA the introduction of the 'bargaining unit' and the duty placed on the employer to bargain with one union and the union to bargain for all employees placed employees in many industries in a strong position to negotiate formal union security provisions. In Germany where no such support has been given some unions, for example the Textile Workers', the Woodworkers' and the Construction Workers', have consistently pressed for an amendment to the Collective Contracts Act which would permit the negotiation of differentiation agreements.

For these employees, too, employer attitudes towards the closed shop are significant. In the UK the absence of a formal structure for collective bargaining means that many employers regard compulsory union membership as a stabilising factor in labour relations. In the USA in the 1930s the continued resistance of many employers to collective bargaining led to the introduction by the state of measures to promote union growth. In Germany a stable collective bargaining system is

236

already given in the form of a dual system of worker representation. Hence employers nationally oppose any extension of union security since there would appear to be no overt pragmatic reason for supporting it.

A major finding of this study with regard to public policy and the closed shop is, therefore, that a distinction must be made between those areas of employment where closed shops tend to develop naturally with or without the encouragement of employers and those areas where direct legal intervention has a definite impact. Unquestionably in the USA the Wagner and Taft-Hartley Acts had a significant effect on union growth and security. In the same way it would seem that in Britain TULRA encouraged the introduction of formal closed shops and that the Employment Act may restrict their growth. In West Germany the existing legislation makes it extremely difficult for weaker unions to achieve greater union security by means of differentiation. It is important to note that in all three countries closed shop prone groups are to be found in those sectors of the economy where employment opportunities are declining. Given these changes in the structure of employment the focus of attention has shifted to industries and services where the closed shop has not been traditional and where the law and public policy have to be taken into account.

The fundamental problem of the closed shop is the same everywhere, and there are important similarities between the ways in which trade unions have attempted to achieve a degree of union security in the three countries under review. There are, of course, also significant differences between one country and another which mean that direct translation of public policy towards the closed shop across national boundaries is either impossible or undesirable. However, these differences do not mean that comparative studies in the area of union security and the closed shop are invalidated, but that they have to be used with discretion.

Reference

1   See Kahn-Freund, O., 'On Uses and Abuses of Comparative Law', *Modern Law Review*, January 1974, vol.37, no.1, pp. 1-27.

Bibliography

Parts I, II and V

Books

Addison, J.T. and Siebert, W.S., *The Market for Labor: An Analytical Treatment*, Goodyear Publishing Co. 1979.

Allen, V.L., *Power in Trade Unions*, Longmans Green 1954.

Beloff, N., *Freedom under Foot*, Temple Smith 1976.

Bloom, G.F. and Northrup, H.R., *Economics of Labor Relations*, R.D. Irwin 1977.

Brownlie, I. (ed.), *Basic Documents in Human Rights*, Oxford University Press 1971.

Burkitt, B. and Bowers, D., *Trade Unions and the Economy*, Macmillan 1979.

Burton, J., *The Economics of the Closed Shop*, in IEA Readings 17, Trade Unions — Public Goods or Public 'Bads'?, Institute of Economic Affairs 1978.

Campbell, C. (ed.), *Do We Need a Bill of Rights?*, Temple Smith 1980.

Carrothers, A.W.R., *Collective Bargaining Law in Canada*, 1965.

Citrine, N.A., *Trade Union Law*, Stevens 1960.

Closed Shop Agreements, Institute of Personnel Management 1976.

Current Law Statutes 1980.

Dicey, A.V., *Lectures on the Relation between Law and Public Opinion in England during the Nineteenth Century*, 2nd edn, reissued by Macmillan 1962.

Dunlop, J.T., *Wage Determination under Trade Unions*, Macmillan 1944.

Gellhorn, W., *Individual Freedom and Governmental Restraints*, Louisiana State University Press 1956.

Grunfeld, C., *Trade Unions and the Individual in English Law*, Institute of Personnel Management 1963.

Haggard, T.R., *Compulsory Unionism, the NLRB and the Courts*, University of Pennsylvania 1977.

Hawkins, K., *Handbook of Industrial Relations Practice*, Kogan Page 1979.

Hayek, F.A., *The Constitution of Liberty*, Routledge and Kegan Paul 1960.

Jacobs, F.G., *The European Convention on Human Rights*, Clarendon Press 1975.

Jenkins, P., *The Battle of Downing Street*, Charles Knight 1970.

Kahn-Freund, O., *Labour and the Law*, 2nd edn, Stevens 1977.

Kahn-Freund, O., *Labour Relations, Heritage and Adjustment*, Oxford University Press 1979.

Macbeath, I., *The Times Guide to the Industrial Relations Act*, Times Newspapers 1972.

McCarthy, W.E.J., *The Closed Shop in Britain*, Blackwell 1964.

McCulloch, J.R., *A Treatise on the Circumstances which Determine the Rate of Wages and the Condition of the Labouring Classes*, G. Routledge 1854.

Mulvey, C., *The Economic Analysis of Trade Unions*, Martin Robertson 1978.

Paterson, P., *An Employer's Guide to the Industrial Relations Act*, Kogan Page 1971.

Petro, S., *The Labor Policy of the Free Society*, Ronald Press 1957.

Rees, A., *The Economics of Trade Unions*, Nisbet/Cambridge University Press/University of Chicago Press 1962.

Rideout, R., *Principles of Labour Law*, Sweet and Maxwell 1979.

Rowley, C.K. and Peacock, A.T., *Welfare Economics: A Liberal Restatement*, Martin Robertson 1975.

Thomson, A.W.J. and Engleman, S.R., *The Industrial Relations Act, A Review and Analysis*, Martin Robertson 1975.

Webb, S. and B., *History of Trade Unionism*, 1920 edn.

Webb, S. and B., *Industrial Democracy*, Longmans Green 1902.

Wedderburn, K.W., *The Worker and the Law*, Penguin Books 1965.

Wedderburn, Lord, 'Discrimination in the Right to Organise and the Right to be a Non-Unionist', in Schmidt, F. (ed.), *Discrimination in Employment*, Almquist and Wiksell International 1978.

Weekes, B., Mellish, M., Dickens, L. and Lloyd, J., *Industrial Relations and the Limits of the Law*, Blackwell 1975.

Articles, reports, statutes, etc.

Benedictus, R., 'Closed Shop Exemptions and their Working', *Industrial Law Journal* 1979.

Bennett, J.T. and Johnson, M.H., 'Free Riders in US Labour Unions: Artifice or Affliction?', *British Journal of Industrial Relations*, July 1979.

'Characteristics of Major Collective Bargaining Agreements', 1 July 1976. Bureau of Labor Statistics 1979, Bulletin 2013, US Department of Labor.

'The Check-off System: A Review of Some Recent Agreements', *Industrial Relations Review and Report*, no.196, March 1979.

'Department of Employment Survey of Management Attitudes towards the Industrial Relations Act 1971', *Industrial Relations Review and Report* nos 83 and 84, July 1974.

Dirksen, E.M., 'Industrial Freedom versus Compulsory Unionism: A Constitutional Problem', *De Paul Law Review*, vol.XV, no.2, 1966.

Drake, C.D., 'The Trade Union and Labour Relations (Amendment) Bill', *Industrial Law Journal* 1976.

Elliott, J., *The Financial Times*, 18 December 1975.

Gennard, J., Dunn, S. and Wright, M., 'The Content of British Closed Shop Agreements', *Department of Employment Gazette*, November 1979.

Gennard, J., Dunn, S. and Wright, M., 'The Extent of Closed Shop Arrangements in British Industry', *Employment Gazette*, January 1980.

Gennard, J., Gregory, M. and Dunn, S., 'Throwing the Book — Trade Union Rules on Admission, Discipline and Expulsion', *Employment Gazette*, June 1980.

Gennard, J., Dunn, S. and Gregory, M., letter to the *New Statesman*, 20 June 1980.

Hanson, C.G., 'The Exercise of Economic Power by the Trade Unions' in *Recht und Macht in Politik und Wirtschaft*, Swiss Institute for International Studies 1976.

Hart, M., 'Why Bosses Love the Closed Shop', *New Society*, 15 February 1979.

Hepple, B.A., 'The Right to Work at One's Job', *Modern Law Review*, November 1974.

'An Independent Review of the Independent Review Committee', *Industrial Relations Review and Report* no.173, April 1978.

'The Independent Review Committee — The Success of Voluntarism?', *Industrial Relations Review and Report* no.208, September 1979.

Johnson, P., 'Towards the Parasite State', *New Statesman*, 3 September 1976.

Kahn-Freund, O., 'The Industrial Relations Act — Some Retrospective Reflections', *Industrial Law Journal*, 1974.

Kassalow, E.M., 'Will West European Unions Embrace the Closed Shop?', *Monthly Labor Review*, July 1979.

McAlister, A., 'Labor, Liberalism and Majoritarian Democracy', *Fordham Law Review*, vol.31, 1963.

Price, R. and Bain, G.S., 'Union Growth Revisited', *British Journal of Industrial Relations*, November 1976.

Wedderburn, K.W., 'Labour Law and Labour Relations in Britain', *British Journal of Industrial Relations*, July 1972.

Weekes, B., 'Law and the Practice of the Closed Shop', *Industrial Law Journal*, 1976.

Wigham, E., *The Times*, 4 June 1976.

Code of Practice: Closed Shop Agreements and Arrangements, Department of Employment 1980.

The Conservative Manifesto 1979.

House of Commons *Hansard*.

House of Lords *Hansard*.

Report of the Royal Commission on Trade Unions 1869.

Report of the Royal Commission on Trade Unions and Employers' Associations 1968.

Report of Inquiry into certain Trade Union Recruitment Activities (The Leggatt Report), Cmnd. 7706, 1979.

Green Paper on Trade Union Immunities, Cmnd. 8128, 1981.

Rule Book of the National Union of Railwaymen.

TUC Guides to Negotiating Procedures, Conduct of Disputes, Union Organisation, February 1979.

TUC Annual Reports for 1969, 1976, 1978, 1979 and 1980.

Trade Disputes Act 1906.

Trade Union Act 1913.

Industrial Relations Act 1971.

Trade Union and Labour Relations Act 1974.

Employment Protection Act 1975.

Trade Union and Labour Relations (Amendment) Act 1976.

Employment Protection (Consolidation) Act 1978.

Employment Act 1980.

Cases

Allen v Flood (1898) AC1.
Cave and Cave v British Railways Board (1976) IRLR 400.
Crofter Hand Woven Harris Tweed v Veitch (1942) AC 435.
Drury v Bakers' Union (1973) IRLR 171.
Goodbody v British Railways Board (1977) IRLR 84.
Himpfen v Allied Records (1978) IRLR 154.
Home Counties Dairies Ltd. v Woods (1976) IRLR 380.
Hynds v Spillers French Baking Ltd. and SUBAW (1974) SLT 191.
Jones v Vauxhall Motors (1972) ITR 250.
Langston v AUEW (1973) ICR 211, ICR 180 (1974) ICR 510.
Mogul Steamship Co. v McGregor Gow (1892) AC 25.
Newell v Gillingham Corporation (1941) 1 All ER 552.
Quinn v Leathem (1901) AC 495.
R. v Burn (1872) 12 Cox C.C. 87.
Reynolds v The Shipping Federation (1924) 1 Ch. 28.
Rook v North Eastern Electricity Board, Industrial Tribunal Report
    No. 23558/79.
Rookes v Barnard (1964) AC 1129.
Saggers v British Railways Board (1977) IRLR 266, (1978) IRLR 435.
Sarvent v Central Electricity Generating Board (1976) IRLR 66.
Strover v Chrysler (UK) Ltd. (1975) IRLR 68.
Taff Vale Railway v Amalgamated Society of Railway Servants (1901)
    AC 426.
Taylor v Co-operative Retail Services Ltd. Appeal No. 233/80 of the
    Employment Appeal Tribunal, October 1980.
White v Riley (1921) 1 Ch.1.
Young, James and Webster v United Kingdom, Application Nos 7601/
    76 and 7806/77 to the European Commission of Human Rights.

Bibliography and list of cases to Part III

Books

Bellace, J.R. and Berkowitz, A.D., *The Landrum-Griffin Act, Twenty
    Years of Federal Protection of Union Members' Rights*, Labor Re-
    lations and Public Policy Series no.19, University of Pennsylvania,
    Industrial Research Unit 1979.
Bloom, G.F. and Northrup, H.R., *Economics of Labor Relations*,
    Irwin, Illinois, 8th edn. 1977.

Estey, M., *The Unions, Structure, Development and Management*, 2nd edn., Harcourt Brace Jovanovich Inc. 1977.

Haggard, T.R., *Compulsory Unionism, the NLRB and the Courts: A Legal Analysis of Union Security Agreements*, Labor Relations and Public Policy Series No.15, University of Pennsylvania, Industrial Research Unit 1977.

Kahn-Freund, O., *Labour and the Law*, 2nd edn., Stevens 1977.

Marsh, A., *A Concise Encyclopedia of Industrial Relations*, Gower Press 1979.

Meyers, F., *Right to Work in Practice, The Fund for the Republic*, New York 1959.

Millis, H.A. and Brown, E.C., *From the Wagner Act to Taft-Hartley*, University of Chicago Press 1950.

Stockton, F.T., *The Closed Shop in American Unions*, John Hopkins University Studies in Social Sciences, 29th series, 1911.

Sultan, P., *Right-to-Work Laws*, Californian Institute for Industrial Relations, Monograph no.2, 1958.

Toner, J.L., *The Closed Shop*, American Council on Public Affairs 1942.

Articles, reviews and government publications

Anderson, J.C., Busman, G. and O'Reilly, C.A., 'What Factors influence the Outcome of Union Decertification Elections?' *Monthly Labor Review*, November 1979.

The Bureau of National Affairs Inc., Washington DC 20037, B-14,120 172, 1977.

Cohen, S., 'Operating Under Right-to-Work Laws', *Labor Law Journal*, August 1958.

Dworkin, J.B. and Extejt, M.M., 'The Union-Shop Deauthorisation Poll: a new look after 20 years', *Monthly Labor Review*, November 1979.

'American Union-busting: Crisis? What Crisis?, *The Economist*, 17 November 1979.

Elliot, R.D., 'The Impact of Right to Work Laws on Union Activity', a National Right-to-Work Legal Defense Foundation Study, unpublished 1979.

Essinger, J., 'The Right-to-Work Imbroglio', *North Dakota Law Review*, vol.51, 1975.

Geddes, P., 'The New American Waterfront', *The Listener*, 6 December 1979.

Gilbert, D., 'A Statistical Analysis of the Right-to-Work Conflict', *Industrial and Labor Relations Review*, vol.19, July 1966.

Haggard, T.R., 'A Clarification of the types of Union Security Agreements Affirmatively permitted by Federal Statutes', *Rutgers Camden Law Journal*, vol.5, 1974.

Hammerman, H., 'Minority Workers in Construction Referral Unions', *Monthly Labor Review*, May 1971.

Hirsch, B.T., 'Unionization and the South: Do Right-to-Work Laws Matter?', *North Carolina Review of Business and Economics*, April 1978.

Kahn-Freund, O., 'The Impact of Constitutions on Labour Law', *Cambridge Law Journal*, 35(2), November 1976.

'Legislative History of the Labor Management Relations Act, 1947', Report No.105.

Lumsden, K. and Peterson, C., 'The Effect of Right-to-Work Laws on Unionization in the United States', *Journal of Political Economy*, vol.83, no.6, 1975.

Miller, R.L., 'Right to Work and Compulsory Union Membership in the US', *British Journal of Industrial Relations*, July 1976.

Moore, W.J., 'Membership and Wage Impact of Right-to-Work Laws' and comments by Palomba, N.A. and Kuhn, J.W., *Journal of Labor Research*, vol.I, no.2, Fall 1980.

Morgan, C.A., 'The Union Shop Deauthorization Poll', *Industrial and Labor Relations Review*, October 1958.

Novit, M.S., 'Right to Work: Before and After the Indiana Experience', *Business Horizons*, October 1969.

Page, W.P. and Delorme, C., 'Economic Efficiency and Right-to-Work Laws: An Issue in a Muddle', *Southern Economic Journal*, vol.37, 1970-71.

Pollitt, D.H., 'Right to Work Law Issues: An Evidentiary Approach', *North Carolina Law Review*, vol.37, 1959.

Prosten, R., 'The Rise in NLRB Election Delays: Measuring Business's New Resistance', *Monthly Labor Review*, February 1979.

Roomkin, M. and Juris, H.A., 'The Changing Character of Unionism in Traditionally Organized Sectors', *Monthly Labor Review*, February 1979.

Rose, J.B., 'What Factors Influence Union Representation Elections?', *Monthly Labor Review*, October 1972.

Ross, P. and Taft, P., 'The Effect of the LMRDA Upon Union Constitutions', *New York University Law Review*, vol.43, part 2, April 1968.

Soffer, B. and Korenick, M., 'Right to Work Laws and Location', *Journal of Regional Science*, vol.3, no.2, 1961.

Summers, C., 'American and European Labor Law: The Use and Usefulness of Foreign Experience', *Buffalo Law Review*, vol.16, 1966.

Theodore, R., 'Union Security Provisions in Agreements, 1954', *Monthly Labor Review*, June 1955.

Theodore, R., 'Union Security and Checkoff Provisions in Major Union Contracts 1958-59', Bulletin No. 1272, United States Department of Labor, Bureau of Labor Statistics, March 1972.

Troy, L., 'Trade Union Membership 1897-1962', National Bureau of Economic Research, Occasional Paper 92, 1965.

United States Department of Labor, Bureau of Labor Statistics, Characteristics of Major Collective Bargaining Agreements, 1 July 1976, Bulletin 2013, 1979.

United States Department of Labor, BLS, National and International Labor Unions in the United States, 1969, BLS Bulletin 16651, 1970.

United States Department of Labor, Directory of National and International Unions in the US, 1973.

United States Department of Labor, Bureau of Labor Statistics, Handbook of Labor Statistics 1975, Reference edition, Bulletin 1865.

United States and Public Welfare Proceedings of 2nd Annual Industrial Relations Conference, Industrial Department AFL-CIO, 1958.

University of Chicago Law Review, 'Closed Shop Union Bylaws Under the NLRA', vol.37, summer 1970.

Cases

Adair v US, 208 US 161, 1908.

AFL v American Sash and Door Co., 335 US 538, 1949.

American Newspaper Publishers Association v NLRB, 193 F 2d 782, 7th Cir. 1951.

Beck v Communications Workers of America, Civil No. M-76-839, Report filed 18 August 1980.

Brotherhood of Railway and Steamship Clerks v Allen, 373 US 113, 1963.

Commonwealth v Hunt, 45 Mass (4 Met) Ill, 1842.

Coppage v Kansas, 236 US 1, 1915.

Ford Motor Co. of Canada v UAW, Lab. Arb. 439, 17 LRRM, 2782, 1946.

Glasser v NLRB, 395 F 2d 401, 2d Cir. 1968.

Gray v Gulf, M & O RR, 429 F 2d 1064, 5th Cir. 1970.

Hammer v Dagenhart, 24 US 251, 1918.

IAM Lodge 508, 190 NLRB 61, 1971.

International Association of Machinists v Street, 367 US 740, 1961.

International Typographical Union v NLRB, 365 US 705, 1961.

J.J. Hagerty 153 NLRB 1375, 1965.

Kaiser v Price-Tewell Inc., 235 Ark. 295, 359 SW 2d 449, 1962.

Keystone Coat, Apron and Towel Supply Co., 121 NLRB 880, 1958.

Laborers' Local 107 v Kunco Inc., 472 F 2d 456, 8th Cir. 1973.

Lincoln Fed. Labor Union v Northwestern Iron and Metal Co., 335 US 525, 1949.

Local 1625, Retail Clerks v Schermerhorn, 373 US 746, 1963.

Local 60, United Brotherhood of Carpenters and Joiners v NLRB 365 US 651, 1961.

Longshoremen's and Warehousemen's Local 6 (Sunset Line and Twine Co.) 79 NLRB 1487, 1948.

Meade Electric Co. v Hagberg, 159 NE 2d 408, Ind. 1959.

Mountain Pacific Chapter, 119 NLRB 883, 41 LRRM 1460, 1950. Enforcement denied 270 F 2d 425, 44 LRRM 2802, 9th Cir. 1959.

Musicians Local 802, 176 NLRB 76, 71 LRRM 1228, 1968.

NLRB v General Motors Corp, 373 US 734, 83 Sup. Ct. 1453, 1963.

NLRB v Gissel Packing Co. 395 US 575, 1969.

NLRB v Jones and Laughlin Steel Corporation, 301 US 1, 1936.

NLRB v Local 138, Operating Engineers, 385 F 2d 874, 2d Cir. 1967.

NLRB v Television and Radio Broadcasting Studio Employees Local 804, 315 F 2d 398, 52 LRRM 2774, 3d Cir. 1963.

NLRB v Tom Joyce Floors Inc. 353 F 2d 768, 9th Cir. 1965 re Northland Greyhound Lines Inc., 80 NLRB 288, 1948.

Oil, Chemical and Atomic Workers' Union v Mobil Oil Corp., 96 SC 2140, 1956.

Operating Engineers Local 542 v NLRB, 329 F. 2d 512, 3d Cir. 1964.

Otten v Baltimore and Ohio Railroad Co. 132 F Supp. 836, EDNY 1952, Aff'd. 205 F 2d 58, 2d Cir. 1958.

Painters' Local 567 v Tom Joyce Floors Inc, 81 Nev 1, 398 F 2d 245, 1965.

Plumbers and Pipefitters Local 231, 115 NLRB 594, 1956.

Radio Officers' Union v NLRB, 347 US 17, 1954.

Railway Employees' Department v Hanson, 351 US 225, 1956.

Retail Clerks Local 1625 v Schermerhorn, 373 US 746, 1963.

Schermerhorn v Local 1625, Retail Clerks, 141 S 2d 269, 1962.

Seamprufe Inc., 82 NLRB 892, 1949, enforced 186 F 2d 671; cert. denied, 342 US 813, 1951.

Sea Pak v Industrial Employees, SD Georg 1969, 300 F. Suppl. 1197; Aff'd 423 F 2d 1229, 5th Cir, 1970, 400 US 985, 1971.

Steele v Louisville and Nashville Railroad, 323 US 192, 1944.

Teamsters Local 357 v NLRB, 356 US 667, 47 LRRM 2906, 1961.

re Union Starch and Refining Co., 87 NLRB 779, 1949, enforced 186 F 2d 1008, 7th Cir, 1951, Cert. denied, 342 US 815, 1951.

United States v Darby, 312 US 100, 1940.

United States v Hutcheson, 312 US 219, 1941.

re Western Electric Co, 84 NLRB 1019, 1949.
Wicks v Southern Pacific R.R., 231 F 2d 130, 1956, Cert. denied, 351 US 946, 1956.
Wyandotte Chems. Corp., 108 NLRB 1406, 1954.

Bibliography and legal rulings to Part IV

Books in German

Abendroth, M., Beckenbach, N., Braun, S., Dombois, R., *Hafenarbeit: Eine industriesoziologische Untersuchung der Arbeits – und Betriebs – verhältnisse in den bremischen Häfen*, Campus, Frankfurt 1979.
Altvater, E., Hoffmann, J., Semmler, W., *Vom Wirtschaftswunder zur Wirtschaftskrise*, Olle and Walter, Berlin 1979.
Bergmann, J., Müller-Jentsch, W., *Gewerkschaften in der Bundesrepublik*, vol.2, Campus, Frankfurt 1977.
Bergmann, J. (ed.), *Beiträge zur Soziologie der Gewerkschaften*, Suhrkamp, Frankfurt 1979.
Biedenkopf, K., *Grenzen der Tarifautonomie* 1964.
Bötticher, E., *Die gemeinsamen Einrichtungen der Tarifvertragsparteien*, Heidelberg 1966.
Däubler, W., *Das Grundrecht auf Mitbestimmung*, EVA, Frankfurt/Cologne 1973.
Däubler, W., *Arbeitsrecht*, Rowohlt, Hamburg 1976.
Gamillscheg, F., *Die Differenzierung nach der Gewerkschaftszugehörigkeit*, Berlin 1966.
Hueck, A., *Tarifausschlussklauseln und verwandte Klauseln im Tarifvertragsrecht*, Munich 1966.
Hueck, A., *Tarifliche Differenzierungsklauseln*, Düsseldorf 1967.
Hueck, A., Nipperdey, C., *Grundriss*, 5th edn.
Hueck, A., Nipperdey, C., *Lehrbuch des Arbeitsrechts*, vol.II (7th edn. 1967).
IMSF Autorenkollektiv, *Mitbestimmung als Kampfaufgabe*, Pahl Rugenstein, Cologne 1972.
Jacobi, O., Müller-Jentsch, W., Schmidt, E., *Gewerkschaften und Klassenkampf, Kritisches Jahrbuch 1975*, Fischer, Frankfurt 1975.
Jacobi, O., Müller-Jentsch, W., Schmidt, E., *Arbeiterinteressen gegen Sozialpartnerschaft, Kritisches Gewerkschaftsjahrbuch*, Rotbuch Verlag, Berlin 1979, p.7.
Jühe, R., Niedenhoff, H.U., Pege, W., *Gewerkschaften in der Bundesrepublik Deutschland*, Deutscher Instituts-Verlag, Cologne 1977.

Kolb, J., *Metallgewerkschaften in der Nachkriegszeit,* Frankfurt am Main 1970.

Kroll, J., *Arbeit und Soziales,* Presse Taschenbuch, 1979.

Nikisch, A., *Arbeitsrecht* 1951.

Peters, J., *Arbeitnehmerkammern in der Bundesrepublik?,* Olzog, Munich 1973.

Schaub, G., *Arbeitsrechtshandbuch,* Beck, Munich 1977.

Schmidt, E., *Die verhinderte Neuordnung,* EVA, Frankfurt 1970.

Seitenzahl, R., Zachert, U., Pütz, H.D., *Vorteilsregelungen für Gewerkschaftsmitglieder,* WSI Studien Nr. 33, Cologne 1976.

Söllner, A., *Arbeitsrecht,* Stuttgart 1978.

Teschner, E., *Lohnpolitik im Betrieb,* Campus, Frankfurt am Main 1977.

Zachert, U., *Tarifvertrag,* Bund, Cologne 1979.

Articles and dissertations in German

Assmann, J., 'Rechtsfragen zum Gesamthafenbetrieb', dissertation, Cologne University 1965.

Bayer, H., 'Bedingungen und Erfolge gewerkschaftlicher. Angestelltenrekrutierung in ausgewählten Wirtschaftsbereichen', *WSI Mitteilungen,* Heft II, 1978.

Bayer, H., 'Die Integration heterogener Mitgliedergruppen in Industriegewerkschaften 1960-1975', *Soziale Welt,* Heft 3 Jahrgang 30, 1979.

Beer, W., 'Die Mitbestimmungssituation im Steinkohlenbergbau', *Das Mitbestimmungsgespräch* 1973.

Blum, N., 'Reform der Gesellschaft durch Reform der Gewerkschaft', *Gewerkschaftliche Monatshefte* 1978/9.

Fuhrmann, J., *Polierstudie — Eine Untersuchung über Arbeitsplatz, Tätigkeit, Rolle und Position von Polierern und Schachtmeistern im Baugewerbe,* internal publication of the IGBSE, Frankfurt (date unknown).

Gernandt, O., 'Die negative Koalitionsfreiheit', *der Arbeitgeber,* February 1954, pp. 154-6.

Herbammer, S., Bischoff, J., Lohau, P., Maldauer, K.H., Steinfield, F., 'Organisationsgrad und Bewusstsein', *Gewerkschaftliche Monatshefte* 11/79, pp. 709-20.

Humml, K., 'Einkommenssituation, Lohnstruktur und Lohnpolitik in der chemischen Industrie', *WSI Mitteilungen* 2/1980, pp. 85-96.

Müller-Jentsch, W., 'Streiks und Streikbewegungen in der Bundesrepublik 1975-1978', in Bergmann, J. (ed.), 1979.

Nipperdey, H.C., 'Rechtsgutachten für den BDA über Lohnabzug für Gewerkschaftsmitglieder und die Vergütung von gewerkschaftlichen Tarifkommissionsmitgliedern durch den Arbeitgeber', Cologne 3 May 1963.

Streeck, W., Treu, H.E., Bayer, H. (a) *Organisationsstrukturelle Wandlungsprozesse in westdeutschen Gewerkschaften 1960-1975* (2 vols), unpublished research project, University of Münster 1978.

Streeck, W., 'Gewerkschaften als Mitgliederverbände Probleme gewerkschaftlicher Mitgliederrekrutierung', in Bergmann, J. (ed.), 1979.

Treu, H.E., 'Gewerkschaftliche Organisation in einer schrumpfenden Branche', *Soziale Welt*, Heft 1/2, 1977.

Treu, H.E., 'Probleme der gewerkschaftlichen Mitgliederrekrutierung in ausgewählten Industriezweigen', *Soziale Welt*, Heft 4, 1978.

Wiedenhofer, H., 'Fragen der Integration gewerkschaftlicher Tarif-und Betriebspolitik', *Gewerkschaftliche Monatshefte*, 11/1979.

Wiedenhofer, H., *Probleme Gewerkschaftlicher Interessenvertretung*, Verlag Neue Gesellschaft, Bonn 1979.

Wlotzke, O., 'Zur Zulässigkeit von Tarifverträgen über den Schutz und die Erleichterung der Tätigkeit gewerkschaftlicher Vertrauensleute', *Recht der Arbeit*, 1976.

Zachert, U., 'Mitbestimmung ohne Gewerkschaften', *Gewerkschaftliche Monatshefte* 6/1979.

Newspaper articles

Handelsblatt, 5 December 1978.
Handelsblatt, 66, 1979.
Spiegel, Nr. 6, 1978.
Die Zeit: Zeit-forum 'Marsch in den Gewerkschaftsstaat?', 29 November 1974 and 6 December 1974.
Die Quelle, Funktionärszeltschrift des deutschen Gewerkschaftsbundes, 11/78.

English books

Brownlie, I. (ed.), *Basic Documents on Human Rights*, Oxford University Press 1971.
Herding, R., *Job Control and Union Structure*, Rotterdam, University Press, 1973.

Marsh, A., Hackmann, M., Miller, D., *Workplace Relations in the Engineering Industry in the UK and the Federal Republic of Germany, A Comparison*, Anglo-German Foundation for the Study of Industrial Society 1981.

Schmidt, F. (ed.), *Discrimination in Employment*, Stockholm 1978.

Articles, research papers in English

Beyme, K. von, 'The changing relations between Trade Unions and the Social Democratic Party in West Germany', *Government and Opposition*, 13, 4.

Erd, R., Müller-Jentsch, W., 'Innovation in the Printing Industry in the Federal Republic', Research paper (B0179/4E), Anglo German Foundation for the Study of Industrial Society, 1978.

Kahn-Freund, O., 'The Impact of Constitutions on Labour Law', *Cambridge Law Journal*, November 1976, p.269.

Lenhoff, A., 'Compulsory Unionism in Europe', *The American Journal of Comparative Law*, 1956, p.32.

Miller, D., 'Trade Union Workplace Representation in the Federal Republic of Germany: An analysis of the Postwar Vertrauensleute policy of the German Metalworkers' Union (1952-77)', *BJIR*, November 1978.

Streeck, W., 'Qualitative Demands and the Neo-Corporatist Manageability of Industrial Relations', *BJIR*, vol.XIX, no.2, July 1981.

Streeck, W., Seglow, P., Bayley, P., 'Railway Unions in Britain and West Germany. Structural sources of cross national differences and similarities', *International Institute of Management Discussion Paper 78/80*, Berlin 1978.

Streeck, W., 'The Organisational Stabilisation of West German Unions during the Last Decade', *IIM Discussion Paper 78/15*, Berlin 1978.

Legal rulings

BAG *Arbeitsrechtsammlung* 5,50; 6,90; 7,23; 8,484.

BAG Arbeitsrechtliche Praxis (AP) Nr 1 on Section 4 Collective Contracts Act (TG), decision of 1 March 1956, BAG AP Nr 5 decision dated 26 April 1961.

Federal Labour Court Decision 29 November 1967, BAG 20 175: AP Nr 13 zu Art 9 GG.

BAG AP Nr 7 re. s.4. Collective Contracts Act. Decision dated 14 February 1968 and confirmed by a further decision 26 April 1961 in BAG AP Nr 5.

Decision of the Federal Constitutional Court 18 December 1974 Nr 24, 297 ff.

Stuttgart Labour Court Decision 4 Ca 15/75, 6 February 1975.

Statutes

The Hessen Constitution 1946.

The Bremen Constitution 1947.

The Works Councils Law 10 April 1946 of the Control Commission (*Gesetz 22 des Kontrollrates*). The Works Constitution Acts 1952 and 1972.

Collective Contracts Law of the Economic Council 9 April 1949, (*Tarifvertragsgesetz des Wirtschaftsrates*).

The West German Constitution 1949.

Federal Statute to establish a special category employer for dockworkers — Port Authority (*Bundesgesetz über die Schaffung eines besonderen Arbeitgebers für Hafenarbeiter, Gesamthafenbetrieb von 3.8.1950*).

Codetermination Act for the Iron and Steel and Coal Industries (*Montanmitbestimmungsgesetz 1951*).

Legal Aid Act: Beratungshilfegesetz, 18 June 1980.

Collective agreements

Blanket agreement for the leather industry (*Manteltarifvertrag für die ledererzeugende Industrie*), 4 October 1977.

Blanket agreement for manual and staff employees in the chemical industry (*Manteltarifvertrag für die gewerblichen Arbeitnehmer und Angestelltenn der chemischen Industrie*), 1 May 1978.

Blanket agreement for the co-operative societies of West Germany (*Mantelarifvertrag für die Mitarbeiter der Konsumgenossenschaften der Bundesrupublik Deutschlands*), 30 November 1973.

An agreement to establish a friendly society and foundation for the employees of the corsetry industry (*Tarifvereinbarung über die Errichtung eines Vereins und einer Stiftung für die Arbeitnehmer der Miederindustrie*), 25 March 1974.

An agreement to provide an additional pension fund for the bakery trades between the Hotel, Foodstuffs and Catering Union and the Federation of Bakery Employers (*Tarifvertrag über die Errichtung einer Zusatzversorgungskasse für das Bäckerhandwerk zwischen der Gewerkschaft NGG und dem Zentralverband des Deutschen Bäckerhandwerks*), 17 April 1970.

An agreement to provide a joint training fund for employees in the bakery and confectionery trades (*Tarifvertrag über die Errichtung eines "Förderungswerkes für die Beschäftigten im Bäckerhandwerk" zwischen der Gewerkschaft NGG und dem Zentralverband des Deutschen Bäckerhandwerks*), 17 April 1970.

Works agreement to regulate terms and conditions of salaried employees not covered by collective agreements (Ruhrkohle AG *Betriebsvereinbarung für AT Angestellte bei der Ruhrkohle AG*), October 1978.

Statistical sources

Statistisches Bundesamt der Bundesregierung, *Statistische Jahrbücher*, Wiesbaden.

Presse und Informationsamt der Bundesregierung: *Gesellschaftliche Daten 1979*, Bonn 1980.

Sachverständigenrat zur Begutachtung der gesamtwirtschaftlichen Entwicklung, *Herausforderung von Aussen, Jahresgutachten 1979/80*, Kohlhammer, Stüttgart/Mainz 1979.

Recht der Arbeit 1976 and 1979.

Official documentation

Minutes of the 8th Congress of the DGB, 1969.

Minutes of the 10th Congress of the DGB, Hamburg 1975.

DGB Aktionprogramm 13 June 1979.

Bundesvereinigung der Deutschen Arbeitgeberverbände, *Katalog der zu koordinierenden lohn — und tarifpolitischen Fragen — von 12.10.1965, in der Fassung von 15.12.1968, von 6.5.1975, und von 16.3.1978.*

CDU — Bundesgeschäftsstelle. *Dokumentation über den Missbrauch gewerkschatlicher und politischer Macht durch SPD — und Gewerkschaftsfunktionäre,* Parts I and II, Bonn.

Stoiber, E., *Rohmaterialen zur DGB Diskussion*, CSU 1979.

Index

American trade unionism (cont.)
effect upon organisation 175-82, 181-2; maintenance of membership during term of contract 122, 162, 168; management opposition to 180; membership 1900-78 113, 157, 180-1; need to organise white-collar workers 181; 'preferential shop' 122; relative weakness 120-1; seniority and hiring in 170, 171; terminology 121-3; union security 6, 112, 115, 121-3, 128-9, 161-8; 'union shop' 122, 131-2, 133, 134, 146, 162, 166, 168; workers covered by collective bargaining agreements 162; workforce location and 'job situs' 149

Anderson, J.C. et al. 183n

Apprenticeships 13-14, 112

Arbeitgeber, die 206

Arizona: emphasises right not to belong to union 145

Arkansas: 'right to work' legislation 148

Associated Society of Locomotive Engineers and Firemen 55

Association of Scientific, Technical and Managerial Staffs (ASTMS): agreement with BP Chemicals 72

Auto Workers Union (US) 178; expelled from AFL-CIO 118, 121

Bakers' Union 33, 34, 54; signs agency shop agreements 33

Bayer, H. 230n

Beer, W. 231n

Bellace, J.R. and Berkowitz, A.D., 142n

Benedictus, R. 76, 82n

Bergmann, J. 217n; and Müller-Jentsch, W. 217n

Beyme, K. von 200n

Biedenkopf, K. 206n

Bloom, G.F. and Northrup, H.R. 123n, 124n, 156, 160n 182n

Blum, N. 200n

BP Chemicals: agreement with ASTMS 72

Britain: Conservative victory in general election 1979 86; general elections 1974 42; 'winter of discontent' 1978-9 86

British Journal of Industrial Relations 41n, 200n

British Rail 60: cases of conscientious objection to union membership in 55-8; closed shop in 55, 58, 59; dismissed employees' appearance before European Commission of Human Rights 99-102; dismissed employees' case goes to European Court 101-2; UMA with TSSA 73

British Shipbuilders: UMA with Confederation of Shipbuilding and Engineering Unions 74

British trade unionism: agency shops 31-4, 54, 55; compared with American and W.German 4-5, 187, 193, 198, 236-7; growth of members 19-20; opposition to Industrial Relations Act 1971 32, 33, 40; origins to 1965 19-26; progress 1867-75 21-3; progress

Codetermination Act 1951 (W. German) 189; provisions of 190, 224; system under 7, 224, 225

Cohen, S. 182n

Colberg, M.R. 160n

Committee for Industrial Organization (CIO): amalgamates with AFL 118; founded 117

Commission on Industrial Relations 34

Confederation of British Industry (CBI) 96

Confederation of Christian Unions (W.German) 189

Confederation of Shipbuilding and Engineering Unions: UMA with British Shipbuilders 74

Conservative Party 95; 'Fair Deal at Work' 31; pledge to change law on closed shop 86

Conspiracy and Protection of Property Act 1875 23, 24

Construction Workers Union (W.German) 193, 209, 216, 236

Criminal Law Amendment Act 1871 22

Däubler, W. 207n, 216n

Department of Employment: *Industrial Relations Review and Report* no.84 36; surveys employers' attitudes to s.5 of Industrial Relations Act 1971 34-5

De Paul Law Review 16n

Dicey, A.V. 16; on problem of individual and right of association 11

Dirksen, E.M. 16n

Disraeli, Benjamin: passes Acts favourable to unions 23

Donaldson, Sir John 37, 38

Donovan Commission 28, 40, 60, 61; Ministry of Labour evidence before 29, 31; on apprenticeships 14; on closed shop 28-31; on compensation for 'unfair dismissal' 38; on conscientious objections to union membership 29-30, 54; on necessary changes in union rule books 30, 38, 39, 50-1

Donovan, Lord 28

Drake, C.D. 52n, 96n

Dworkin, J.B. and Extejt, M.M. 183n

Electricity Supply Union 46

Elliot, R.D. 156, 160n

Elliott, J. 67, 81n; on closed shop 68

Employers: attitude of American employers to unions 180; attitude to s.5 of Industrial Relations Act 1971 34-6, 38; reaction to closed shop 7, 8, 13, 14, 79, 236

Employers and Workmen Act 23

Employers Federation (BDA), West German 197; attitude to union security 214-5

Employment Act 1980 5, 50, 63, 86, 104, 107; closed shop enactments 87; Code of Practice on closed shop 86, 87, 88, 93-4, 96; enlargement of conscience clause for non-unionism 89-91; likely effectiveness 94-5, 96; on compulsion to join union 89; on unfair dismissal 87, 88, 91;

Employment Act 1980 (cont.) on 'union-only' sub-contracts 88-9; protects employees from dismissal on formation of UMA 92-3; sets standard for worker approval of UMAs 91, 96; SLADE clause 89

Employment Appeal Tribunal: cases brought under TULRA 48, 49, 57-8

Employment Gazette 96n

Employment Protection Act 1975 5, 86

Employment Protection (Consolidation) Act 1978 89, 93, 104; on ballots as to UMAs 107; on dismissal relating to union membership 105-7

Engleman, S.R. 41n

Equity (trade union) 34

Erd, R. and Müller-Jentsch, W. 230n

Essinger, J. 153, 160n

Estey, M. 124n

European Commission of Human Rights 60; case of TULRA and dismissed BR employees before 99-102; finding against UK 99, 101

European Convention on Human Rights 60; and TULRA 99-102; articles comprising 99-100

Federal Corrupt Practices Act 1947 (US) 136

Federal Post Office (W.German): informal closed shop in 226

Financial Times, The 81n

Fine Arts Union (W.German) 189, 219

Florida: 'right to work' legislation 143, 145, 147

Foodstuffs, Tobacco, Hotel and Catering Union (W.German) 211; agreements discriminating in favour of workers 222

Fordham Law Review 16n

Free Nation 81n

Gallup: 1959 poll on closed shop 83

Gamillscheg, F. 199n, 206n, 230n

Geddes, P. 183n

Gennard, John 68, 71, 95; Dunn, S. and Wright, M. 'The Content of British Closed Shop Agreements, 63n, 75; Dunn, S. and Wright, M. 'The Extent of Closed Shop Arrangements in British Industry' 69; Gregory, M. and Dunn, S. 96n

Georgia: check-off legislation 149

Georgia State Bar Journal 160n

German Labour Front (Nazi) 187, 201

Gernandt, O. 206n

Gewerkschaftliche Monatshefte 200n

Gilbert, D. 160n

Gladstone, W.E. 22

Government and Opposition 200n

Hagelstange, T., 'Die Entwicklung der Mitgliederzahlen der DGB — Gewerkschaften' 194

Haggard, T.R. 15n, 149, 159n, 182n; on question of individual v. group 9

Hailsham, Lord 90

Hammerman, H. 182n

Sultan, P. 159n
Summers, C. 124n
Supreme Court (US) 130, 131, 134, 146, 149, 175; and labour legislation 119-20; as guardian of constitution 119; on hiring halls 169; ruling on agency shop 147; upholds 'right to work' laws 145, 146

Taff Vale case 24
Taft-Hartley Act 1947 (US) 32, 116, 118, 120, 121, 138, 139, 140, 171, 237; amends Wagner Act 118, 125; authorises agency shop 133-4; defines 'employee' and 'employer' 125-6; effect on union organisation 175; meaning of union membership under 132-3, 134-5, 168-9; on authorisation and deauthorisation votes by union members 135-6, 175, 179; on check-off arrangements 136, 149; on political expenditure and members' rights 136-7; on religious objections to union membership 137-8; on right to refrain from union membership 126; opposed by unions 118; prohibits closed shop 130, 131, 161, 169; protection for employee against unfair practices 126-7; provisions concerning union security agreements 128-9; provisions subservient to state labour laws 143-4, 145, 146; sanctions union shop 131-2, 162; thirty-day grace period for joining union 135
Taft, Senator 134

Teamsters Union (US) 178; corruption in 121; expelled from AFL-CIO 118, 121
Teachers' Union (W.German) 188, 189
Texas: disregard of 'right to work' legislation in 173; union density 153
Textile Workers' Union (W. German) 203, 211, 216, 229, 236; gains differentiation between members and non-members 220-1
Theodore, R. 182n
Thieblot, A.J. 'Patterns and Trends in Labor Organization' 174
Thomson, A.W.J. 41n
Times, The 34
Toner, J.L. 123n
Trade Disputes Act 1906 24, 95; effect of *Rookes* v *Barnard* on 25-6; unions given immunity from torts under 24
Trade Disputes Act 1965 26
Trade Regulations 1869 (German) 201
Trade Union Act 1871 21, 120; 'Charter of Trade Unions' 21; nullified by Criminal Law Amendment Act 1871 22
Trade Union and Labour Relations Acts 1974 and 1976 (TULRA) 7, 42, 43, 71, 89, 92, 93, 236; and European Convention on Human Rights 99-102; cases brought before tribunals under 48-50, 55-9; encourage UMAs 75, 76, 80, 91; give employees right to join union 43; objections to union membership under 54-

West Germany: Codetermination Act 1951, *see* separate entry; Collective Contracts Acts 189, 191, 192, 196, 211, 213-4, 222, 236; Constitution (Basic Law) 1949 10, 187, 188, 192, 198-9, 201-6 *passim*, 210; debate on union power 1970s 197-8; Federal Constitutional Court 204, 205; Federal Labour Court 196, 202, 203, 204, 209, 210, 220, 221, 222; law on human rights 10-11, 192, 204; Reich Labour Court 210; Staff Representation Act 225, 226; worker chambers in 205-6; Works Constitution Acts 1952 and 1972 189, 190, 191, 196, 197, 209, 214, 223-7 *passim*

Westphalian Clothing Employers' Association 203, 221

Wholesale and Retail, Banking and Insurance Union (HBV), (German) 211, 220

Wiedenhofer, H. 199n, 217n

Wigham, E. 68, 76

Willis, R.N. 160n

Wilson, Harold 42

Wlotzke, O. 200n

Wood and Plastics Union (W. German) 211, 236

Works Councils Act 1920 (German) 191

Yorkshire Bank 33

Zachert, U. 217n, 230n

Zeit, die 200n